D1624576

STRIKE FROM THE AIR

For my grandchildren
Rex and Beatrix (Bebe) Treadwell

STRIKE FROM THE AIR

THE EARLY YEARS OF THE US AIR FORCES

TERRY C. TREADWELL

AIR WORLD

AIR WORLD

STRIKE FROM THE AIR
The Early Years of the US Air Forces

First published in Great Britain in 2020 by
Air World
An imprint of
Pen & Sword Books Ltd
Yorkshire – Philadelphia

Copyright © Terry C. Treadwell, 2020

ISBN 978 1 52677 645 7

The right of Terry C. Treadwell to be identified as Author of this work has been
asserted by him in accordance with the Copyright, Designs and Patents Act 1988.

A CIP catalogue record for this book is available from the British Library.

All rights reserved. No part of this book may be reproduced or transmitted in any form
or by any means, electronic or mechanical including photocopying, recording or by any
information storage and retrieval system, without permission from the Publisher in writing.

Typeset by SJmagic DESIGN SERVICES, India.
Printed and bound in the UK by TJ Books Limited

Pen & Sword Books Limited incorporates the imprints of Atlas, Archaeology,
Aviation, Discovery, Family History, Fiction, History, Maritime, Military, Military
Classics, Politics, Select, Transport, True Crime, Air World, Frontline Publishing, Leo
Cooper, Remember When, Seaforth Publishing, The Praetorian Press, Wharncliffe
Local History, Wharncliffe Transport, Wharncliffe True Crime and White Owl.

For a complete list of Pen & Sword titles please contact

PEN & SWORD BOOKS LIMITED
47 Church Street, Barnsley, South Yorkshire, S70 2AS, England
E-mail: enquiries@pen-and-sword.co.uk
Website: www.pen-and-sword.co.uk

Or
PEN AND SWORD BOOKS
1950 Lawrence Rd, Havertown, PA 19083, USA
E-mail: Uspen-and-sword@casematepublishers.com
Website: www.penandswordbooks.com

MIX
Paper from
responsible sources
FSC® C013056

Contents

Introduction

This book is about the part played by United States aviators and their aircraft in the First World War and in their little-known involvement in the Polish/ Soviet War of 1919–20.

The first part of the book covers the development of the aviation section of the army with balloons and the part they played in the War Between the States (the American Civil War). Also covered is the first use of aircraft when General Pershing attempted to track down the revolutionary Pancho Villa after he had crossed the Mexican border into the United States and killed a number of American citizens. Then came the development of naval aircraft during the American invasion of Veracruz resulting in the first American aircraft to be hit by gunfire.

With the advent of the First World War the book tells how America was drawn into the conflict and the adventurers who went to France and joined the Lafayette Escadrille, the Royal Flying Corps and the Royal Naval Air Service before joining the newly-created United States Air Service. Also covered are some of the individuals, including the first black aviator Eugene Bullard and the loners like Frank Luke. The part played by the US Navy and Marine Corps is also covered.

At the end of the First World War a group of American pilots joined together to form a squadron, the Kościuszko Squadron, which fought against the Russians in the Polish/Soviet War. The squadron had to fly captured German and Austro-Hungarian aircraft and, combined with inadequate fuel, spares, supplies and back-up ground crews, these men overcame the language barriers and all the other logistical problems to make a serious contribution to the defeat of the Russian army.

The final part of the book contains a number of escape reports by USAS pilots and observers, which gives a real insight into the conditions to which they and other Allied soldiers and airmen were subjected in German prison camps during the First World War.

Chapter One

The establishing of a balloon section by the Signal Corps in 1891 heralded the birth of the United States Army Air Service. The Franco-Prussian war in 1870 had brought the balloon into the forefront of military use in Europe when, during the conflict, the city of Paris was cut off from the outside

First communication balloon to ascend from Paris while under siege by the Germans.

world by surrounding German forces. Extensive use was made of balloons during this period to carry letters and dispatches out of Paris and keep contact with the rest of France and her army. These letters and dispatches were mostly carried at night to prevent the balloons being attacked by the Germans. So successful were these flights that at the end of the war a great deal of interest was shown by other European countries, including Germany, in the use of the balloon for military purposes. Officers from various European countries were sent for training at the French Aérostation in order to gain specialist knowledge so that they too could develop their own military balloon corps.

Balloons had also been used during the American Civil War of 1861–65 when, at the outset, a number of experienced balloonists, among them Thaddeus Lowe, John LaMountain and John Wise, offered their services to the Union army. The Confederates tried their hand at ballooning as well, mainly to counter the balloons of the Unionists. One type of balloon used by the Confederates was of the Montgolfier style, which was made of rigid cotton and known as a 'hot smoke' balloon. The attempt worked, but their handling techniques were poor due to their lack of experience and the balloon was subsequently lost and finally captured and destroyed by the North. Another style used by the Confederates and referred to as the 'silk dress balloon' consisted of aerostat envelopes made of multi-coloured dress-making silk which, when gas was available, was used effectively over Richmond. Initially

Balloonist John Wise.

it was attached to a railway locomotive and as the battle moved so did the train, but when it went beyond the tracks it was attached to a tugboat called the *Teaser*. The *Teaser* transported the balloon down the James River and launched the balloon at several observation positions before the tugboat ran aground and was captured by the Unionists. Another 'silk dress' balloon was constructed but was lost in a high wind; once again handling techniques and lack of experience were the cause of the problem. The lack of supply materials made it impossible to replace it.

The first recorded successful military observation flight was made during

Observation balloon being filled with hydrogen.

the Cape Hatteras Expedition in August 1861, when John LaMountain discovered a number of concealed Confederate camps during an ascent above the Cape. The information was of great interest to the expedition's commander, General Butler, whose forces were able to destroy the camps with limited casualties to his men.

In Washington, President Lincoln had taken an interest in the use of the balloon during the war and summoned Thaddeus Lowe to him. Lowe talked with the president, hoping to convince him of the usefulness of a balloon corps. Then on 24 July 1861, Lowe was asked to make an observation flight from Fort Corcoran to allay rumours of a Confederate force marching on the capital. This was done successfully and Lowe was able to report that there was no large Confederate force anywhere near. Then, just before the Battle of Manassas, President Lincoln sent Lowe to General Winfield Scott, Commander-in-Chief of the Union armies, to see if the balloon would be of use as an observation platform.

It soon became clear, however, that General Scott was not one of those inclined towards the use of the balloon during wartime and there is no record of any flights taking place before or during the battle. The Union army took a terrible beating and both sides lost large numbers of troops. Lowe was sent for by Lincoln to ask whether or not he thought the balloon might have made a significant difference to the outcome. Lowe, of course, said that in his opinion the balloon may have been able to give the ground forces information on the movements of the Confederate forces, but now they would never know.

President Lincoln sent Lowe, with a personal message card, to meet again with General Scott:

> Will Lieut. Gen. Scott please see Professor Lowe once more about his balloon?
>
> A. Lincoln
> 25 July 1861.

On three separate occasions Scott refused to see Lowe for a variety of reasons. Angry, Lowe went to see Lincoln, who personally escorted Lowe to Scott's headquarters. Scott, on being confronted by the president, agreed to look very seriously at the formation of a balloon corps.

Thaddeus Lowe was offered a position with a salary of $30 a day for every day his balloon was used, but he wanted more. He wanted a regular salary and the position of military aeronaut, coupled with a commission to build a balloon. With support from various quarters, this was finally agreed and Lowe, now Chief of the Balloon Corps, set about building his balloon, named Intrepid. The balloon was of 25,000 cubic feet, made of India silk with linen cordage and rigging. The 1st Balloon Corps had its first balloon.

The usefulness of this new balloon was highlighted when on 24 September 1862 at Falls Church, Virginia, Thaddeus S. Lowe directed Union artillery on the Confederate army from a tethered balloon by means of a crude telegraph system (flags). The use of the balloon during this particular battle enhanced the accuracy of the cannon fire to a large degree, playing a significant part in the outcome, and again it also served well as an observation platform. At the crossing of the Rappahannock River on 11 December 1862, the balloon was used to great effect, enabling the Union army to cross almost unhindered. During the Battle of Fair Oaks the balloon was paramount in being one of the main reasons for the Union army's success. The service developed slowly and although a number of balloons were used, only nine other aeronauts were ever employed and none of them was given military status. The army, although accepting their services, refused to accept them into their ranks. Thaddeus Lowe was the one exception, which highlighted the barrier between the old ways and progress. At one time Thaddeus Lowe had seven balloons in the corps ranging from 15,000 to 32,000 cubic foot capacity.

Moving the balloons to different places started to become a problem. As a large number of the battles appeared to be happening around the Potomac

Above: Thaddeus Lowe inflating his observation balloon during the American Civil War.

Right: Professor Lowe launching his balloon named Intrepid.

The balloon Intrepid lifting off.

River area, it was decided to operate observation stations along its banks. Supplying the various stations was carried out by means of a coal barge that was towed by a tug, or occasionally by means of paddles or oars. The Balloon Corps made full use of this barge to transport their balloon and equipment to the various areas of war, thus creating in effect the first 'aircraft carrier'.

The Rough Riders on San Juan Hill.

After the Civil War, the Balloon Corps was shuttled between various departments of the army, the Topographical Engineers, the quartermaster and then the Corps of Engineers, where it slowly faded into obscurity. Change was not something liked by the army, and although somewhat grudgingly it accepted that the balloon had played a part in the war, the diehards were not convinced that the balloon had a future in the military.

It wasn't until 1891 that radical new thoughts started to open the minds of the United States military hierarchy. The Americans up to this point had showed little or no interest in the balloon, even though it had proved its worth during the Civil War. However, the American army in Cuba during the Spanish-American War of 1898 used one balloon. The whole episode was a debacle. The troops arrived on 22 June 1898, but the balloon corps did not arrive until 28 June. The equipment for the balloon was contained in seven wagons and when it was finally unpacked, it was found that the varnish had softened to the degree that nearly all the panels of the balloon were stuck together. Only after extensive repairs had been made and the balloon inflated was it possible to make any ascents. Even so, there was a

Left: Balloon used at the Battle of San Juan Hill.

Below: The Wright Brothers' first flight in 1903.

great deal of trepidation on the part of the observers as to whether or not the repairs would hold. Three ascents were made altogether, one of which was during the famous Battle of San Juan Hill in which it successfully directed artillery fire, but only a matter of days later the balloon was totally destroyed by enemy gunfire when it was flown close to the enemy lines. Interest in the balloon once again waned rapidly and its development was put on hold.

While the rest of the Western world was still concentrating on the use of balloons, in America two brothers, Wilbur and Orville Wright, were about to turn the world of aviation upside down. On 17 December 1903, 4 miles south of Kitty Hawk, North Carolina, the two brothers carried out the first confirmed powered flight of an aeroplane. This almost immediately relegated the balloon into second place and opened the way for a new concept of aerial transport, be it for war or peaceful purposes.

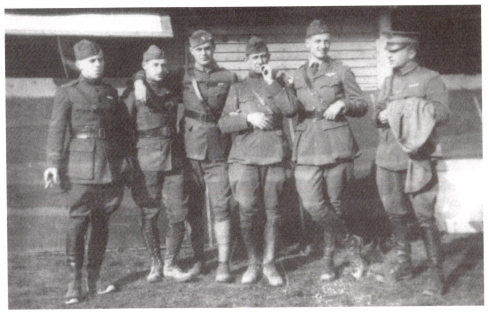

Right: Colonel Charles deForest Chandler USAS.

Below: Officers of the 1st Observation Group.

9

Within the United States military, however, the balloon was now, somewhat belatedly and surprisingly, starting to attract attention again as an observation platform and Congress found some money for balloon development. A small balloon facility was opened at Fort Myer, Virginia to look into the possibilities of the use of the balloon within the military. After a great deal of study by a group of dedicated enthusiasts such as army Major Frank Lahm – the first American to receive a balloonist's licence – and in 1907 an Aeronautical Division was created within the Office of the Chief Signal Officer in Washington by Captain Charles deForest Chandler.

One year later, the near-defunct balloon facility at Fort Myer was transferred to Fort Omaha, Nebraska and a balloon school opened under the command of newly-promoted Major Charles DeF. Chandler. The location of the school was perfect, there was no smoke from nearby cities or towns to pollute the air and it was situated on a large plain, giving the students and instructors a superb panoramic view. It was also relatively close to the General Staff College at Fort Leavenworth, Kansas, where officers could be billeted while attending courses at the balloon school.

In France, the French had developed the Caquot observation balloon, named after its inventor French army Captain Albert Caquot. The balloon was a near oval shape with fins on the tail that enabled the balloon to attain excellent stability at heights of up to 4,000ft and in winds of 60 miles per hour, thus creating an extremely stable observation platform. Nicknamed 'the Elephant' by its ground crews, the Caquot balloon was made of a very strong rubberized fabric which enabled it to resist a certain amount of sustained machine-gun fire. The only drawback was that it was inflated by means of highly flammable hydrogen gas which, if ignited, would turn the balloon almost instantaneously into a raging inferno.

In the meantime, the development of the aircraft in the United States had continued its slow plodding progress after the initial excitement and speculation as to what this new machine could offer had almost disappeared. In 1907, the president of the American Aero Club, Cortlandt Bishop, sent an article from the magazine *Scientific American* to President Teddy Roosevelt. Roosevelt was impressed and asked the US War Department to look into the use of the aircraft as a military machine, but it was ultimately left to the Europeans to look upon this new invention as a weapon of war. America had given the world the first aeroplane and then, to all intents and purposes, appear to have abandoned it as a serious military machine. They had watched with great interest the development of the air forces of the European nations as they fought over the skies of Europe, but they

Rescuers going to the crash of the Wright Flyer at Fort Myer in which Orville Wright was injured and Lieutenant Thomas Selfridge killed.

themselves had done very little to form their own air force. Fortunately there were a number of people in America who had the foresight to see that the aeroplane had an important part to play as a leading weapon of war and took measures to see that their country would not be left behind.

Wright Flyer being removed from its hangar at Fort Myer, 1919.

Wright Flyer being demonstrated at Fort Myer.

The War Department had a number of meetings with Wilbur Wright regarding the purchase of an aircraft. At the beginning of 1907 they invited tenders for an aircraft with the following specifications:

1. The aircraft should have a speed of at least 40mph,
2. Carry two persons with a combined weight of 350lb,
3. Have enough fuel for at least a one-hour duration,
4. Be able to fly non-stop for 125 miles,
5. Be controllable in flight in any direction and return to its starting-point and alight without damage.

Of the forty-one bids submitted, only three were accepted. Trials were started at Fort Myer in Virginia in August 1908 and the Wright Brothers Flier had been modified to carry two persons and the pusher engine power increased to 30hp. During the trials one of the bracing wires on the Wright Flyer came loose and was struck by the propeller, causing it to crash. Orville Wright, who was flying the aircraft, was seriously injured but his passenger, Lieutenant Thomas E. Selfridge, was killed. The following year, after the Wright Flyer had been rebuilt and modified, it was flown once again by Orville Wright, this time very successfully. The army awarded the Wright

Lieutenant Benjamin Foulois.

Curtiss JN-2 being prepared for flight at North Island airfield, San Diego, California.

Brothers a $25,000 contract and at the end of August they delivered the army's first aircraft: Aeroplane No.1.

As part of the contract the Wright Brothers had to give flight instruction to two army officers, Lieutenants Frank Lahm and Frederick Humphreys, and they completed their training at College Park, Maryland. A third officer, Lieutenant Foulois, joined them for training but the winter weather caused the whole programme to be moved to Fort Houston, San Antonio, Texas, where Foulois completed his flight training. The army now had three qualified pilots, but because of lack of funding all three were returned to their units where they stayed until 1911 when the training was reactivated and five new aircraft purchased. Aircraft No.1 by this time was worn out and was taken out of service, but today it is on display in the Smithsonian Institute.

In 1912, with the arrival of summer, operations were moved back to College Park where several other pilots were trained. It was also being used to carry out tests, which included altitude flights to over 4,000ft, a number of cross-country flights, aerial photography and the testing of a new bombsight. At the end of November, the school had grown to fourteen officers (all pilots), thirty-nine enlisted men and nine aircraft, a mixture of Wright, Burgess and Curtiss. With the arrival of winter the school moved once again: the Wright aircraft and their crews this time to Augusta, Georgia, and the Curtiss aircraft with their crews to Glenn Curtiss's private airfield on North Island, San Diego. The airfield on North Island was later given to the army by Glenn Curtiss and became the army's Aviation School.

The army's safety record up to this point was not good. Twenty-eight aircraft had been purchased, nine had been destroyed in crashes and of the forty men who had been trained as pilots, eleven had died in aircraft-related accidents. At the beginning of 1914 an investigation into the fatal accidents resulted in the remaining eleven Curtiss and Wright pusher-type aircraft being condemned as unairworthy and the type being unsuitable for military use. This in effect left the army with only five aircraft and they were all in need of servicing and repairs. Luckily Glenn Martin had a sports plane that was easily converted into a dual-control trainer and so the army immediately placed an order for seventeen of these aircraft. Known as the 'J' model, it became the forerunner of a series of aircraft affectionately known as the 'Jenny'.

Following legislation that recognized army aviation as a permanent member of the military organization, it was placed under the umbrella of the Signal Corps. By July 1914 the aviation section had 60 officers and 260 enlisted men and despite continuing lack of funds, by 1915 they had expanded considerably.

Chapter Two

Interest in aviation as far as the navy was concerned was nurtured by Captain Washington Irving Chambers, USN, later regarded by many as the father of US Naval Aviation. Chambers had attended the International Air Meet at Belmont Park, New York during October 1910 and had met designers, manufacturers and pilots. So impressed was Chambers that he persuaded the Department of the Navy to part with $25,000 for the acquisition of two aircraft. Chambers wasted no time in getting things moving and one month later on 14 November 1910, aided by a civilian pilot named Eugene Ely from the Curtiss plant, carried out the first ship-to-shore flight.

A specially-built structure was constructed over the forecastle of the scout cruiser USS *Birmingham* (CL-2) that was anchored off Old Point Comfort, Virginia. Eugene Ely, in a 50hp Curtiss pusher, opened the throttle of the engine and roared down the 83ft long, 24ft wide platform with a downward slope of 5 degrees, and into the air. The aircraft dropped momentarily, the propeller just clipping the water, and then climbed into the air. Ely had intended to fly to New York, but because of some minor damage to the tips of the propeller, headed the aircraft for the shore and made a safe landing. Chambers had proved that the aircraft was a viable investment, but he still had to convince the sceptics.

Captain Irving Washington Chambers, USN.

While these doubters were still pondering over the flight, Chambers arranged for a second demonstration, only this time the aircraft was to <u>land</u> on the deck of a ship, then take off again. On 18 January 1911, Ely took off from a field at Tanforan, just south of San Francisco, and headed for the armoured cruiser USS *Pennsylvania* (ACR-4). The ship, which was anchored off Hunter's Point in San Francisco Bay, had had a somewhat larger platform built over its stern. Like the platform built on the USS *Birmingham* it was built with a 5-degree slope, but in addition there were twenty-two ropes stretched across the deck, each weighted down with 50lb sandbags. The idea was that the three pairs of steel hooks fitted on the undercarriage bar beneath the aircraft would catch the ropes and bring the aircraft to a halt. The demonstration was a complete success, but it was still to take a number of years and more experiments before the sceptics were completely convinced.

After these flights, Glenn Curtiss offered flight training to a naval officer at no charge to the navy. The navy, quick to take advantage of

Eugene Ely taking off from the USS *Birmingham*, the first flight taken from a ship.

such an offer, sent Lieutenant T.G. 'Spuds' Ellyson to San Diego to carry out flight training. After successfully completing flying training he was awarded his brevet and became Naval Aviator No.1. The navy then set up a small flight training camp at Annapolis, Maryland under the command of Lieutenant Ellyson and purchased three hydroplane aircraft, two Curtiss and one Wright. As part of the purchasing agreement, both companies had to train one pilot and one mechanic. The first of these newly-qualified naval aviators to arrive was Lieutenant John H. Towers (later Admiral Towers) to set up the training schedule.

The navy was also the first American military force to display the aircraft's practical use. On 6 October 1912, Lieutenant John H. Towers, flying a Curtiss A-2 floatplane, took off from the water at Annapolis and remained in the air for six hours, ten minutes and thirty-five seconds, emphasizing the use of the aircraft for reconnaissance purposes.

The US Marine Corps had been watching the navy's progress carefully and the Corps' commandant, Major General William P. Biddle, decided that it would be a good idea if the Corps had their own pilots. The first to arrive at Annapolis for training was Lieutenant Alfred A. Cunningham

Eugene Ely landing on board the USS *Pennsylvania*.

Eugene Ely about to touch down on the deck of the USS *Pennsylvania*.

Eugene Ely being congratulated by Captain Pond of the USS *Pennsylvania* after his historic landing aboard the ship. Note the inflated bicycle tyres.

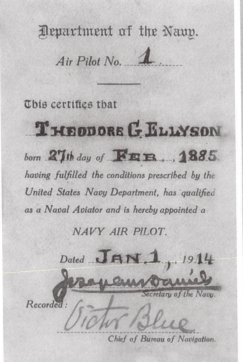

Lieutenant 'Spuds' Ellyson's pilot's licence as No.1 aviator in the US Navy.

on 22 May 1912, but he was told that there were no serviceable aircraft. He then sought permission to travel to Marblehead, 20 miles north of Boston, to the Burgess Company, where they were building Wright hydroplanes. The instructors there took him on and after only two and a half hours of instruction, he soloed on 20 August 1912. The second of the Marines to report for training was Lieutenant Bernard L. Smith, who reported to Annapolis. The three aircraft there were now serviceable and, like Cunningham, Lieutenant Smith passed after only three hours of instruction.

As part of Fleet manoeuvres in January 1913, the United States navy set up an aviation camp on Fisherman's Point, Guantanamo Bay, Cuba. The aircraft flew scouting missions and carried out spotting sorties looking for mines and submerged submarines. So successful were they that a great deal of interest was generated within the navy towards this new addition to the navy's operational capabilities, but unfortunately the major and influential interest that was needed to push it forward was missing.

At the end of 1913, however, thirteen naval aviators had successfully completed their training, including three Marine Corps pilots. Because of the interest now being taken in flying, the majority of those who passed out were retained as instructors, but the interest in aviation generated by the camp was to be its downfall. It was becoming too small, and so in January 1914 the United States navy opened its first Naval Air Station at Pensacola, Florida. The camp at Annapolis was closed down and the staff, including the Marine Corps personnel, was moved to Pensacola. The training of pilots and ground crews was informal, had no sense of discipline or purpose and consisted mainly of graduates from Annapolis. The curriculum was unstructured, only covered the technical side of aviation and for some unknown reason omitted fundamental navigation and seamanship. It has to be remembered, though, that aviation was something completely new and there were very few skilled personnel to teach the students. Everyone was on a learning curve, including the instructors. Slowly but surely, the curriculum was tightened up and the standard of instruction improved.

The first American army squadron, 1st Aero Squadron at Fort Sam Houston, Texas, consisting of eight aircraft made up of Curtiss JN-3s and R-4s, had been put together in 1913 when it was feared that there was going to be a revolution in Mexico. The pilots – Lieutenants Eric L. Ellington, Loren H. Call, Charles J. Boeha, Fred Seydel, Ralph Jones, H.M. Kelly, Moss L. Love, Townsend F. Dove and J.C. Morrow – had been taken from the aviation school at San Diego to make up the squadron, which was formed at Columbus, New Mexico and put on standby in case they were needed. Then in April 1914 the squadron, under the command of Lieutenant (later Brigadier General) Benjamin Foulois, was ordered to Galveston, Texas to take part with the navy in the assault on Veracruz. When they arrived at Fort Crocket, Galveston, they were told that the ships that were to take them to Mexico had sailed without them. Furious, Lieutenant Foulois and the 1st Aero Squadron turned around and headed back to the school at San Diego without even unpacking their aircraft. In reality the whole mission had no chance of success had it even begun. The aircraft could not fly over the Sierra Madre Mountains that rose to 12,000ft and would not have been able to withstand the violently turbulent air currents that whirled around the Sierras.

The rumblings of revolution continued in Mexico, and it was left to the US Navy to become involved. The first message that mobilized the Naval Aviation section into action was sent to Pensacola on Sunday, 19 April 1914. It was sent to Captain William Sims while he was having lunch aboard the

Members of the 1st Aero Squadron.

Members of the 1st Aero Squadron. Left to right: Lieutenants Clinton Russell, John Brooks and Captain Benjamin Foulois. The gentleman on the right is unknown.

JN-2 taking off from Columbus, New Mexico.

Aeronautical Training Ship, the cruiser USS *Birmingham*, with her captain Lieutenant Commander Henry 'Rum' Mustin. The message read:

**DIRECT COMMANDING OFFICER
AERONAUTIC STATION**

**REPORT YOU FOR SERVICE ONE
AEROPLANE SECTION**

**CONSISTING TWO FLYING BOATS OR
HYDROAEROPLANES**

ONE SPARE BOAT OR PONTOON TWO SPARE MOTORS. TWO HANGARS, TENTAGE FOR PERSONAL AND OTHER NECESSARY SPARES AND OUTFITS. LIEUTENANT TOWERS IN CHARGE WITH LIEUTENANT SMITH AND ENSIGN CHEVALIER AND TEN MECHANICIENS.

Lieutenant Commander Mustin went on deck to inspect the facilities required for such a mission. The USS *Birmingham* had been in the public eye on 14 November 1910 when Eugene Ely had flown a Curtiss pusher from her deck, only this time aircraft were going to have to fly from her deck

American ships in the bay at Veracruz, Mexico.

under battle conditions. If successful, it would be a great boost for naval aviation; if not, it could spell the death knell. However, it was decided to use floatplanes instead as the ships would be anchored off Veracruz. After his initial inspection, Mustin realized that the ship had no facilities for hoisting

Lieutenant Bellinger's aircraft being lowered into the water for an observation flight.

the aircraft in or out of the water, so lowering booms were quickly installed on the mainmast to serve as derricks.

The unstable situation in Mexico suddenly reached its zenith when a message was received in Washington that a German merchant ship was to dock on 21 April at Veracruz with a cargo of weapons and ammunition for General Victoriano Huerta's troops.

The USS *Birmingham*, with an aviation detachment aboard consisting of three pilots, three aircraft and twelve enlisted men all under the command of Lieutenant John H. Towers, was immediately dispatched to join the Atlantic Fleet forces operating off the coast of Tampico. Meanwhile, the USS *Mississippi*, under the command of Rear Admiral Frank Jack Fletcher with a second aviation detachment aboard, was dispatched to assist in the military operations at Veracruz. On 21 April 1914, the Fleet landing force lost nineteen men to snipers from the revolutionary army when they attempted to seize Veracruz.

The city of Veracruz was a contrast of extremes. The pastel-painted buildings with their green and pink balconies set against a background of deep azure blue skies presented a beautiful sight, but the vast majority of

Crew about to go on an aerial flight over Veracruz.

the city had no sanitation, disease was rampant and the whole area reeked repulsively of rotting refuse and human waste. This cesspool of a city was what the US Navy and Marines were about to try to take.

The USS *Mississippi* launched her first observation flight, an AB-3 flying boat flown by Lieutenant (junior grade) P.N.L. Bellinger,[1] over the harbour of Veracruz to search for mines. Two days later Bellinger made a second flight, this time accompanied by an observer Ensign W.D. LaMont, to photograph the harbour.

On 2 May 1914, the USS *Mississippi* launched a third flight, this time in a Curtiss C-3 (AH-3) floatplane, to search for enemy troops reported near El Tejar. After flying for more than fifty minutes they returned to the ship having seen nothing but American army troops, but what they had done was record the first American aerial mission under military conflict conditions. Four days later, on 6 May 1914, Bellinger, with Lieutenant (junior grade) Saufley[2] as observer, flew a reconnaissance flight over enemy positions near Veracruz. Their aircraft was hit by rifle fire from the 'invisible' enemy; the first marks of combat on a US naval aircraft.

Over the next few days, Bellinger and Saufley carried out several more observation flights over the town, more as a show of strength than a serious threat, but fortunately without any further incidents. The flights were merely token gestures in support of the 'bluejackets' who were already in the town mopping up resistance.

An aviation camp was set up on the beach and the work of scouting the area continued. After flying a number of missions during the next month with no results, the number of flights was reduced to one per day. The crews of the aircraft were looking for ghosts and they knew it. The navy felt that it was a waste of time and effort to continue, but were told that they would have to stay until the army was able to get some of their Air Service aircraft there. However, this was not the first time aircraft had been considered for

---

1. Bellinger later commanded one of the four NC aircraft, the NC-1, in the US Navy's successful attempt to be first to fly across the Atlantic, although only one, the NC-4, was to complete the trip. Bellinger also became an admiral in the Second World War.

2. Lieutenant (junior grade) Saufley was to lose his life in an AH-9 on 9 June 1916 when his aircraft crashed into the sea off Santa Rosa Island, Pensacola. It happened during an endurance flight after the aircraft had been in the air for eight hours and fifty-one minutes. The cause is not known, but was possibly engine failure.

USN aircraft flying over Veracruz with USN ships at anchor in the harbour.

use in a military capacity against the Mexicans. The first recorded use was in February 1911 when a US government pilot carried out a reconnaissance flight over the rebel forces at Ciudad Juárez but did not carry out any aggressive action.

The results from the Veracruz incident made nonsense of the attempt to provide air support for ground troops, and highlighted the lack of commitment at the time by the American government to the future of air power. However, it did spur the aircraft manufacturers (only twelve of the manufacturers were capable of producing what could loosely be called military aircraft at that time) into later looking at the problem with serious intent. Some 400 aircraft were produced during 1916, and not one could be considered to be a pure military aircraft.

Then early in 1916, one José Doroteo Arango Arámbula, also known as Francisco 'Pancho' Villa, appeared on the scene in Mexico. Pancho Villa was born in 1878 in the small village of San Juan del Rio in the Mexican state of Durango. He began his career as a bandit in Northern Mexico in the early 1900s, rustling cattle and holding up stagecoaches. By 1910 he had turned his 'talents' into fighting a revolution, being largely responsible for the overthrow of President Porfirio Díaz, who went into exile in May 1911, and becoming the sworn enemy of General Venustiano Carranza, head of the de facto Constitutionalist government of Mexico.

Uneducated as he was, Pancho Villa could see that there was a place for the aircraft as an observation platform and possibly a bomber. With this in mind he invited an

Pancho Villa.

American by the name of Edwin C. Parsons, later to become a member of the famous Lafayette Escadrille, to come to Mexico and train some of his officers to fly. Parsons, the son of a wealthy businessman from Springfield, Massachusetts, had been taught to fly by the aircraft manufacturer Glenn L. Martin and had been working in the film industry as a stuntman/pilot among other things. At the beginning of 1913, together with a friend of his, another pilot by the name of Jean de Villa, Parsons went to Mexico to train some of Pancho Villa's officers to fly. For nearly a year the two Americans desperately tried to train the officers but to no avail. The major problem facing the two instructors was the simple act of getting the potential aviators just to set one foot inside the cockpit. They were terrified of the machine and only one of the officers could be said to have grasped the rudiments of flying. After a number of accidents, which angered Pancho Villa, mainly because he couldn't understand why they happened, the two Americans

Pancho Villa on horseback.

decided to leave. Their decision was hastened when a friendly German agent operating in Mexico warned the two men to leave, as Pancho Villa was about to embark on a dangerous game that would involve the United States.

The two men headed for the border under the pretence of getting spares for the aircraft and never returned. It was while in Philadelphia some months later that Parsons heard of the formation of the Escadrille Américaine and so headed for France.

Later in 1914, Villa joined forces with Emiliano Zapata and marched into Mexico City, forcing General Carranza to flee to Veracruz. There Carranza joined forces with General Álvaro Obregón Salido (later to become the thirty-ninth president of Mexico) and nine months later retook the capital. The revolutionaries had, in fact, used an aeroplane piloted by a Mexican officer, Captain Gustavo Salinas, in an attack on General Victoriano Huerta's troops in April 1914. He had dropped a number of crude bombs on

Above left: Edwin C Parsons.

Above right: Emiliano Zapata, Villa's right-hand man.

Captain Gustavo Salinas (second left) with his aircraft.

Huerta's troops while they were defending the port city of Mazatlán, none of which caused any serious damage. In September of 1915, Pancho Villa then attacked Carranza's garrison at Agua Prieta and suffered heavy losses; his army of followers was decimated. Carranza, using aeroplanes flown by American mercenary pilots, repulsed this attack. Among these pilots was Didier Masson, a Frenchman who was also later to become a member of the legendary Lafayette Escadrille. Masson at one time even tried dropping a can of dynamite down the funnel of Huerta's one and only gunboat, the first attempt by an American aircraft to carry out an aerial bombing attack, but it was woefully unsuccessful. Mexico can lay claim to being one of the first countries to use aircraft in warfare, even though their pilots in the main were American mercenaries.

Although this was a Mexican problem, the garrison at Agua Prieta was on the US/Mexican border a few miles from Douglas, Arizona. So concerned were the residents of the town that the governor of Arizona asked the US Army for help, who then dispatched the 1st Aero Squadron to San Antonio, Texas. Pancho Villa in the meantime had fled back north

Above left: Didier Masson (left) with two unknown French pilots.

Above right: Didier Masson.

to regroup and reassess his situation. On 11 January 1916, Pancho Villa and a heavily-armed army of horsemen stopped a train not far from the town of Chihuahua and murdered nineteen Americans who were on board. Carranza, now recognized by the Americans as the legitimate ruler of Mexico, made a determined effort to finish Villa and went after him with a vengeance. The fact that America officially recognized Carranza as President of Mexico so incensed Villa that on 9 March 1916, with between 500 and 1,000 men (the exact figure is not known), he attacked the town of Columbus, New Mexico, burning homes, killing eighteen American soldiers and civilians, and wounding seven others. This was the first foreign invasion of the United States since 1812, and the last. The United States Cavalry chased Villa back across the border. On 10 March 1916, President Woodrow Wilson ordered General John 'Black Jack' Pershing to mount a Punitive Expedition of some 10,000 troops and the 1st Aero Squadron into Mexico to find and destroy Pancho Villa. For more than a year the army and 1st Aero Squadron pursued Villa through deserts and over mountains, but to no avail.

STRIKE FROM THE AIR

During General Pershing's Punitive Expedition, the 1st Aero Squadron, consisting of eight Curtiss JN-3s under the command of Captain Benjamin D. Foulois, had been assigned to provide some form of air support. The aircraft were based on the Johnson Ranch, Casas Grandes where the reconnaissance flights took off. As gun platforms the Curtiss JN-3 aircraft were totally ineffective, but in the area of communications, reconnaissance and courier work they had a role to play. Because of the vast distances and the number of troop columns that were spread out across the terrain, the only way Pershing could keep in touch with his commanders was by using aircraft. Radios at the time were of very low power and the mountains created static, which made transmissions almost inaudible and consequently ineffective. The mountains protecting the Casas Grandes of Mexico were up to 12,000ft high, but because of the hot, dry air and the violent turbulence it created, the Curtiss JN-3s were unable to fly over them. In fact, most of the time they had great difficulty in staying airborne even close to the ground, but despite all these difficulties the 1st Aero Squadron managed to prove that the aircraft did have its place in war, although not to General Pershing's full satisfaction.

Pilots of the 1st Aero Squadron while on the hunt for Pancho Villa.

Curtiss JN-3 at Johnson's Ranch at Casas Grandes.

The expedition lasted just over a year and it was not only the soldiers and airmen that took a beating from the torturous heat and terrain, but also the aircraft, whose wings and undercarriage suffered badly from the sagebrush and heavy landings on the rough terrain. In fact, at the end of the expedition, only two of the original eight aircraft could actually be flown and they were deemed unsafe to fly. The aircraft and their pilots were returned to their base at Columbus, New Mexico, reflecting on what they had learned. The then Secretary of the Navy, Josephus Daniels, announced to Congress that the point had been reached 'where aircraft must form a large part of our forces for offensive and defensive operations.'

In May 1917, the balloon school was put under the command of Major Frank Lahm (Major Chandler having been posted to Washington to the Office of the Chief Signal Officer), but in September, Major Lahm, together with Major Chandler, was sent to France to observe balloon training and combat deployment on the Western Front. During this period Lahm and Chandler carried out a number of missions themselves, taking the observation balloons to heights of over 1,500ft. They had watched helplessly from the ground on a number of other occasions when German fighter aircraft attacked defenceless balloons, highlighting the dangers that the balloonists and their ground crews faced every time they ascended to carry out spotting and reconnaissance missions.[3]

The body of Pancho Villa hanging out of his car after being assassinated.

---

3 Pancho Villa was never captured. He was assassinated, together with his secretary Colonel Miguel Trillo and three of his bodyguards, on 11 July 1923 in Guadalupe, a suburb of Hidalgo del Parral, Chihuahua, Mexico, while slowly driving in his Dodge automobile through the town towards his ranch at Canutillo. Seven assassins armed with rifles stood in front of his car and opened fire, among whom was Jesús Salas Barraza, who said on his release after serving only six months of a twenty-year sentence: 'I'm not a murderer, I rid humanity of a monster.' The remaining six assassins were also sentenced to twenty years but only served six months.

Chapter Three

It is often thought that it was the sinking of the 32,000-ton ocean liner RMS *Lusitania* off the coast of Ireland by the German submarine *U-20* on 7 May 1915 that brought the United States of America into the First World War, but it was only one of a number of incidents that was responsible. The *Lusitania* incident arose when the commander of the *U-20*, *Kapitänleutnant* Walther Schwieger, had seen a ship some 14 miles distant and identified her, according to his 1914 copy of *Jane's Fighting Ships* and the *Naval Annual*, as

The submarine *U-20* that sank RMS *Lusitania*.

U-20.

an armed merchant cruiser believed by Germany to be in use as a troopship. In his boat's log Schwieger wrote the following:

> 2:20 P.M. Directly in front of us I sighted four funnels and masts of steamer at right angles to our course, coming from south-southwest and going toward Galley Head. It is recognised as a passenger steamer.

> 2:25 P.M. Have advanced eleven metres toward steamer, in hope it will change course along the Irish coast.

> 2:35 P.M. Steamer turns, takes direction to Queenstown, and thereby makes it possible for us to approach it for shot. We proceed at high speed in order to reach correct position.

> 3:10 P.M. Torpedo shot at distance of 700 metres, going 3 metres below the surface. Hits steering centre behind bridge.

As Schwieger peered through his periscope, he continued to dictate for the log to his First Officer *Oberleutnant* Rudolph Zentner who stood beside him:

> Unusually great detonation with large cloud of smoke and debris shot above the funnels. In addition to torpedo, a second explosion must have taken place. (Boiler, coal or powder?)

RMS *Lusitania* leaving New York on her fateful voyage.

RMS *Lusitania*.

Kapitänleutnant Walter Schwieger of *U-20*.

Bridge and part of the ship where the torpedo hit are torn apart and fire follows. The ship stops and very quickly leans over to starboard, at the same time sinking at the bow. It looks as though it would capsize in a short time. There is great confusion on board. Boats are cleared and many of them lowered into the water. Many boats, fully loaded, drop down into the water bow or stern first and capsize. The boats on the port side cannot be made clear because of the slanting position. At the front of the ship the name LUSITANIA in gold letters can be seen. The chimneys are painted black. The stern flag is not hoisted. The ship was going about twenty miles an hour.

Twenty minutes later the liner plunged to the bottom of the Atlantic, leaving 1,198 passengers and crewmen, among them 35 children and 135 Americans (among the latter was the multi-millionaire Alfred G. Vanderbilt) to die in its cold waters. There were 761 survivors of this horrendous attack. Schwieger maintained that he never realized that the ship was the *Lusitania* until, on looking through his periscope, he saw the ship's name in gold letters on the bows as she was sinking.

On his return to Wilhelmshaven, Germany, Schwieger was warmly congratulated by other members of the submarine fraternity, but received a severe reprimand from the Kaiser for having sunk the liner. This angered many of the submarine commanders, as they maintained that Schwieger was just following the orders issued by the Kaiser's military advisors <u>and</u> with his full knowledge.

On 1 May, the day the *Lusitania* had left New York on her fateful voyage, an American oil tanker, the SS *Gulflight*, was struck by a torpedo from the German submarine *U-30* commanded by *Kapitänleutnant* Erich von Rosenberg-Gruszczynski off the Scilly Isles. Three of the tanker's crew were killed in the incident. The captain, Alfred Gunter, died later of a heart

The American tanker *Gulflight* sinking at the bows.

The American tanker *Gulflight* showing the torpedo damage to her bows.

attack and two other crew members died when they jumped overboard, and although the ship was severely damaged, she managed to limp back to port under her own steam. The Germans claimed it was a case of mistaken identity and apologized profusely, but the *New York Times* bannered the incident as a 'Flagrant violation of our rights'.

These violations were further aggravated by the sinking of the 15,000-ton White Star transatlantic passenger liner SS *Arabic*, again off the coast of Southern Ireland, on 19 August 1915 by the German submarine *U-24* under the command of *Kapitänleutnant* Herbert Schneider. The liner, with 429 passengers and crew aboard, was en route to New York when she was torpedoed. Forty-four passengers died in the incident, three of them Americans, when the liner sank in less than ten minutes after being struck by the torpedo. The German explanation, which the Americans totally rejected, was that the submarine was in the process of a perfectly 'legitimate' act of war, sinking the British merchant ship SS *Dunsley* by shellfire when the SS *Arabic* appeared on the scene.

According to the German U-boat commander Schneider, the liner appeared to change her course and he was convinced that his submarine was about to be rammed and had fired a torpedo at the *Arabic* in self-defence. This incident was followed shortly afterwards by the sinking of the 10,920-ton liner SS *Hesperian* off Fastnet on 6 September 1915 by the submarine *U-20* with the loss of thirty-two lives. The *U-20*, commanded by *Kapitänleutnant* Schwieger who earlier that year had sunk the RMS *Lusitania*, again pleaded mistaken identity. No sooner had the crisis over these atrocities been averted than news about the sinking of the Italian liner

The liner SS *Arabic*.

Above: SS *Dunsley*, sunk by the submarine *U-24*.

Right: *Kapitänleutnant* Schneider, commander of the submarine U-24 that sank the SS *Arabic*.

SS *Ancona* by the Austro-Hungarian submarine *U-38* under the command of *Kapitänleutnant* Max Valentiner came through. The Austro-Hungarian Empire was allied to Germany at the time, and the incident was particularly brutal in as much as the liner was fired upon and sank while the passengers were in the process of trying to escape into the lifeboats.

Although these terrible acts of aggression on unarmed ocean liners and an oil tanker had a significant impact upon America's relationship with Germany, it was an accumulation of these and a number of other incidents that collectively would be instrumental in bringing the United States of America into the war. The final act of treachery and deception, however, was the interception of the now infamous Zimmermann telegram.

The telegram, from Arthur Zimmermann, Germany's Foreign Minister, to the German Ambassador von Eckardt in Mexico, had been intercepted by British Naval Intelligence. The head of British Naval Intelligence at the time was Admiral Sir Reginald Hall who, together with his small team of cryptologists, decoded the message and handed it over to the American ambassador in London, Walter Page. At the same time the British team also handed over the 'key' to unlocking Germany's cryptic messages,

Arthur Zimmermann and the coded telegram.

TELEGRAM RECEIVED.

FROM 2nd from London # 5747.

"We intend to begin on the first of February unrestricted submarine warfare. We shall endeavor in spite of this to keep the United States of America neutral. In the event of this not succeed- ing, we make Mexico a proposal of alliance on the following basis: make war together, make peace together, generous financial support and an under- standing on our part that Mexico is to reconquer the lost territory in Texas, New Mexico, and Arizona. The settlement in detail is left to you. You will inform the President of the above most secretly as soon as the outbreak of war with the United States of America is certain and add the suggestion that he should, on his own initiative, invite Japan to immediate adherence and at the same time mediate between Japan and ourselves. Please call the President's attention to the fact that the ruthless employment of our submarines now offers the prospect of compelling England in a few months to make peace." Signed, ZIMMERMANN.

The decoded Zimmermann telegram.

thus enabling the United States Intelligence organization to decode any German messages intercepted by them. It was said later that the decoding of the message was to have consequences that no one at the time could ever have envisaged.

The sending of the Zimmermann Telegram to the Mexican government in an attempt to

Admiral Sir Reginald Hall.

persuade Mexico to declare war on America was an attempt to postpone or slow down the transportation of armament and other war supplies to the British and their allies who were at war with Germany. If this could be achieved, then by doing so, it would tie up large numbers of American troops and arms and dramatically slow down the supplies to Europe. Germany's intention was to strangle the supply lines by carrying out unrestricted submarine warfare that they hoped would force Britain and France into submission. With encouraging successes on the Eastern Front, the German high command believed that they would be able to divert large numbers of troops to the Western Front, forcing the British and French to capitulate before American forces could be trained and shipped to Europe. The Zimmermann message read as follows:

Cartoon showing a German talking with a Mexican regarding making war together.

We intend to begin on the first of February unrestricted submarine warfare. We shall endeavor in spite of this to keep the United States of America neutral. In the event of this not succeeding, we make Mexico a proposal of alliance on the following basis: make war together, make peace together, generous financial support and an understanding on our part that Mexico is to reconquer the last territory in Texas, New Mexico, and Arizona. The settlement in detail is left to you. You will inform the President of the above most secretly as soon as the outbreak of war with the United States of America is certain and add the suggestion that he should, on his own initiative, invite Japan to immediate adherence and at the same time mediate between Japan and ourselves. Please call the President's attention to the fact that the ruthless employment of our submarines now offers the prospect of compelling England in a few months to make peace.

Signed,
Zimmerman.

The Mexican president, Venustiano Carranza, instructed a military commission to undertake a feasibility study of a war with America in an attempt to regain New Mexico and Arizona. It took the commission just a matter of days to conclude that it would not be possible to sustain an attack against American forces; neither would it be desirable for a number of reasons. The main reasons were as follows:

1. America was too powerful and too well armed.
2. The promise of financial and military aid from the Germans was extremely tenuous, especially in light of information stating that they would be unable to provide Mexico with enough gold to support the country's economical structure. Even if some financial aid was given, the Mexican government would have to purchase weapons, ammunition and other essential war supplies from neighbouring South American countries. These were the countries that had organized the Niagara Falls peace conference in 1914 to avoid a full-scale war between the United States and Mexico over the United States occupation of Veracruz. If Mexico were to enter war against the United States, it would strain relations with those nations.

3. The attempt would also put foreign relations with other countries in jeopardy.

President Venustiano Carranza decided that neutrality was the best option for Mexico and refused to even consider the offer.

The decoded Zimmermann telegram was immediately flashed to President Wilson, and despite the strenuous denials of the German government, essentially ended the uneasy peace that had existed between America and Germany.

On 3 February 1917, President Woodrow Wilson announced to the American Congress that all diplomatic relations with the German Empire had been severed. Even at this stage there was still uncertainty as to whether or not the United States would actually go to war, but on 18 March 1917 news came that was to inflame the American people even more. It was announced from London that three American steamships, the *City of Memphis*, *Illinois* and *Vigilancia*, had been sunk by a German submarine. The *City of Memphis* and *Vigilancia* were sunk without warning, resulting in a total loss of life of those on board. The exception was the oil tanker *Illinois* that was steaming through the English Channel on 18 March 1917 on her way home to Texas. She had a large pair of American flags and the initials 'U.S.A.' painted on her sides. A German submarine stopped the tanker, boarded, plundered and then destroyed her by setting off bombs in the oil compartments. The fate of the crew remains a mystery, but it is unlikely that the submarine commander would have killed them in cold blood; more likely they were left to their own fate in their lifeboats, which in the minds of many was tantamount to the same thing.

Two months later, on 2 April 1917, President Wilson asked Congress to declare that a state of war existed between the United States and Germany. By 6 April 1917, both houses had passed the resolution and the United States officially declared war. Some 25,000 men of the National Guard, along with some 2,000 sailors, were ordered to stand by and ready themselves for war. Congress then debated whether or not to introduce a draft system, but as one opponent, Champ Clark, the Speaker of the House of Congress, announced: 'In the estimation of Missourians, there is precious little difference between a conscript and a convict.' However, an act was passed ordering that men in their twenties must register for the draft of 5 June 1917 and on that day 9,660,000 men registered. On the morning of 20 July Secretary of War Newton D. Baker reached into a large glass jar containing 10,500 numbers, the largest number in any registration district, and took out

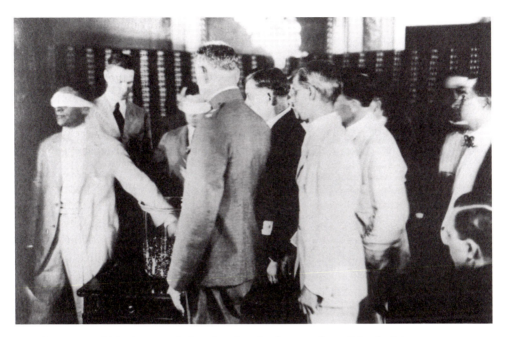

Secretary of War Newton Baker drawing the first number of the draft lottery.

a capsule bearing the number 258. The man holding that number in each district throughout the United States was the first to be called.

The problem that the United States of America now faced was that they were totally ill prepared for a war of this magnitude. They had been involved in a number of wars previously – e.g. the Spanish-American War, the Mexican War and the Philippine Insurrection – but they were no more than skirmishes compared to the war on which they were about to embark. The Germans, on the other hand, were a warring nation and had been at war in Europe for three years. They were well trained, well-equipped and battle-hardened, while the Americans were none of these. The United States had not used their inventiveness and ingenuity to any extent and up to this point had just been willing to sit and observe all that was happening in Europe.

Funds were made available to the president, and America was about to embark on the biggest test of its resources and manpower since the War of Independence, only this time Britain was to be its ally, not its enemy. By the time the war ended, America would have contributed in excess of $35,000,000,000 to the allied effort, 75,280 of her men would have been killed in action, 201,847 wounded and 8,668 would be prisoners of war or missing, all in a matter of just 18 months. The cost in resources was to be enormous, but the cost in human lives and suffering was to be incalculable.

It was also a time of anguish and heart-searching for the American people, mainly because of its multi-national population, which of course included a large number of Germans. It was discovered later that a number of German/Americans had returned to Germany to fight against Britain and France and, ultimately, their adopted country America. There was also a faction in America that encouraged the war, not out of any form of patriotism or hatred of the Germans, but because they were munitions and military hardware manufacturers and could see the means of making enormous profits.

There was a considerable amount of opposition from many groups in America, especially those that had family members whose ancestry was German. A great deal of pressure was put on the government to try to dissuade them from entering the war and for a while the government resisted the urge to get involved, but then the incidents described earlier occurred, forcing the United States to take action and join her ally Great Britain in the fight against Germany.

The American ambassador in Berlin, Mr James W. Gerard was recalled at the beginning of February, and the German ambassador to the United States, Count Johann von Bernstorff, had his passport returned and was asked to leave the country. The German government reacted immediately by cutting the telephone wires to the American Embassy in Berlin, interfering with all the mail, withholding the ambassador's passport and removing all his diplomatic privileges. They gave their reason for these acts as 'Holding the Ambassador hostage for the proper treatment of their Ambassador, Count Bernstorff, and the crews of the German ships in the United States.' The Americans replied that all official German property would be 'immune from seizure and their persons from molestation so long as they behaved themselves'. Encouraged by this, and the fact that they realized they were only aggravating the situation, the Germans released the American ambassador and his staff, who immediately returned to the United States. The Germans, now faced with an even greater adversary, went after nearly all the shipping in the Atlantic and among these a number of unarmed merchant ships, including the British hospital ship HMHS *Llandovery Castle* that was sunk by the submarine *U-86*.

On the night of 27 June 1918, the German submarine *U-86* had sighted the clearly-marked hospital ship 116 miles off Fastnet Rock, off the coast of southern Ireland. The ship was torpedoed and the ship's

Right: James Gerard, US
Ambassador to Germany, after
being recalled.

Below: HMHS *Llandovery
Castle*.

U-86 commanded by *Fregattenkapitän* Helmut Patzig who torpedoed HMHS *Llandovery Castle*.

crew took to the lifeboats. Fortunately there were no wounded aboard, but there were fourteen nurses. After surfacing, the commander of the submarine, *Fregattenkapitän* Helmut Patzig, spoke to the captain of the *Llandovery Castle*, Captain R.A. Sylvester, demanding to know about the eight American airmen that were on board. It was pointed out by Captain Sylvester that there were seven Canadian medical officers aboard and that was probably where the confusion lay (it was never discovered how the Germans knew who was on board). *Fregattenkapitän* Patzig, according to Captain Sylvester, turned away in anger, fired upon the survivors and then ran down the remaining lifeboats, smashing them like matchwood and spilling those left alive into the water. In all, 234 hospital staff, including the 14 nurses and 34 crew members died at the hands of *Fregattenkapitän* Helmut Patzig and his crew. The only survivors were those in the captain's lifeboat.

This unparalleled act of inhumanity caused outrage around the world, and there were violent anti-German demonstrations in Britain, America, Australia and South Africa. During some of the riots a number of German businesses were attacked and set on fire, but these effects were offset against another incident that this time concerned the Royal Navy. It came about through an attack on 18 August 1915 by the German submarine *U-27*, commanded by *Kapitänleutnant* Bernhard Wegener, on a British/Irish crewed cargo

Fregattenkapitän Helmut Patzig.

ship, the 6,359-ton SS *Nicosian*, which was carrying 780 mules and 80 American muleteers to Britain. The crew and muleteers had taken to the lifeboats after their ship had been stopped by *U-27* and were watching the submarine attempt to sink their vessel when a Royal Navy Q-ship (armed decoy ship used as an anti-submarine weapon) HMS *Baralong* arrived and sank the submarine with gunfire. Eleven members of the U-boat's crew, who survived the shelling, swam towards the now abandoned cargo ship instead of towards the *Baralong*. The crew of the Q-ship shot six of them as

SS *Nicosian*.

The Q-ship HMS *Baralong*.

they tried to get aboard; the remaining five, who had managed to clamber aboard the cargo ship, were later shot by British Marines after they had boarded the vessel. The damage to the *Nicosian* was slight and after a makeshift crew had been put back on board, a tow line was rigged between the two ships and the long haul to Avonmouth Docks, Bristol, began. They were joined later by an armed yacht that continued to escort both ships into port.

The incident, which was related to the US authorities some months later by the muleteers, caused an outcry from the German authorities and the pro-German press in the United States regarding the 'barbarity' of the British Royal Navy. This had come about when some of the surviving muleteers complained about the way the survivors of the U-boat had been shot after they had made their way aboard the *Nicosian*. The fact that the *Baralong* had saved the lives of the muleteers and the crew of the *Nicosian* seemed to have eluded all the survivors. This incident was further aggravated one month later, when HMS *Baralong* sank the submarine *U-41* with only two survivors. These two crewmen complained bitterly about the harsh treatment they said they had received at the hands of the Royal Navy. *U-41*

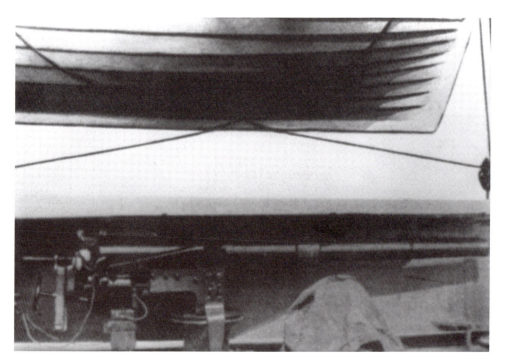

One of the concealed guns on the *Baralong*.

One of the concealed guns exposed and being readied for firing.

The German submarine
U-41 being approached
by the *Baralong*.

The German submarine *U-41* being shelled by the Q-ship *Baralong*.

SS *Urbino*.

was in the process of trying to sink the unarmed cargo ship, SS *Urbino*, when the *Baralong* arrived on the scene. Others conjectured that some public feeling at this stage was being aimed unfairly against the Royal Navy and, as a consequence, appeared to have forgotten about the war being waged by German submarines on unarmed liners and their civilian passengers, many of which were Americans. Cargo ships and their crews were the main targets, and the atrocities carried out on the crews of some of these unfortunate ships by some of the crews of these submarines angered people all over the world.

Chapter Four

In 1916 the US Congress had made available some funds for the development of the National Guard Aviation Units, a number of which were already in service using privately-owned aircraft. The first to take advantage of the funds was New York State, and within a matter of months the 1st Aero Company, NYNG (New York National Guard) based at Mineola was formed, with twenty-six officers and twelve enlisted ranks. With additional funding from the Aero Club of America, Mineola soon became the recognized airfield to which students from the Curtiss School at Newport News, Virginia and the Thomas School at Ithaca, NY, were sent to be qualified as Reserve Military Aviators. Because of the increased need for facilities to train these new

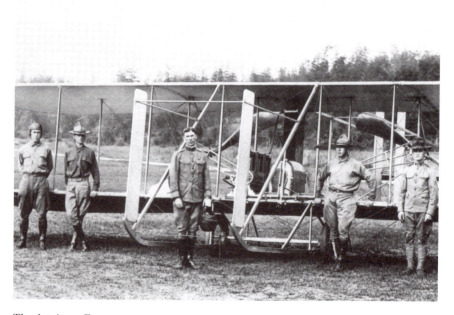

The 1st Aero Company.

aviators, the Governors Island Aviation School in New York was moved to Mineola to be amalgamated with the 1st Aero Company.

The number of foreign nationals who were living in France at the time of the outbreak of war and who volunteered to join the French military was overwhelming. The problem was that if they joined the French military, they would have to give up their national citizenship and become French citizens. To overcome this problem it was decided that if they were to join the Foreign Legion, also known as the Légion Étrangère, they could retain their own citizenship.

The beginning of May 1916 saw the appearance of the Lafayette Escadrille. The squadron was named after the Marquis de Lafayette who had helped the Colonials in their fight for independence against King George III of England in 1777. Now the Lafayette Escadrille was to fight alongside the British in their battle against the Germans. The Lafayette Escadrille was a French/American squadron flown by American volunteer pilots and regular French military pilots. It was to leave its mark in the First World War, helping to lay the foundations of an air force that was to become a world leader in later years.

The squadron started life in 1916 when young American adventurers decided to go and fight in the war in Europe. Some joined the RFC (Royal Flying Corps), while others joined the Foreign Legion. After training

Members of the Lafayette Escadrille. Left to right: Alfred de Laage de Meux, Choteau Johnson, Lawrence Rumsey, James McConnell, William Thaw, Raoul Lufbery, Kiffin Rockwell, Didier Masson, Norman Prince and Bert Hall.

Members of the Lafayette Escadrille. Left to right: James McConnell, Kiffin Rockwell, Georges Thenault, Norman Prince, Victor Chapman.

Members of the Lafayette Escadrille. Left to right, front: Didier Masson, Stephen Bigelow, Charles Johnson, William Thaw, Georges Thenault, Edwin Parsons, Thomas Hewitt, Harold Willis, Willis Haviland. Left to right, rear: Ray Bridgeman, Kiffin Rockwell, Henry Jones, David Peterson, William Dugan, Douglas MacMonagle, Walter Lovell, Antoine Maison de Rouge.

as pilots, they joined with French pilots in the Service Aéronautique. Initially there was a certain reluctance on the part of the French to accept American volunteer airmen. This had come about when earlier in the war, a German airman had joined the Service Aéronautique by means of a forged American passport. He caused considerable damage by feeding back intelligence on French air activities and aircraft before being discovered and shot as a spy.

In later years more than 4,000 men would lay claim to having flown with the Lafayette Escadrille, but in reality only 38 Americans and 4 French officers ever officially numbered among its flying personnel. (A complete list of all those who served in the Lafayette Escadrille appears at the end of the book.) What also set these men apart was the fact that they were nearly all college-educated and nearly all came from well-to-do families. They could have spent the rest of their lives in comfort, but chose to fight either out of a love of adventure or out of a sense of idealism.

William Thaw II, it is said, first proposed the idea of an all-American squadron of volunteers. Thaw had learned to fly at the Curtiss Flying School at Hammondsport, New York in 1913 and soon made himself a reputation as a pilot who could take chances and survive. His background was that of a young man who came from an extremely wealthy family and enjoyed all the comforts that money could buy. His father was a director

of a number of large companies including the Pennsylvania Railroad and allowed his son virtually unlimited funds. It was while on a visit to the Riviera that war broke out and Thaw immediately offered his services as an aviator to the French government. They turned him down on the grounds that they had more volunteers to fly than they had aircraft. They also did not want any foreigners in their army at that point in the war.

Thaw would not take no for an answer, and together with forty-two other Americans, he went to the Hôtel des Invalides on 21 August 1914 and enlisted in the Foreign Legion as a common *soldat*. He convinced the French authorities that he had served with the American forces in Mexico and explained his lack of drill

William Thaw.

experience by saying that he had been part of a guerrilla outfit. He was enrolled into the Second Regiment of the Foreign Legion and was sent to the Champagne sector. One American, Herman Chatkoff, who was trying to enlist, actually went as far as telling the French sergeant who was asking about any previous service he may have had that he had served for five years in the Salvation Army. He was sent to Battalion C of the 2nd Regiment. Within four weeks of joining the Foreign Legion, the American contingent, with only the basics of training, was sent to the front.

The Americans, with their 100lb of equipment on their backs, the straps of which were soon cutting into their shoulders, joined up with 4,000 other Legionnaires of various nationalities and were force-marched towards Reims. Soon every muscle in their aching bodies was screaming for rest and their feet were painful and swollen. Just before evening they reached Hautevillers where they were to be quartered for the night. Taking off their boots, they were greeted by the sight of large blisters and blood. A veteran Legionnaire showed them how to deal with the problem by taking a needle and strong thread and pushing it through the blister, cutting off the thread and leaving it to act as a drain. After treating all the blisters in the same fashion, he covered their feet in tallow, smeared more on the inside of their socks and their boots. Somehow it worked, and the following morning the battalion marched to the front.

It was while at the front, holding a section of the line at Verzenay, that Thaw came up with the idea of an all-American squadron of fighter aircraft after a squadron of German fighters had flown overhead. He voiced his ideas among the other American pilots that he knew, but that was as far as it got.

However, Thaw was not the only American who had had ideas about an all-American squadron. Norman Prince, a graduate lawyer from Harvard University who, like Thaw, had learned to fly in 1913, offered his services to the French government and was accepted. The idea never came to fruition until Thaw, after his second attempt at joining the French Aviation Service was successful, met up with Norman Prince and Bert Hall. One thing led to another, and the French authorities decided to include the American volunteers into one of their squadrons for training.

After a great deal of training, which took longer than normal because of the language barrier, the original members won their brevets, then other American volunteers arrived. After some discussion by representatives of both the American and French governments and the promise of financial support from a group of wealthy American businessmen, Squadron N.124

was formed. The fact that Paul Ayres Rockwell, brother of Kiffin Yates Rockwell and cousin of Robert, had married the daughter of Georges Leygues, President of the French Foreign Affairs Committee, may also have had something to do with it.

In July 1915, Dr Edmund Gros and Jarousse de Sillac hosted a luncheon party at the home of a friend, Senator Gaston Menier. The list of guests included Colonel Bouttieux, Leon Bourgeois and a guest of honour, General Auguste Hirschauer, the head of French military aeronautics. Before the day was over, General Hirschauer had agreed in principle to the formation of an all-American squadron. Yet with more and more Americans arriving in France to join in the war, it was decided to implement the proposal for an all-American squadron and the L'Escadrille Américaine was formed. However,

Above: American group of airmen. Left to right: Victor Chapman, Elliott, Cowden, Bert Hall, William Thaw, Lieutenant Delage, Norman Prince, James McConnell, Kiffin Rockwell, Captain Thenault.

Right: Dr Edmund Gros.

after protests by the German Ambassador in France and other pro-German groups in the United States who said it was the Escadrille des Volontaires and in violation of the Hague Convention (Article 6, Chapter 1, Convention V), the name was changed to the L'Escadrille Lafayette or 'Lafayette Flying Corps', although its official name was Escadrille de Chasse Nieuport (N)124. Among the founders of this soon-to-become-famous Lafayette Escadrille were Captain Georges Thenault, Lieutenants Alfred de Laage de Meux, Victor Chapman, Norman Prince, James McConnell, Kiffin Rockwell, William Thaw, Elliott Cowdin, Clyde Balsley, Charles Johnson, Bert Hall and Lawrence Rumsey.

With the creation of the new squadron it was decided to have the distinctive head of a Seminole Indian Chief (this was later replaced with the head of a Sioux Indian Chief), painted on the side of the fuselage of the SPAD (Société Pour l'Aviation et ses Dérivés) VII.CI aircraft and it became the official insignia of the legendary Lafayette Escadrille. The squadron was supported and financed by many wealthy and influential Americans

Above left: Captain Georges Thenault, CO, Lafayette Escadrille.

Above right: James McConnell.

Above left: Kiffin Rockwell, William Thaw and Paul Pavelka with the Lafayette Escadrille's mascot, the lion cub Whisky.

Above right: Elliott Cowdin.

Lawrence Rumsey.

Alfred de Laage de Meux.

who believed that the United States should be actively engaged in the war as an ally of Britain and France. For some there was an alternative and ulterior motive in as much as they saw ways and means of turning the war into a profitable enterprise by manufacturing war materials.

Among another of the founders of the squadron was Weston Birch 'Bert' Hall. Hall was born on a farm in Higginsville, Missouri in 1885, the son of a former Confederate soldier. Hall left America and went to France in search of adventure and became the 'American in Paris', a Paris taxi driver. He became disillusioned with his job and joined the Foreign Legion out of a sense of 'there has to be more to life than being a taxi driver.' He applied to join the French Air Service and during an interview with the commandant, Hall told him that he had flown combat missions with the Turkish Army during the Balkan War. He then asked to borrow an aircraft in which to demonstrate his flying ability. He was given a Blériot and with the commandant and others watching, he started the engine and careered across the grass before lurching momentarily into the air and then crashing into the side of a canvas hangar. A furious commandant, shouting that Hall knew nothing about flying at all, confronted a sheepish Hall as he clambered from the wreckage. Hall agreed, and then said that he thought he could

Insignia of the Lafayette Escadrille: Sioux chief.

Bert Hall with his Nieuport C.1.

master the art of flying but realized it was a bit more complicated than he thought. For some unknown reason the commandant liked his openness and nerve, and sent him for flying training. Hall soon began to regale his fellow trainees with stories about his war exploits, so much so that an investigation was ordered into his background. Nothing was found, not even a birth certificate, so two security men were assigned to befriend Hall and find out what they could. They were concerned after an incident concerning another American, F.C. Hild, who had deserted during flying training and returned to the United States. He gave interviews to a number of newspapers describing the poor training and equipment of the Service Aéronautique and it was suspected that he had given information to the Germans at their embassy in Washington. Nothing was ever found out about Hall's background and he continued his flying training. During his career, Bert Hall embellished his exploits to the extent that it was hard to know where the truth actually lay.

Initially the group of American businessmen who were behind the formation of the 'L'Escadrille Américaine' were called the Franco-American Committee. The name was later changed to the Lafayette Flying Corps Committee with William K. Vanderbilt as honorary president, Jarousse de Sillac as president and Dr Edmund Gros as vice-president, and it was they who conceived the idea of financing an American fighting unit in the French Air Service. The idea was to have American heroes in French uniforms, fighting for freedom in this new and colourful element of warfare. This, it was hoped, would lend publicity to the raising of funds in America to support the cause. This was a very 'Hollywood'-sounding description and one that was to rapidly disillusion those who later fought in the war.

The First World War, whichever way one looked at it, was a war for artillery and infantry, and the balloons and aircraft were, according to the sceptics, only there for support. The heavy artillery, in these early years, caused more devastation than bomber aircraft ever did, but it was the reconnaissance flights and artillery spotting missions carried out by the aviation section that was primarily responsible for the success of the artillery. By the end of the war, the aviation section had proved its worth beyond all doubt and had been grudgingly accepted by the sceptics as 'having done their bit'.

When America declared war on Germany, there were only five United States aviation officers in Europe: three were at French flying schools undergoing instruction; one was the assistant military attaché in London; and the remaining one was Major William (Billy) Mitchell who was acting as an observer in Spain. With the onset of the war, Mitchell immediately made his way to Britain entirely on his own initiative and set up a meeting with Major General Trenchard. With the help of Trenchard, Mitchell constructed a plan that he could present to General Pershing. The plan consisted of two types of air force: one was in effect a development of pursuit squadrons; the other bomber squadrons. It was because of General Trenchard's contribution and influence that the plan in principle was accepted and a board of officers convened to create the Air Service, AEF (American Expeditionary Force).

The board, however, was more inclined to create an independent strategic air force than an air force that was controlled by the army. General Pershing realized this and saw the air force as part of the army under his control. He dismissed the idea proposed by the board, which had been guided and very impressed by the British and French strategic bombing squadrons, and insisted that units were trained for missions in support of and in participation with the army.

Brigadier General William 'Billy' Mitchell, USAS.

Although there were moves to try to give the air force some independence, aside from the odd occasional pursuit and bombardment missions, they stayed under the auspices of the army throughout the war. In fact, it wasn't until September 1947, after the end of the Second World War, that the army relinquished its hold over the air force.

The United States navy, in the meantime, had not restricted their direction and movements solely towards the sea. On the declaration of war against Germany, naval aviation strength stood at 48 officers and 239 enlisted men, all with aviation experience of one kind or another. They had fifty-four aircraft – all training types – plus one free balloon, one kite balloon, one very suspect dirigible and one air station. The navy had started training pilots and crews some six years earlier, but had fallen into a limbo period over the last year, mainly because of the number of accidents that had befallen their students. In the main, this was not the fault of the instructors or students but of the aircraft themselves. It has to be remembered that the aircraft industry in America, like their counterparts in Europe, was still at the learning stages of development and some of the aircraft coming out of the factories left a lot to be desired in the military sense. In fact, the main source of American aircraft was in Europe; e.g. Britain and France.

More than $3 million had been set aside by Congress for the US Navy's Naval Flying Corps, as it was known in the Naval Appropriation Act of 29 August 1916, but unfortunately none of the funding appeared to find its

Lieutenant Kirk Booth of the US Signal Corps being lifted on a man-carrying kite.

way into the navy's coffers. The Naval Flying Corps had not been officially established, and although suitable sites for air bases had been selected along the East Coast, all were in the planning stages. Late in 1916 the first of the Curtiss N-9s were delivered to the navy and experiments were started with shipboard catapults aboard the USS *North Carolina*, the USS *Huntingdon* and the USS *Seattle*. In Britain, France, Germany, Italy and the Austro-Hungarian Empire naval aviation was being actively encouraged, leaving the United States woefully behind, but interest was growing and a number of wealthy young men at the various universities in America decided to buy their own aircraft and hire instructors to teach them. Among these was F. Trubee Davison of Yale University who formed the First Yale Unit, which was later incorporated into Aerial Coastal Patrol Unit (CPU) No.1. This CPU was the brainchild of Rear Admiral Robert E. Peary and Henry Woodhouse, both ardent believers in naval aviation who raised money from individual contributions to form the National Coastal Patrol Commission. This encouraged Curtiss and other enterprising manufacturers to set up flying training schools, not only for pilots but for mechanics and engineers to keep the aircraft flying.

Lieutenant Frederick Trubee Davison, USNAS.

Although Davison had a number of students at Yale ready to learn to fly, he still had the problem of finding enough aircraft and instructors to meet their needs. Just outside New York on Long Island, a Philadelphia merchant by the name of Rodman Wanamaker operated a flying school at Port Washington. After lengthy consultations with him, Davison managed to persuade him to let them use his Curtiss flying boat and one instructor by the name of David McCulloch. McCulloch was to later join the navy and gain fame as the co-pilot of the NC-3 flying boat on the US Navy's successful attempt to become the first to fly the Atlantic Ocean, although only one of the four NC aircraft, the NC-4, made it.

The summer of 1917 saw the first twelve members of the First Yale Unit at Locust Valley clambering all over the Curtiss flying boat, maintaining it, cleaning it and learning to fly. By the end of the summer four of the students had flown solo and the remaining eight were ready. Towards the end of the year, the students were invited to take part, as members of the Aerial Coastal Patrol, in manoeuvres off Sandy Hook with battleships, destroyers and coastal boats. So successful were the manoeuvres, and so impressed with the standard of flying by the Yale faculty were the military and civilian hierarchy, that the faculty was given two more seaplanes and additional funding. In March 1917, the whole unit was transferred to West Palm Beach, Florida to take advantage of the weather and to finalize the remainder of their flying training. All members of the First Yale Unit were enrolled into the US Navy and a naval lieutenant placed in command. One month later the unit returned to Long Island and began the business of flight training in readiness for war.

The US Marine Corps had not been idle, and aviation essentially started for them on 22 May 1912 when the first Marine aviator, First Lieutenant A.A. Cunningham, reported for his initial flight training at Annapolis, Maryland. After receiving his ground instruction, Cunningham was posted to the Burgess Company and Curtiss Aircraft Factory at Marblehead, Massachusetts for flight training itself. On 1 August 1912, after two hours of training he soloed, even though he had only witnessed two landings prior to his own. Cunningham became Marine Aviator No.1 and designated Naval Aviator No.5. Two more Marines followed that year – Lieutenant Bernard L. Smith and Second Lieutenant William M. McIlvain – but it wasn't until June 1915 when the next Marine, First Lieutenant Francis T. Evans, reported for training, followed on 31 March 1916 by

The First Yale Unit of the USN Air Reserve.

Curtiss flying boat of the First Yale Unit being used in training.

Slipways at Huntingdon, Long Island, New York used by the First Yale Unit.

First Lieutenant Alfred Cunningham, USMC.

First Lieutenant Roy Geiger. These five Marine aviators were to form the nucleus of USMC aviation.

Both Smith and Cunningham contributed enormously to the experimental and development phases of Marine Corps aviation, although they had different concepts on how the aviation side should be used. Cunningham favoured total support of the Marine Corps, whereas Smith saw Marine Corps aviation supporting both the navy and the Corps.

During January and February 1914, Lieutenant Smith and Second Lieutenant McIlvain (Marine Aviator No.3), together with ten enlisted mechanics, one flying boat and one amphibian, were involved in a combined fleet and landing force exercise at Culebra, Puerto Rico. The two pilots flew daily missions over the island carrying brigade officers to show them the ease, speed and field of vision offered by aerial reconnaissance. The aviation contribution to the exercise was a complete success, so much so that the Marine Corps took up Lieutenant Smith's recommendation that an advanced base consisting of five aviators and twenty enlisted ground crewmen be set up.

On 7 April 1917, the day after the United States had declared war on Germany, the president directed that control of the US Coast Guard be transferred from the Treasury Department to the US Navy. The first two Coast Guard aviators, Second Lieutenant Charles E. Sugden and Third Lieutenant Elmer F. Stone, had been trained at NAS Pensacola at the end of 1916. Some months later, a further sixteen Coastguardsmen were trained as pilots and assigned to the US Navy's Aviation Division. When the United States entered the war the following year, a number of these Coast Guard pilots were posted to France and fought with honour. Among these was Lieutenant Charles Sugden, USCG, who became commanding officer of NAS Ile Tudy, France and was awarded the French Chevalier of the Legion of Honour. At the end of the war all Coast Guard personnel returned to serve under the jurisdiction of the US Treasury Department.

April 1917 also saw the formation of the Marine Aeronautical Company's Advance Base Force at the Marine barracks in the Philadelphia Navy Yard, under the command of Captain A.A. Cunningham. The company was made up from the Marine Aviation Section at US Aeronautical Station, Pensacola, Florida and from the Marine Corps Reserve Flying Corps, and consisted of 34 officers and 330 enlisted men with two Curtiss R-6 seaplanes and one Farman land version.

The Marine Aeronautical Company was divided into two units, the 1st Marine Aeronautic Company and the 1st Aviation Squadron, commanded by Captain Francis T. Evans and consisting of ten officers and ninety-three enlisted men. The 1st Marine Aeronautic Company moved to the Navy Coastal Air Station at Cape May, New Jersey on 14 October 1917 for seaplane and coastal patrol training. The 1st Aviation Squadron, commanded by Captain McIlvain, consisting of 24 officers and 237 enlisted men, was posted from Philadelphia to start flight training at the Army Aviation School at Hazelhurst Field, Mineola, Long Island, New York in the same month. Because of the increasingly inclement weather, the 1st Aviation Squadron moved south to the US Army's Gerstner Field at Lake Charles, Louisiana.

After extensive training, the 1st Marine Aeronautic Squadron, complete with its complement of 10 Curtiss R-6 seaplanes, 2 N-9 seaplanes, 6 Curtiss HS-1 flying boats, 12 officers and 133 enlisted men, boarded the USS *Hancock* in the Philadelphia Navy Yard. Their destination was Ponta Delgada in the Azores, where throughout the war they maintained a constant daylight patrol of the Western Approaches. They were the first fully trained and equipped flying unit from the United States to operate overseas.

The squadron carried out patrols around the waters that surrounded the islands from dawn to dusk, and the only sighting they had of the enemy was on 11 September 1918. A Curtiss R-6 was on patrol with pilot Lieutenant Walter Poague and his crew member Gunnery Sergeant Zeigler when they sighted a German U-boat on the surface. They circled, then came in to attack and drop their one and only bomb. Unfortunately, not only did the bomb miss, but it also failed to explode and the two flyers could only watch as the submarine's crew leisurely battened down the hatches and then submerged out of sight.

A further unit from within the 1st Aviation Force was formed, under the command of Captain Roy Geiger, USMC. This unit, consisting of four officers and thirty-six enlisted men, was ordered to Miami, Florida, where they took over a small airfield owned by the Curtiss Flying School. After extensive training and the influx of a number of fully-trained pilots from the US Navy, the 1st Marine Aviation Force was mobilized for France and its first taste of war. On 1 April 1918, Captain McIlvain's squadron arrived in Florida to join up with Captain Roy Geiger's squadron. The nucleus of the 1st Aviation Force was for the first time all together at one location. The force was then shaped into four squadrons and designated A, B, C and D. The first three squadrons set sail for France on 18 July 1918 aboard the USS *DeKalb*, with the remaining one, D Squadron, staying in Miami to set up a training programme.

After a long delay, when it was discovered that there were no aircraft available for the Marines, they were assigned to fly with British crews

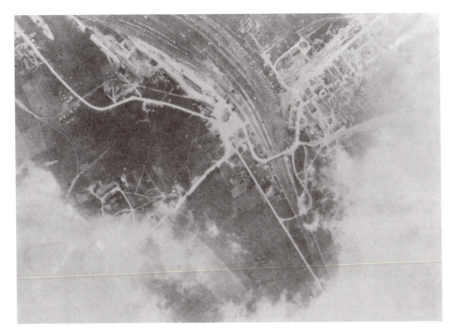

The 96th Aero Squadron bombing the German-held railway yards at Dommary-Baroncourt. This was the first American bombing mission.

while arrangements were made for the supply of planes. On 12 October the force joined the Day Wing of the Northern Bombing Group with their own aircraft and although their time was limited before the Armistice was signed, they carried out a number of important bombing raids. One raid in particular on 14 October 1918 concerned eight Airco DH.4s on a bombing mission to carry out a raid on the German-held railway yards at Tielt, Belgium. On the way back from the raid, which was not very successful, twelve German fighters jumped the formation. One of the bombers was separated from the others and singled out for attack. The gunner, Gunnery Sergeant Robert G. Robinson, managed to shoot down one of the attackers before he himself was hit. Despite his wounds, Robinson continued to fight while his pilot, Second Lieutenant Ralph Talbot, weaved all over

Second Lieutenant Ralph Talbot, MoH.

Second Lieutenant Ralph Talbot, MoH standing in front of his Curtiss JN-4.

the sky. Sergeant Robinson was hit twice more and was rendered unconscious. Talbot shot down another of the fighters with his forward-firing fixed guns, and then decided that discretion was the better part of valour and put his aircraft into a steep dive. Levelling off at an altitude of 50ft, Talbot roared over the German lines and landed safely at a Belgian airfield, where his gunner was taken to hospital for treatment. Robinson recovered and, together with Talbot, was awarded America's highest honour, the Medal of Honor. Sadly Talbot was killed on 26 October 1918, carrying out an engine test on an old worn-out DH.4. The engine failed on take-off, with the result that the aircraft plunged into an embankment at the end of the field and exploded into flames on contact.

During the relatively short period of time that US Marine Aviation was involved in the war, they carried out 57 missions and dropped a total of 33,932lb of bombs at a cost of 4 pilots killed plus 1 pilot and 2 gunners wounded. They accounted for four German fighters and claimed eight more possibles.

The wreckage of Second Lieutenant Talbot's aircraft at Le Fresne.

The crash scene just minutes after Second Lieutenant Talbot's crash.

While the Marine Corps were getting to grips with their squadrons, the navy was showing a renewed interest in the use of airships as a reconnaissance and fleet patrol craft. On 20 April 1917 the US Navy carried out trials on their new airship, the DN-1. The tests were carried out at NAS Pensacola, together with a floating hangar for the airship. The first flight of the navy's first airship, a B-Class model designated DN-1, was successful after making the trip from Chicago, Illinois where it was made to Akron, Ohio. It was flown by a Goodyear pilot by the name of R.H. Upson. A second flight in the airship, this time by the navy and flown by LCDR Frank R. McCrary, USN was made from Pensacola but was a dismal failure. Further tests were unsatisfactory and after just three flights the project was cancelled. Even after extensive modifications and testing, the results were the same and only two more flights followed before the airship was finally grounded for the last time.

However, the lighter-than-air programme supported by the Goodyear Tire and Rubber Company was slowly gaining momentum. Goodyear had agreed with the navy that they would provide the facilities and the equipment; all the navy had to do was provide the trainees. The school opened on a field located at Fritch Lake (later called Wingfoot), 3 miles from the town of Akron. It consisted of a hangar 400ft x 100ft x 100ft, tool and equipment shops, classrooms and barracks for the students and quarters for the officers. Within six months, the first eight men had qualified and were designated Naval Aviators (Dirigibles), but it was to be a further two months before they were assigned to their units.

US Navy Airship No. 1 approaching its floating hangar.

The navy had learned a great deal from the fiasco and so a Dr Jerome Hunsaker was asked to develop a theory of airship design, the result being the very successful B-type airships. Lieutenant John Towers had returned from Europe having inspected British designs and, using reports from attachés on British airship operations, the navy was prepared to seek bids for blimps from American manufacturers. On 4 February 1917 the Secretary of the Navy directed that sixteen non-rigid airships of Class B be procured. After a meeting with the Chief of the Bureau of Construction and Repair and representatives of Goodyear, Goodrich, Baldwin Company, Connecticut Aircraft Company, Curtiss Aeroplane and Motor Corporation and the US Rubber Company, it was agreed that the order for sixteen dirigibles was beyond the capability of any one company. The conference resulted in a committee to coordinate on sharing raw materials, information and experience. Ultimately Goodyear manufactured nine envelopes, Goodrich made five and Curtiss assembled fourteen of the gondolas for the airships. Connecticut Aircraft worked with US Rubber for its two envelopes and with the Pigeon Fraser Company for its gondolas. The Curtiss-built gondolas used by Goodyear and Goodrich used modified Curtiss JN-4 fuselages powered by Curtiss OXX engines. The ones made by Connecticut Aircraft were powered by Hall-Scott engines. All the B-Class airships were delivered to the navy between August 1917 and September 1918.

Later another training base was set up at Pensacola, Florida. One of these airships was built by the Baldwin Company that produced the Baldwin

Airship No.1. Its first test flight was from Fort Meyer, Virginia in 1908, but like many other of the companies it was just the one. As crews became more competent, coastal patrols from naval air stations were commenced. The airships operated from NAS's Chatham, Massachusetts, Cape May, New Jersey, Rockaway Beach and Montauk Point, New York, and Key West, Florida. Although the airships that carried out these coastal patrols proved to be an extremely useful weapon, not one was ever used in Europe. Trained LTA (Lighter Than Air) pilots were sent to NAS Paimboeuf in France, where they carried out familiarization training in French airships before going on active service patrols.

The use of manned kite balloons on battleships and destroyers for observation purposes was a direct spin-off from the airships. These balloons, unlike the airships, were tethered to the ships and had no directional movement, other than up and down, save that of the ship's own movement. Their purpose was to spot for enemy warships or submarines, but was controlled by the weather. If the seas were relatively calm, then the observation kite balloon was launched, but if there were high seas running or it was foggy, then it was impracticable.

The Baldwin Dirigible No.1 on a test flight over Fort Myer.

Kettering Bug, the proposed idea for a guided missile.

Experiments were also started with a guided missile programme after the Secretary of the Navy had allocated funding of $50,000. The work centred on the use of aerial torpedoes in the form of automatic gyroscopically-controlled aircraft. The results were at first encouraging, but the longer they went on the more expensive they became and the project was shelved. It was resurrected during the Second World War, but only used on a couple of occasions.

The first national insignia designed for United States aircraft was ordered to be placed on all naval aircraft. It was a red disc within a white star on a blue circular field on the wings and red, white and blue vertical stripes with blue forward on the rudder. One of the main reasons for the insignia was the increasing number of incidents in which US aircraft were fired upon by their own troops and it was deemed necessary to educate the ground troops in what was considered the then simplest way.

* * *

In February 1913, the chairman of the House Committee on Military Affairs, Republican James Hay, had proposed a bill that would have created a separate Air Corps. However, the Assistant Secretary of War at that time,

Henry S. Breckinridge, saw military aviation as 'merely an added means of communication, observation and reconnaissance, which ought to be coordinated with and subordinated to the general service of information and not erected into an independent and uncoordinated service.'

He also emphasized the point that aviation was still in its infancy, that it was destined for a long time to be an auxiliary of the line and that its immediate future would therefore be best handled by the Signal Corps. Breckinridge also stressed the fact that the Signal Corps had the technical information, expertise and qualified personnel to handle all of aviation's needs. In his view, young aviators did not possess the scientific knowledge and the maturity required. This sweeping statement was later proved to be totally without foundation and regarded by many to be unjust and offensive to the young aviators who were later to lay down their lives. The proposed bill was defeated, and control of military aviation passed to the army's Signal Corps under the command of Colonel George P. Scriven.

Thus the formative years of the United States Army Air Arm, or United States Air Service (USAS) as it would later become known, were as part of the US Signal Corps. One year later the USAS was placed under the command of Lieutenant Colonel George O. Squier and consisted of 131 officers, only 56 of whom were flyers, and 1,087 enlisted men. Squier was a mature disciplinarian, and despite being a non-flyer, was ideally suited to the position after seeing air action when he had been the military attaché in London at the beginning of the war. Just after the American declaration of war, two of his subordinate officers, Captains Edgar Gorrell and Benjamin Foulois, drew up a proposed budget for the rapidly-expanding Air Service. They drew the charts on large pieces of grocery wrapping paper acquired from a local grocery store that showed a required budget of $600,000,000, a figure greater than that required for building the Panama Canal. Fortunately Squier had seen first-hand the war in Europe and realized that this figure was not going to be excessive. He persuaded the then Secretary of War Newton D. Baker that it was not an outrageous figure, leaving him to persuade the president and then in turn members of Congress that the amount was necessary and not excessive.

Squier realized that the Air Service was in desperate need of aircraft and facilities, so he persuaded the government to purchase a cotton field near San Antonio, Texas for the express purpose of training aviators. It was called Kelly Field, and by the end of the war 5,182 officers and 197,468 enlisted men had been trained there. He also presided over the acquisition of aircraft from Great Britain, the De Havilland 4, and arranged for them to be built in the United States under licence, but with the twelve-cylinder Liberty engine installed.

Of the number of officers initially in the Air Service, only twenty-six of them were in fact pilots; the remainder were engineers or administrative officers. Among the pilots were William Thaw II, Didier Masson and Raoul Lufbery, who had fought the Germans since 1914 and would do so until the end of the war. William Thaw had joined the Foreign Legion at the beginning of the war as a private in Battalion C, 2nd Regiment. After serving with the Legion for a while, Thaw transferred to Escadrille D.6 as a *soldat mitrailleur* (machine-gunner). However, he wanted to fly, and after convincing the authorities that he had done some flying back in the United States, was sent to the French military aviation school at Saint-Cyr late in 1915 where, after training, he was awarded his brevet. He was flying Caudron G.IIs with Escadrille C.42 based at Nancy when word came through that an American unit was to be formed because of the increased number

Raoul Lufbery in French uniform.

of American pilots joining up. Thaw immediately asked to be transferred and within a very short time, because of his experience, was promoted to the rank of lieutenant colonel in the USAS. In less than four years William Thaw had risen from private in the French army to a lieutenant colonel in the American army and been given command of the 3rd Pursuit Group, US Air Service; a truly remarkable achievement, but then he was a rather remarkable man.

Raoul Lufbery, on the other hand, had been born in France, the son of an American father and a French mother. His education was that of a French schoolboy and after his mother had died, he was left in the care of his grandmother while his father returned to the United States. After many years of working his way around the world, he returned to the United States to try to find his father but without success. He joined the US Army and fought in the Philippines against the natives who were in revolt at that time.

After three years Lufbery left the army and went to Saigon where he met and joined up with the French aviator Marc Pourpe as his mechanic. The two of them toured the Far East giving exhibitions and finally ended up in Paris at the onset of the First World War. Raoul Lufbery then joined the Foreign Legion, but because of his experience and knowledge, was almost immediately sent on detached duty to the Service Aéronautique. When his friend Pourpe was killed while trying to land in fog, Lufbery volunteered for training as a pilot and was posted to the Aviation School at Chartres. On graduating with the rank of sergeant he was posted to Bombardment Squadron No.106, where he served with distinction until May 1916 when he was transferred to the Lafayette Escadrille. Within a few months he had proved himself to be one of the most skilled pilots in the squadron and had shot down six aircraft by the end of the year. By the beginning of 1917 he was among the highest-scoring pilots of the Lafayette Escadrille, and in August 1917 was commissioned *sous-lieutenant* and had been awarded the Légion d'Honneur, Médaille Militaire, Croix de Guerre with ten Palms and the British Military Medal. He was also becoming a household name in the United States. With the entrance of the United States into the war, great pressure was put upon Raoul Lufbery to transfer to the United States Air Service, and with great reluctance he agreed. His one regret was that although any military decorations he had been awarded by the French would be accepted by the USAS, the number of 'kills' he had made (more than twelve confirmed) would not. Nevertheless, Lufbery transferred to the USAS on 10 January 1918 with the rank of major and was given temporary command of the 94th Pursuit Squadron.

Didier Masson was French and had emigrated to California in 1905. In 1909 he learned to fly and became an exhibition pilot. Then in 1913 he went to Mexico and joined General Salido's campaign against General Huerta. Masson was placed in charge of Salido's air force; in fact, he <u>was</u> the air force as the general only had one aircraft, a battered Curtiss JN-3 biplane. At the outbreak of the First World War,

Left: Raoul Lufbery in USAS uniform.

Below: Members of the 94th Aero Squadron, USAS.

Masson returned to France and joined the infantry, but after a few months in the trenches he applied for the Service Aéronautique and was accepted. He was awarded his military pilot's brevet on 10 May 1915.

Another American adventurer who came from the Foreign Legion was Eugene Jacques Bullard, one of only two known black aviators to serve in the First World War. The other was *Feldwebel* Marcel Pliat, a Frenchman who fought with the Imperial Russian Air Service as an observer/gunner. Eugene Bullard was born in Columbus, Georgia in 1895. His father, who was a freed slave, told him that Europe was the place to go to escape racial prejudices, specifically France. In 1912 Eugene stowed

Eugene Jacques Bullard.

away on a German freighter that was headed for Britain. Once in Britain, broke and penniless, he turned to boxing to make ends meet and became quite successful. However, he still wanted to go to France, so in 1913 he headed across the Channel into France and ultimately to Paris. Work was difficult to find and soon he was once again broke and penniless so in 1914 he joined the Foreign Legion's 170th Infantry Regiment known as the 'Swallows of Death'. While with the 170th Infantry, he was sent to Verdun where, during the bitter fighting, he was wounded twice. During this action Bullard distinguished himself, for which he was awarded the Médaille Militaire and the Croix de Guerre. Later, when asked why he had joined the Foreign Legion, Bullard replied: 'Well, I don't rightly know, but it must have been more curiosity than intelligence.' This probably summed up the reasons why many young Americans joined up to fight at the time.

At the end of 1916, while at Fort Douaumont, Eugene Bullard asked to be transferred to the flying corps. An American friend bet him $2,000 that he could not get into the corps. Eugene Bullard went to Tours to start his training and from there to Avord in central France. It was while there that he met James Norman Hall, who was later to fly with the legendary Lafayette Escadrille. It is interesting to note that he remembered Eugene Bullard with a great deal of affection, saying in a letter to a friend:

> This democracy is a fine thing in the army and makes better
> men of all hands. For instance, the corporal of our room is an

American pilots at the French Flying School at Tours being trained on very flimsy Morane trainers.

American, as black as the ace of spades, but a mighty white fellow at that. The next two bunks to his are occupied by Princeton men of old Southern families. They are best friends with him. This black brother has been in the Foreign Legion, wounded four times, covered with medals for his bravery in the trenches, and now uses his experience and knowledge of French for the benefit of our room, the result being that the inspecting lieutenant said we had the best-looking room in the barracks.

After graduating and gaining his brevet, Eugene Bullard collected the $2,000 from a delighted but grudging friend. He served with Spa.93 and later Spa.95 from August to November 1917, scoring one confirmed 'kill' and one possible. Just after his last mission, it is said that Bullard requested to leave the flying corps and to be returned to the Foreign Legion's 170th Infantry after being turned down for transfer to the Lafayette Escadrille. It was said that the discipline in the flying corps had proved too much for him and that that was the reason for his request, but another report says that he was sent back to the infantry after striking a superior officer while on leave. The discipline in the Foreign Legion is legendary; consequently

Above left: Eugene Bullard, the only black pilot in the USAS when with the French Air Service.

Above right: Eugene Bullard with his pet monkey Jimmy.

it is hard to believe that the discipline in the flying corps was harsher. The truth is more likely to be somewhere between the issue of his colour, the incident with the superior officer and the fact that he only held the rank of corporal and to transfer to the Lafayette Escadrille he had to hold the rank of at least a first lieutenant. Also one of the major sponsors of the Lafayette Escadrille was a man called Dr Edmund Gros whose racist views were well-documented.

After leaving the flying corps Eugene Bullard went back to the Foreign Legion but when America entered the war, American pilots who were already fighting with the French were invited to transfer to the USAS, but Bullard was never asked. After the war he was awarded fifteen medals by the French including being made a Knight of The Legion of Honour, France's highest decoration. When the Second World War started in 1939, Bullard owned a bar by the name of 'Le Grand Duc' frequented by German soldiers. During this period he worked for French Intelligence, gaining information from his German customers. Yet when America entered the war, American pilots who were already fighting with the French were invited to transfer to the USAC, but once again Eugene Bullard was never asked so he cycled all the way to Portugal and returned to America via a Red Cross ship. He applied once again to fight for his country, but was not accepted as he was deemed to be too old. He died in 1961, but it was not until 1992 that he was officially recognized by the United States for his part in the First World War by being awarded a posthumous promotion to the rank of first lieutenant in the USAF. Nothing is known regarding the other black aviator, *Feldwebel* Marcel Pliat, as to whether or not he survived the war.

James Norman Hall, who had befriended Eugene Bullard, was another of the college graduates who went to Europe to join in the war. Hall joined the 9th Battalion of the Royal Fusiliers in Aldershot, Hampshire in May 1915, before being sent on active service to the Western Front. He was discharged from the British army because of his father's illness and returned to America. In July 1916 he returned to France with the intention of working on his book *Kitchener's Mob*, but enlisted in the French Air Service instead. On finishing his training he was posted to the Lafayette Escadrille and continued to serve until it became the 103rd Aero Squadron, at which point he joined the USAS and was given the rank of captain. He served with distinction until he was shot down on 7 May 1918 and taken prisoner, which he remained until the end of the war. He then returned to America where, together with his friend Charles Nordhoff, he wrote a two-part volume on the story of the Lafayette Escadrille. He became the author of fifteen books, one of which was the epic story *The Mutiny on the Bounty*.

Prior to the United States entering the war, a large number of Americans who wanted 'in' crossed the border into Canada and joined the Royal Flying Corps (RFC) and the Royal Naval Air Service (RNAS) under the guise of Commonwealth citizens. They had their primary training at Camp Borden, Ontario, before being shipped across the Atlantic for further training in Britain or France. From there they were dispatched to various squadrons in France. Later, just after America entered the war, 300 cadets selected from various American universities and about 800 enlisted men from the Signal Corps were sent to Camp Borden for training; they were called the Toronto Group. The initial training was not quite what the American volunteers had expected. They suddenly came up against the British military drill system and a discipline that was harsher than anything they had experienced before, but they realized there was purpose behind it all and soon became accustomed to its rigours.

Curtiss JN-4 at Camp Borden, Canada.

Ten squadrons were to be formed and the flying training, because of the harsh winters in Canada, was split between Camp Borden in Ontario and Taliaferro Fields in Texas. Because of the lack of equipment and aircraft, only eight of the ten squadrons materialized: Nos 17, 22, 27, 28, 139, 147, 148 and 183. Two of the squadrons, Nos 17 and 148, were assigned to the Royal Flying Corps although flown by American pilots. Nos 22, 27, 139 and 147 were assigned to the 1st and 2nd Pursuit Groups of the USAS and No.183 Squadron was later re-formed as part of the 278th Observation Squadron. The remaining squadron, No.28 Pursuit Squadron, was assigned to the 3rd Pursuit Group.

Another group of Americans who wanted to fly was selected from graduates from the universities of Illinois, Texas and California and the School of Military Aeronautics at Princeton in August 1917. These volunteers were known initially as the 'Italian Detachment' (later known as the Oxford Group), as they were destined to be sent to Italy for flight training. Among the first of the Princeton students who went to Camp Borden, Canada for flight training was one James Forrestal, whose name was later to become synonymous with US naval aviation and after whom, many years later, one of the largest aircraft carriers ever built was named.

The group's first stop was in fact in England, where their orders were changed and they were sent to Oxford University for ground school training.

After finishing the course, the Oxford Group, as they then became known, were sent for primary, then advanced flight training at various RFC bases in England, then on to the School of Aerial Fighting at Turnberry in Scotland where, upon graduating, they were given commissions to lieutenant and placed in a pool of RFC/RAF pilots ready for posting to squadrons on the Western Front.

Among this group of pilots and observers was Lieutenant Elliott White Springs, the son of an extremely wealthy Southern cotton-mill owner. Springs was picked out by Major William (Billy) A. Bishop, VC as an extremely promising fighter pilot, and in May 1918 had him posted to No.85 Squadron RFC under his command and tutelage. Despite his playboy image, Elliott White Springs learned quickly and soon became one of the squadron's top exponents of aerial fighting. By the end of June 1918, he had raised his tally of 'kills' to four, but on 27 June was shot down and injured. After spending some weeks in hospital he returned to his unit, only to find that he had been posted to the 148th Pursuit Squadron with promotion to captain on 1 August 1918. Six more victories by the end of the month raised his score to ten and earned him the award of both the DSC

American members of 85 Squadron, RFC at Hounslow, England.

Members of 85 Squadron USAS: D.V. McGregor and Elliott White Springs (standing); Horn, Thompson, Lawrence Callaghan, McGrider (kneeling).

American pilots of 85 Squadron RAF about to fly to France from Hounslow, England. Left to right: Elliot White Springs, Augustus Horn, Longton, Lawrence Callaghan, Guy Thompson, Harry Brown.

(Distinguished Service Cross) from the British and the DFC (Distinguished Flying Cross) from the Americans. He was to end the war with a total of sixteen victories.

Elliott White Springs was to later write the classic First World War book *War Birds: The Diary of an Unknown Aviator*. It was later established that the 'unknown aviator' was in fact his friend Lieutenant John McGavock Grider, who had kept a diary of his and fellow pilots' lives up to the point of his death in June 1918. Elliott White Springs had been given the diary and continued to update it, only embellishing it somewhat. Nevertheless, it gave an extremely accurate insight into the life of a First World War aviator.

The 93rd Pursuit Squadron was formed late in August 1917 at Jefferson Barracks, St Louis. It was formed out of the pick of the students who had just graduated and been immediately posted to Kelly Field for general army drill training. On completion of this the squadron moved to England, where the pilots and ground crews were assigned in groups to various Royal Air Force establishments for further training on engines and airframes. In May 1918, the squadron was regrouped and sent overseas to Issoudun in France, where they were greeted by their commanding officer Major Huffer, a very experienced pilot. John Huffer was another American who had joined the USAS via the Foreign Legion. Born in Paris to American parents, he enlisted in the Foreign Legion in 1915, but within six months had applied to join the French Air Service and was sent to Avord for flight training. Three months later after completing his training he was posted to Escadrille

Issoudun airfield.

Major Jean Huffer and Raoul Lufbery deep in conversation.

N.62 as a reconnaissance pilot flying Farmans. He joined Escadrille 62 in October 1917 flying SPADS over the Western Front. He was promoted to major in November 1917 following his transfer to the USAS and given command of the 94th Aero Squadron. He was later transferred to the 1st Air Depot at Colombey-les-Belles as Assistant Operations Officer, where he immediately arranged further training for the ground crews within the engine repair shops there, while the pilots attempted to get in some flying hours on French aircraft. In July 1918 the squadron moved to Vaucouleurs and into the war. He also saw service as the CO (Commanding Officer) of the 93rd Aero Squadron where he served until the Armistice.

At the end of May 1917, a second Yale unit had been formed under the leadership of Ganson Goodyear Depew of Buffalo, New York, who presented the idea to Admiral W.S. Benson who was Chief of Naval Operations (CNO) at the time. The twelve members of the unit were enlisted into the United States Naval Reserve Force (USNRF) and ordered to report to Lieutenant Wadleigh Capehart at Buffalo, New York. As was the practice at the time, most of the funding was from private sources. Equipment and a second-hand Curtiss F-boat were purchased. The Second Yale Unit's, or Aerial Coastal Patrol Unit N.2 as it became known, existence was very nearly cut short when on one of the first excursions of the newly-acquired Curtiss flying boat, it crashed, killing the instructor and so badly injuring the passenger that he was invalided out of the service and the war. Ganson Depew acquired another aircraft and flying instructor out of his own pocket and persuaded the naval authorities to give them another chance, which they did.

The trust that the Naval Board had bestowed upon them bore fruit when in the November, all twelve men passed the stringent tests required to acquire their 'Wings of Gold'. The final flying test was to take the Curtiss flying boat up to 6,000ft, cut the engine and glide down in a spiral, then land on the water and taxi to a point not less than 20ft from a marker buoy. Three of the twelve students actually stopped with their aircraft's nose nestling against the buoy. The twelve were granted commissions as ensigns and five were posted overseas to Europe, six to NAS Pensacola and one to Washington D.C. After arriving in Europe, the five new ensigns were posted to Moutchie, France for bombing instruction in French FBA flying boats. Later the same month, three of them were posted to RNAS Felixstowe, where they were introduced to the delights of the twin-engined F2A flying boat.

Felixstowe F.2A being towed on a Thorneycroft lighter.

CHAPTER FOUR

It was at Felixstowe in November 1917 that they took part in 'lighter stunt' experiments with the F2A flying boat. This was developed over the need to carry out long-range reconnaissance flights over the North Sea. The distance from Felixstowe to the Danish coastline of Heligoland was 340 miles, and because the aircraft did not have this kind of range, they could not spot German shipping making journeys northwards up the coast of Denmark.

Wing Captain C.R. Sansom, RN and Wing Commander Porte, RFC, had developed a 'lighter' that could carry an F2A flying boat and be towed behind a destroyer at high speed. The 'lighter' was in fact a barge that settled quite low in the water and was a derivative of the Thames lighter barges that were used to carry materials up and down the River Thames.

Three destroyers towing three lighters with F2As aboard left Felixstowe and proceeded across the North Sea to a point near the Dutch coast. The aircraft were offloaded from the lighters and then took off on patrol.

Felixstowe F.2A
on patrol over the
North Sea.

The three aircraft flew along the coast to the Bight of Heligoland, then back across the North Sea to Felixstowe and returned safely. A number of flights were made using this system and all were very successful. The other two ensigns, who were still in France, were assigned to the Northern Bombing Group (NBG) and carried out ferry flights of Caproni bombers from Italy over the Alps to northern France. These were hair-raising flights as the reliability of these aircraft was always being brought into question.

With the war in Europe becoming more and more intense and the use of aircraft more and more prevalent, it became clear that the growth and organizational structure of army aviation in America was completely inadequate. In May 1917 the Council of National Defense established the Aircraft Production Board, but by the end of the year hardly anything had changed. There were accusations of mismanagement and inefficiency resulting in a new organization known as the Air Service, which consisted of the Division of Military Aeronautics and the Bureau of Aircraft Production. This was endorsed when the president appointed John D. Ryan to become the Director of the Air Service and Second Assistant Secretary of War, giving aviation a very high representation at top government level.

The development of the USAS, as it became known, began to gain momentum as new roles for the air service were put forward. One of the roles that had been put forward by Colonel Edgar S. Gorrell, President of the Stutz Motor Car Company, envisioned a strategic bombing campaign against the German industrial centres deep in the heart of Germany. Gorrell was not just an armchair officer; he had graduated from West Point in 1912, qualified as a pilot two years later and served under Pershing on the Mexican border. Pershing recognized him as a man who understood strategy and put him in charge of 'strategical aviation', whatever that was deemed to be.

Gorrell was sent to Europe as Assistant Chief of Staff of the Air Service, AEF in October 1917 and after becoming aware of General Hugh Trenchard's concepts for strategic bombing, realized that not only would raids on the German industrial centres cause manufacturing problems, but the effect on German morale would also be a major factor. The person who coined the phrase 'It sounds good in theory' must have been thinking of Gorrell's proposal, because on paper the idea certainly had merit but from a practical point of view, there were serious logistical problems. In France the idea was greeted with some scepticism, and it was estimated that it would take a raid of more than 600 bombers to have any long-term effect on the German manufacturing economy. Training for these bombers would start in the United States on old Curtiss 'Jennies' and on completion of this, further training would have to be carried out in England on DH.4s or Handley Page bombers. The length of time required for both sets of training and the logistics of moving that amount of men and equipment around was horrendous. In addition to this, it was realized that these bombers would need fighter escorts, and there were no fighters that had the range to fly to Germany and back escorting the bombers. This was a situation that was to be realized again during the Second World War. Gorrell's answer to this was that the bombers would afford their own protection by sheer weight of numbers and that the raids would be carried out at night. This in itself was enough to squash the idea, but it was discussed in depth and ultimately dismissed. It was thought that the USAS had not developed enough to carry out such a mission; indeed, it was thought that not even the Royal Flying Corps would consider such a raid.

In June 1917, Major Raynal C. Bolling, USAS was sent to Europe to find out first-hand the role expected of the newly-formed United States Air Service. Bolling, an experienced organizer, had set up the First National Guard Aero Company in New York in 1915 and had been a top lawyer with United States Steel before the war. Coupled with this, he was trusted by

Above left: Major Raynal C. Bolling, USAS.

Above right: Major Townsend Dodd, USAS.

General Pershing and well acquainted with aviation. Pershing knew he would ask the right questions and assimilate the answers before bringing advice back to Washington. Within a month of Bolling's return, Major Townsend F. Dodd of the Signal Corps was sent to France with General Pershing and Major Bolling. Dodd was no stranger to command as he had commanded the 1st Aero Squadron in 1916 and had flown with Pershing on Mexican border operations. On arrival in France, Dodd was promoted to colonel, a position he held until September 1917. Bolling and Colonel 'Billy' Mitchell were assigned to organize the Balloon Section of the AEF together with Major Frank Lahm. When Brigadier General William L. Kenly, a field artillery officer, arrived in Paris to set up the Air Service headquarters of the American Expeditionary Force (AEF) on 3 September 1917 and take up the post of Chief of the Air Service, he replaced Colonel Dodd. Raynal C. Bolling, Assistant Chief in charge of Supply, and Colonel William Mitchell, Air Commander, Zone of Advance were moved from the Balloon Section and assigned to Kenly's staff. They had plenty of ideas, but no aircraft.

The relative calm was short-lived when, on 27 November, Brigadier General B.D. Foulois arrived in France complete with a ready-made headquarters staff consisting of 112 officers and 300 men. Within two

Members of the 1st Aero Squadron.

General Billy Mitchell with members of his staff. Left to right: Captain Vallois (French Air Service), Lieutenant Colonel Brereton, Mitchell, Major Joralemon, Captain Marvel, Lieutenant Scawb and Lieutenant Mathis.

days he had replaced Brigadier General Kenly as Chief of Air Staff and moved his own team into the headquarters. The resentment created by the sudden move also caused organizational problems, with one side refusing to cooperate with the other. There were also other obstacles, brought about in the main by jealousy and friction between the aviation and ground staffs.

Many young aviators, with their initial baptism in war, considered themselves to be members of a Corps d'Elite and as Major Frederick Palmer, a senior member of General Foulois' staff, wrote in a letter to a friend:

> Every whim of these flyers was unwritten law to the ground forces on the flying field, who expected to have M'Lord's steed ready for him to mount before he rode forth to the tournament of the skies; and his bath drawn in his pleasant quarters, ready for him on his return. Some of the glamour was rapidly disappearing, as it was discovered that the ability to fly was not uncommon and there were no end of volunteers for aviation. The same could not be said for the common soldier. Aces had their communiqués, whilst the surviving officer of a veteran

battalion which took its objectives amidst suffering horrendous losses, was not mentioned. Ascending, well-groomed and well-fed, to death in a plane seemed quite pleasant when compared to going over the top from filthy trenches, to be mashed up in No Man's Land among putrid corpses.

In reality, after a few months of combat flying, or in some cases only a few days, the glamour rapidly wore off when the young flyers discovered how vulnerable they were when in the air. Aircraft at that time were constructed mainly of wood and covered in a painted fabric that burned furiously when ignited. It was an accepted fact that if either air or ground fire hit the aircraft, their chances of survival if the aircraft caught fire were virtually nil. Some actually chose to jump to their deaths rather than be roasted alive. If the engine was hit, the castor oil that was used to oil the rotary engine would invariably spray all over the pilot, causing him to ingest it through his mouth and nose. This in turn could cause serious intestinal problems.

Back in the United States, Congress had allocated a staggering $640,000,000 to the air programme and then set about convincing the general public and the media that it was justified. This angered General Pershing, who thought that the extra money spent on convincing the public would have been better spent in establishing the Air Service. However, he had problems of his own within the structure of his senior officers, and although his own contemptuous attitude towards the new Air Service had not changed one iota, he had the foresight to realize the potential of such a service. Pershing was convinced that the war would be won on the ground and the Air Arm would just act as a support to the infantry and artillery in a reconnaissance role. The problem with his senior officers was later resolved on 29 May 1918, when he replaced the Chief of the Air Service Brigadier General Kenly with one of his own men, Brigadier General Mason M. Patrick, an old classmate. Pershing also recommended that increased pay and rank for men engaged in flying duties should be abolished. He could see no difference between a man flying an aircraft and a man firing a gun in a muddy trench. In fact, in his opinion, the man in the trench was in many ways worse off, for he was stuck where he was. Although the increased pay for flying duties was never abolished, it was drastically reduced.

General Pershing's view of the usefulness of an Air Service was guided by the number of experienced aviation specialists under his command, which amounted to very few. One of these was Major Frank P. Lahm who was an expert on military balloons. He had received his balloonist's certificate in

1905 and his pilot's rating in 1909. In May 1917, Lahm had been given command of the army's balloon school at Fort Omaha, Nebraska, but in August was sent to France to study French and British balloon training and their operations under battlefield conditions. He was ordered to return to the United States in the December, but General Pershing intervened, saying that Lahm's expertise was required by the AEF.

The need for balloon companies at the front increased. There were only four balloon companies in France at the time supporting the infantry; they were the 1st, 2nd, 3rd and 4th who made up the 2nd Balloon Squadron. Training was of the essence and training under battlefield conditions even more so. In the United States military balloon training was virtually non-existent compared to Europe, even though there had been a balloon section in the US Army Signal Corps in existence since 1891. A number of officers had been sent to Europe at the time to study French *Aérostation*, but unfortunately all the information acquired was soon forgotten, so in 1917 an advanced school was set up at Cuperly-sur-Marne, France, close to the French balloon school at Vadenay. This school didn't last long because during the German offensive of March 1918 it came under intense heavy attack, so it was decided to move it to Sougé, between the Gironde and Dordogne Rivers in south-west France, close to the city of Bordeaux.

Students at the school soon discovered that being a member of a balloon company was not a soft option. Because of the very nature of their role as information-gatherers, the balloons were close to the front and rapidly became a target for enemy artillery, small-arms fire and attacks by aircraft. Not only were the observers in the balloon's basket at risk, so were the ground crews. The balloon had to be filled with 23,000 cubic feet of flammable hydrogen, so around the balloon area there was not only a winch truck, but trucks carrying large numbers of gas cylinders. Because they were regarded as a very serious threat by both sides, balloon companies became important targets and were subjected to heavy shelling with high-explosive shells. As can easily be imagined, the results of a direct hit on one of the trucks carrying the gas cylinders would, at the very least, be catastrophic to those within a considerable range of the vicinity. This danger was highlighted on 16 June 1917, when men of the 4th Balloon Company were in the process of inflating their balloon in preparation to carry out spotting for the 26th Yankee Division's artillery. The men had just broken off for breakfast when German artillery shells rained down around them. Seconds later the Caquot balloon, which was only partially inflated, received a direct hit and exploded. Fortunately there were no

Men of the 10th Observation Balloon Company manually operating the winch.

American observation balloon being launched.

serious casualties, but it decimated the area and dented the pride of the 4th Balloon Company as they were the first American Balloon Company to lose their balloon, but they would not be the last.

After finishing their intensive training from the French, the companies were usually sent to the relatively quiet sectors where they carried out observations for artillery units and were eased into battle conditions.

While at the front, living accommodation for the balloon companies usually comprised just two-man pup tents. Some of the companies spent months living in the most horrendous of conditions and constantly on the move.

On 31 January 1918, four more balloon companies – the 5th, 6th, 7th and 8th – were sent to France. They were supposed to be ready to support the American divisions who were preparing for the great offensive. It was soon discovered, much to the anger of General Pershing, that the companies had only the basic rudiments of ballooning and would have to be sent to the French balloon schools for advanced training. This, of course, could not be done overnight; in fact, it took nearly five months. Although these balloon companies carried out their duties with honour, great courage and fortitude, it was short-lived because they never entered the theatre of war until the conflict was almost over.

Brigadier General Foulois was appointed Chief of Air Service, First Army, with Colonel Mitchell as his deputy. Brigadier General Kenly was promoted

Sopwith Camel of the 41st Aero Squadron, USAS.

Camel F1 in US markings at Martlesham Heath.

to major general and appointed as Director of Military Aeronautics back in the United States. Colonel Mitchell continued to press for advancement of the Air Service; so much so, in fact, that Brigadier General Foulois requested that Mitchell be appointed Chief of Air Service, First Army, and that he himself became the Assistant Chief of Air Service under Brigadier General Patrick. The request was granted in August 1918 and Mitchell, promoted to brigadier general, started to expand the Air Service rapidly. Within two months an Air Service, Second Army was formed under Colonel Frank P. Lahm and just before the Armistice was signed, a Third Army was created.

It has to be remembered that it wasn't until May 1919 that the first aircraft flew across the Atlantic: the US Navy's NC-4 Curtiss flying boat. This meant that almost all the aircraft flown by American pilots in the war were either British or French and any American aircraft had to be transported to Europe by sea. This of course added to the many logistical problems faced by the AEF.

Chapter Five

The 1st Observation Squadron should have been the first American squadron to go into action, but there were no aircraft for them. Instead, it was the 1st Aero Squadron, under the command of Major Ralph Royce, who arrived in France on 3 September 1917. Among the men who boarded the SS *Lapland* in New York were forty-six aviation cadets under the command of Major William O. Ryan. They were to move on to the 8th Aviation Instructional Centre at Foggia in southern Italy, which had recently been created for flight training. The remainder of the cadet pilots were given further training as an observation squadron at the French Air Service School at Avord and equipped with French Dorand AR.1s and 2s, SPAD XIs and the odd Sopwith.

The aircraft were not well received by the squadron, who unaffectionately called them 'antique rattletraps', but they flew a number of missions with them, the first on 11 April 1918. Later the squadron moved to Issoudun for further training, but because of the camp's state of unreadiness, they spent more time building and equipping the camp than in flying training. Major Royce went to Paris in an effort to arrange more flying training for his men. He sent the aviation mechanics to the various aircraft factories around Paris to increase their knowledge and improve their techniques.

In June that year, much to their delight, the squadron was re-equipped with new Salmson 2-A2s. The squadron was then sent to the 1st Corps Aeronautical School at Amanty for observer training. They were then able to use the Toul area that covered the 350-mile front from the English Channel to Switzerland. The area was chosen because it had been relatively quiet for some months and was deemed to be a good sector for breaking in pilots who had little or no combat experience. In January of 1918, Major Royce returned to Amanty to take over as director of the school, as well as being the commanding officer of the 1st Aero Squadron, but still he had the problem of insufficient aircraft and spares. It was during this time that the 1st Aero Squadron claimed the first victory for the USAS. Major Royce sent some of his men to the airfield at Neufchâteau to observe the French Bombardment Group Br.123. On arrival they saw that the group's thirty-two Bréguet XIV aircraft were preparing to leave on a mission. One of the Americans, observer Lieutenant Stephen Thompson, was invited to go along as an observer/gunner. As the aircraft crossed over the French lines into German-held territory, the ack-ack guns opened up, peppering the sky with puffs of black smoke. Then as suddenly as it started, it stopped and the French crews saw that seven Albatros D.III fighters from Jasta 3 were climbing to intercept them. The pilot indicated to Thompson to release all the bombs, which he did. As the fighters closed in, Lieutenant Thompson found it difficult to fire the machine gun with gloves on and so removed them. Seconds later, one of the Albatros fighters swooped down and Thompson opened fire, watching the tracer bullets stitch a line of holes across the cockpit, wounding the pilot. The German aircraft went into a spin and crashed behind the German lines, killing the pilot *Leutnant* Bruno Langer. On landing, Lieutenant Thompson discovered that he had frostbitten hands but he had scored the first victory for the USAS, a fact that was not officially recognized until 1967.

Early in 1917 the American aircraft industry, such as it was, had agreed to deliver more than 20,000 aircraft, but it was obvious from the outset that they were totally incapable of producing such a vast number within such a short period of time. By the beginning of January 1918, the 12 companies capable of producing aircraft had only delivered a total of 800 aircraft, of which only 100 could even be considered for use in combat.

On 21 February 1918, the US War Department announced that it was sending the first American-built warplanes, known as Curtiss 'Jennies', to the Western Front in France. In reality the aircraft were British-designed DH.4s built by Curtiss, which in Europe were now considered to be obsolete.

The first aircraft were shipped from Dayton, Ohio aboard a freighter that was later torpedoed off the Azores, so it wasn't until May 1917 that the first American-built DH.4s arrived in France. Out of a total of nearly 6,200 aircraft delivered to the USAS in France, only 1,200 (DH.4s) came from the United States. The remaining 5,000 (SPADs, Salmsons and Nieuports) came from France and were ostensibly training aircraft. However, in America things were starting to happen, manufacturers were getting their act together and starting to think ahead, especially the engine manufacturers.

The part being played by the few American airmen fighting in Europe was beginning to capture the imagination of the newspapers and the public. More and more young Americans were captivated by the stories of the daredevil fighter pilots in France and consequently the army was

Nieuport 10s and other aircraft at Issoudun airfield.

being inundated with requests for flight training. The government set up a commission headed by General Benjamin D. Foulois to look into flight training, and sent them to Canada to see how the Canadians were producing their military aviators. On their return, the commission found that more than 18,000 Americans had volunteered for flight training. This may seem an overabundance of volunteer aircrew, but it has to be remembered that the life span of an aviator during the First World War was measured in weeks rather than years or even months.

On 20 May 1918, the Airplane Division of the army's Signal Corps was transferred from the control of the Signal Corps and came under the supervision of two different agencies controlled by the Secretary of War, the Bureau of Aircraft Productions and the Division of Military Aeronautics, combined to become the USAS (United States Air Service). It was an unusual alliance and one without precedent, so the choice of who was to head it caused problems. President Woodrow Wilson solved the problem by appointing the former head of Anaconda Copper, Mr John D. Ryan, as director of the Air Service and the Second Assistant Secretary of War.

Although the Americans now had plenty of training aircraft and volunteers, the one thing they were short of was airfields. It was decided by means of a reciprocal agreement between Britain, Canada and the United States that during the summer and autumn months the RFC (Royal Flying Corps) would train ten US squadrons in Canada and in the winter, squadrons would be trained at three airfields in Texas. The pilots carried out their primary training in both Canada and the United States and were awarded their 'wings', but as they had only flown training aircraft, they were shipped overseas to carry out advanced combat training under French and British pilots before being allocated to their respective squadrons.

The following signal was issued to all American servicemen who were to fight in France:

December 3, 1917. Stencil #694

WAR DEPARTMENT
Office of the Chief Signal Officer
Washington
INFORMATION SECTION – AIR DIVISION

The following confidential information is furnished for the use of the Army and Navy and authorized civilians in the service of the Government.

T.H.BANE

Lt. Col., Signal Corps

WARNING TO AMERICAN AVIATORS

Things to avoid if Forced to Land behind German Lines

The following instructions in the form of a warning have been given to British Aviators. American Officers and Aviators should note them and appreciate their importance.

If you are unfortunate to be compelled to land behind the German lines, you may be agreeably surprised by the apparent hospitality and generosity of your welcome there. The German Officers will probably have you stay with them as their guest for a few days at one of their squadrons and will make you most comfortable. You will probably be extremely well entertained with the very best of everything they can offer. An abundance of good champagne from France will oil the wheels of conversation between the officers of the German Flying Corps, and one whom they will probably term a brother officer of the English Flying Corps. They will appear to be very good fellows, straightforward, cheerful and keen on the scientific side of flying, apart from their ordinary work with which they may say they are quite fed up. They will probably lead you to talk about the possibilities of aviation after the war, and profess little interest in aviation as actually applied to war. It may not take much wine to gladden your heart, and to induce you to lay aside your suspicions and reserve, and forget the guile, which lies behind their artless questions.

And so unaccustomed as you are to this form of deceit, you may fall another victim to this clever combination of cunning and hospitality. But though they may succeed for the moment in making a favorable impression, you will afterwards have every reason to remember during this war the Germans have proved themselves to be a cruel and unscrupulous enemy, but they are sound financiers and have an eye to good investment. It does not cost them much to entertain you well, and even if they did expect to get an adequate return for their money in the form of information unwittingly imparted by you.

That's why they will give you all the delights of the 'Carlton' and 'Savoy' with none of the regrets of an overdraft at Cox's and that is why you will be treated as a highly honored guest, instead of being half starved in one of their now notorious prison camps, a treatment which is in fact only postponed until they have squeezed every ounce of useful information out of you. The work is done by experienced men. Quite unknown to yourself one or more of the seemingly irresponsible flying men are highly trained intelligence officers who will sift bits of useful information from your most brilliant 'bon mot' received with the keenest amusement and gratification.

On the other hand, different methods may be employed, though these are not so common with prisoners of the Flying Corps, as with others. You may be browbeaten and ordered to disclose information under pain of suffering penalties, if you refuse. Remember this is only a ruse and they will not carry out their threats. It is more possible that they will respect you for your patriotism and discretion.

It is quite possible that you may be placed in a hut with an officer alleged to be an English prisoner, speaking English fluently and knowing many people in England well, and wishing to have news of everyone and everything, or perhaps he will ask no questions, relying only on your confidence. It will be difficult for you to believe that he is not a companion in misfortune, but this is a common trick of all intelligence services and a very profitable one.

Therefore, be on your guard and remember that in a show like this, it is impossible for any individual not at the head of affairs to say what is of use to the enemy and what is not. Remember that any information you may inadvertently given may lengthen the war and keep you longer in Germany; may cost the lives of many Englishmen, may strain the country's resources even more than they are being strained at present. Don't think this is all imagination and needless caution. The need of it has been bought by experience. No careless or irresponsible feelings ought to weigh with us against anything we can do to hasten the conclusion of the war.

Chapter Six

Early in 1917, the Italian Ministry of Aviation had selected a small remote town in Italy by the name of Foggia as a training field for their expanding air force, but as more and more Americans came into the war, it was decided to use the airfield as a flight training facility for the Americans using Italian instructors. Initially it was thought that upwards of 1,000 pilots would graduate from the school, but as time progressed, budget cuts and an unusually high accident and drop-out rate resulted in only 411 pilots graduating.

The arrival in Italy of the first flight students was initially a novelty for both the Americans and the local townspeople. The Americans' idea of a warm sunny Italy was soon disillusioned by the damp weather that greeted them on their arrival, together with the abundance of mosquitoes and flies. The latter disappeared as soon as the cold weather set in, but things didn't improve for the students. Lieutenant Sherwood Hubble, one of the first arrivals at Foggia, said that the town was a dirty, filthy place where the majority of the townspeople cooked, ate and slept in one room together with their chickens and cows. He further stated that the one aim of the shopkeepers was to relieve the Americans of as much money as they could with grossly inflated prices.

Flying at the school started briskly enough, but as soon as the weather started to deteriorate, the Italian instructors introduced the word '*Domani*' ('Tomorrow') into the flight curriculum. This was one of the main reasons for the low graduation rate.

At the beginning of 1918, a detachment from the US Army Medical Corps descended upon the base and sprayed the area with a pesticide in an attempt to control the mosquito and fly population. The food on the base left a lot to be desired; so much so, in fact, that a number of the students went into the town for their meals. Although a great deal of time and money was put into the training facility at Foggia, it never became the success that was expected of it.

At the beginning of January 1918, the first of the USAS squadrons arrived at the Air Service Concentration Barracks at St Maixent, France. The unit had been set up to evaluate and test the members of the various squadrons over a period of fifteen days, after which they were attached to various units at the front.

There were still problems with aircraft production, however, and the situation was further aggravated when, on 7 February 1918, Brigadier General Foulois received a cable from a Colonel S.D. Waldon of the production service of the Air Service in Washington. The cable stated that the desperately-awaited fifty American-manufactured de Havilland DH.4s with the twelve-cylinder Liberty engine needed to 'be retained in the United States for advanced training where they can be closely observed and the benefit of any troubles or necessary corrections be immediately given to the manufacturers. Do you approve?'

When Foulois presented the cable to General Pershing, to say that Pershing was not best pleased was the understatement of the year. He was furious, and immediately cabled back: 'Send 45 of the DH.4s to the AEF immediately and keep five in the United States for training, observation and corrections.'

One week later, General Pershing received a cable from Colonel Waldon requesting confirmation of Pershing's demand and stating that if that were the case, deliveries would start immediately. The only problem, Waldon explained, was that the aircraft would have no accessories, i.e. no radios, guns, gun sights or electrical apparatus for heating clothing, and these would take an additional two months. What he in fact would get was an aircraft with an engine and nothing else. Washington wanted the aircraft fully equipped and tested before they were sent to the AEF, but Pershing insisted that the only way to test these aircraft was under the conditions in which they would be expected to operate, and by pilots who understood the rigours, stress and strains of combat aircraft.

It was becoming quite obvious that the aviation programme introduced by the US Congress on 24 July 1917 was naïve in its approach. The idea that you could throw bodies and money into a war and win may have been feasible a few centuries back, but this was a war of machines and weapons, the like of which had never been seen and used before. What was also being recognized was that although manpower from the United States was not a problem, aircraft, guns and ammunition were. There were more than 300,000 troops under General Pershing's command and what had not been fully realized by the United States high command was that the war was spread across half of Europe and the logistical demands for both men and armament in the battle areas were great. The lack of aircraft forced the Americans to place their observer graduates with French Escadrilles until such time that American aircraft were available.

Another major problem that was of great concern was the repair and refurbishment of the existing aircraft. Badly-damaged aircraft were cannibalized to such an extent that in one squadron, every aircraft had at least one part of one specific aircraft that had crashed and been cannibalized. In another incident, telephone wires were used to replace the flying wires on a number of aircraft. Problems were arising out of the poor-quality aviation fuel, poor magnetos and spark plugs and lack of proper tools. Messages flashed backwards and forwards between the squadron engineering officers and headquarters, most of which were very aggressive and angry. Both parties felt the frustration, and increased efforts were made to resolve the problems. The message being sent back to the government in America was that the United States was not ready for war. It took a lot more than just money and men; it required appropriate organizational and logistical skills that were geared to a wartime situation and this was totally new to the Americans.

In an attempt to placate General Pershing, the Army Chief of Staff Peyton March sent him a cable stating: 'Every effort is being made to meet your wishes but manufacturing program of equipment, shipping, etc. has not advanced as rapidly as was hoped for in the beginning.'

In fact it was hardly advancing at all and in the formative year it was left to the Allies to supply the aircraft and training for the AEF.

On 15 February 1918, three former members of the Lafayette Escadrille N.471 – Lieutenants Meredith Dowd, Joseph Gill and George Willard – were transferred and joined the 2nd Escadrille Américaine, which was renumbered Esc.N.471 and became known unofficially as the Second Lafayette Escadrille. According to some historians, the squadron accounted for six enemy planes and one balloon, but little else is known about it. How or why it was given the same number as the original Lafayette Escadrille is not known, but it is thought it may have been initiated by the three pilots – Dowd, Gill and Willard – who were transferred to the squadron. There is one other possible explanation, however; the Camp Retranché de Paris Escadrilles numbered from 461 to 470 and the N.471 was created out of increasing demands to defend Paris. It is an accepted fact that both sides were desperate for pilots as the aircrew loss rate was extremely high. It was because of this that the 2nd Escadrille Américaine was created and fifteen other pilots were assigned to the squadron. The ground crews and support personnel were all French and the squadron was put under the command of Lieutenant Le Comte Sanche de Gramont as part of Groupe de Chasse 21, which was under the command of Colonel LeClerc.

The squadron formed up at Le Bourget Field and began the task as 'Defenders of Paris', with particular attention being paid to the night raids carried out by German bombers. The aircraft supplied to the squadron were Nieuport 27s, used at the time as flight trainers. The mechanics soon fitted night landing flares on the lower wings, but these proved to be totally useless. Their tireless patrols were barely more than just a 'flexing of muscles' and the Germans continued to advance; so much so, in fact, that the squadron had to relocate to Château-Thierry, some 37 miles away. Things were now so desperate that orders went out to the pilots to fly low-level along the German trenches and shoot everything that moved. This tactic, of course, was bound to take its toll in casualties, and the first to fall was the commanding officer Lieutenant Comte de Gramont on 3 July 1918. His place was taken by Lieutenant Walter Avery, USAS, who soon proved his worth by taking part in one of the fiercest ground-strafing missions that took place appropriately on 14 July, Bastille Day.

Lieutenant Walter Avery,
148th Aero Squadron, USAS.

For nearly two months the squadron flew virtually continuous strafing missions against the German ground forces, and by the middle of July the tide had been stemmed. The German advance had been halted and they had begun their retreat. The threat to Paris was over and the squadron was disbanded, the Americans being sent to various fighter squadrons. The 2nd Lafayette Escadrille was no more, but it had proved its worth.

The transfer of the American pilots from the Lafayette Escadrille to the various USAS squadrons was held up for a period of more than six weeks. They were regarded as 'civilian pilots' no longer in the service of France but not recognized as members of the US Air Service. The formation of the 103rd Pursuit Squadron on 18 February saw the problem resolved.

The 1st Pursuit Group was formed at Toul with Major Atkinson in charge and consisted of four squadrons, the 27th, 94th, 95th and 147th, together with the 91st and 135th Observation Squadrons, and the 2nd Pursuit Group made up from the inexperienced 13th, 49th, 22nd and 139th Pursuit Squadrons and were assigned to the 1st US Army. The 1st and 12th Observation Squadrons were added later, together with the 1st, 2nd and 4th Balloon Companies. Situated in the north-east of France, the city of Toul was ideal for the 1st Pursuit Squadron to operate from because it had a large railway close by and had a number of hotels, bars and restaurants all within close proximity to the airfield. In addition to this the 1st Air Depot was just south at Colombey, the 1st and 12th Observations were based at Ourches and to the west at Amanty was the 1st Corps Aeronautical School.

A number of Pursuit squadrons belonging to the 1st Pursuit Group became operational at the beginning of 1918: the 95th Pursuit Squadron, 94th Squadron, 27th Squadron and the 147th Squadron. Although the 95th was the first to arrive in France, it was discovered that none of the pilots had had training on the machine guns, so the honour of being the first into action went to the 94th. The squadron, later commanded by Captain Eddie Rickenbacker, had as its emblem the famous 'Hat-in-the-Ring'. However, it was only a matter of weeks before the 95th was in action.

The 95th had arrived at the small village of Villeneuve-les-Vertus on 18 February 1918 under the command of Captain James E. Miller. Miller had been a former staff officer with General Pershing at his headquarters in Paris and had been in charge of Advanced Field No.5 when assigned to command the 95th in place of its temporary commander Raoul Lufbery. The squadron proceeded on to the airfield of Villeneuve, which was some 4 kilometres from the village itself, and waited. The aircraft assigned to the squadron were Nieuport 28s and were awaited with great anticipation but it

Air crew of the 135th Squadron, USAS.

Officers of the 135th Observation Squadron. Rear, left to right: Lieutenant Louis Schlesinger, Wallace Coleman, Carl Stewart, Thomas Bromley, Lawrence Smart. Front, left to right: Charles Fleet, Basil Clarke, Edward Landon, Charles Stoner, Percival Hart.

wasn't until 6 March that they arrived and then without guns. Two American pilots, Majors Davenport Johnson and Millard Harmon, both on temporary assignment to Groupe de Chasse (also known as Groupement Ménard) under the command of Commandant Ménard, were based at Villeneuve and offered to take Captain Miller on patrol over the lines.

On the morning of 9 March 1918, Captain Miller, flying a SPAD borrowed from the French Groupe and accompanied by Harmon and Johnson also flying borrowed French aircraft, took off on patrol. Harmon suffered engine trouble and had to return, leaving only Johnson and Miller. Just outside Craonne they sighted a flight of German two-seater aircraft and attacked. Johnson's guns had jammed, forcing him to break off the attack, but he had not warned the inexperienced Miller that the two-seaters were armed both front <u>and</u> rear. The result was that while attempting to attack from behind, Captain Miller was met with a hail of bullets from the rear gunner and was cut to ribbons.

Captain Eddie Rickenbacker in the cockpit of his SPAD XIII.

Some of the 'Hat in the Ring' Squadron members. Left to right: Lieutenant Eastman, Captains Meissner, Rickenbacker, Chambers and Lieutenant Taylor.

This highlighted the lack of gunnery and aerial combat training, and although the 95th had had some training, it was obviously not enough. Firing at a moving target was one thing, but firing at a moving, twisting target that fired back was something entirely different. The squadron was ordered immediately to Cazeaux for increased target training, but it was soon realized that there was no substitute for the real thing and that was to prove costly in lives and aircraft, for both sides.

Early in January, Brigadier General Foulois had received a cable from the War Department informing him that they had implemented a plan to train aircrews in aerial gunnery and that facilities would be available by 15 May 1918. This was to be in the shape of aircraft with target towing facilities and two-seater aircraft with movable and synchronized guns. He was also told that a school for observers was to be opened at Kelly Field, San Antonio, Texas on 1 March, together with a bombing school at Houston, Texas. In addition to this, a Pursuit school was to be opened at Lake Charles, Louisiana. Foulois realized from past experience that if

The 94th Aero Squadron. From left to right, front row: Lieutenant L. Prinz, Lieutenant H.H. Tittman, Lieutenant F. Ordway, Lieutenant W.W. Smith. Middle row: Lieutenant W.G. Loomis, Lieutenant C.A. Snow, Lieutenant M.E. Green, Lieutenant A.F. Winslow, Captain K. Marr, Lieutenant E.V. Rickenbacker, Lieutenant J.A. Meissner, Lieutenant T.C. Taylor, Lieutenant G.W. Zacharias. Back row: Lieutenant H. Coolidge, Lieutenant A.L. Cunningham, Lieutenant W.W. Chalmers, Lieutenant J.H. Eastman, Lieutenant A.B. Sherry, Lieutenant J. Wentworth, Lieutenant R.Z. Cates, Lieutenant E. Clark, Lieutenant J.N. Jeffers.

Major Davenport Johnson, USAS.

he were to wait for these programmes to be implemented, not only would there be no one to fight in France, but the war would probably end before they materialized. This was a prime example of the lack of understanding between the War Department in the United States and the men fighting the war in France. It was because of this that Foulois activated his own programme at Cazeaux. In the meantime, Captain Davenport Johnson, who had been on temporary assignment to the French Groupe, was ordered by General Mitchell to take over command of the 95th on 20 March 1918.

On 17 July 1918 a member of the 95th Pursuit Squadron, 1st Pursuit Group, was shot down and taken prisoner; his name was Lieutenant George Puryear. He later distinguished himself by becoming the first American airman to escape from a prisoner of war camp. His report can be found at the end of this book.

Slowly but surely the 95th Pursuit Squadron, after completing its gunnery course at Cazeaux, regained its morale and started to make its mark. Then in June Captain David McKelvey Peterson, a former member of the Lafayette Escadrille, replaced Captain Johnson. The squadron pilots were sent on leave to Paris and, while on their way back to the squadron, were diverted to Colombey-les-Belles and from there to Toul, where they joined up with their ground crews and the 94th Pursuit Squadron.

The same gunnery problem had been realized by members of the 1st Corps Observation Group when, while during their final days of training at Neufchâteau, they were invited to visit a French Bréguet bombing group based nearby. Major Royce, the school's commanding officer and also commanding officer of the 1st Aero Squadron, had made arrangements for the students to go on bombing raids with the squadron to gain experience. The pilots of the bombers assumed that all the students had been trained as gunners, and because of the language difficulty confirmation was never established. On one particular raid on Saarbrücken on

Brigadier General Benjamin Foulois, Chief of the USAS.

119

25 February 1918, the bombers were attacked by German Albatros fighters while over the target. Of the eight bombers on the raid, three of them carried American observers from the school. During the attack by the fighters, it was soon realized by the French pilots that their observers had had no combat training whatsoever and had to flee for their lives. One student, Lieutenant Stephen W. Thompson, managed to acquit himself by shooting down one of the Albatros fighters. He admitted later that he was terrified at the time and his legs were shaking so much that he had to brace them against the fuselage. The French pilots were not at all pleased.

This situation only compounded the frustrations being experienced by the army's high command in Europe. The German army had moved its Eastern Front troops westward after the Russian army had collapsed in November 1917. At the beginning of 1918 the German army consisted of 192 divisions of battle-hardened troops as opposed to 49 British, 53 French and 5 American divisions. The American troops up to this point had had insufficient training and were desperately short of supplies. General Pershing realized that to stop the German advance there had to be a concerted effort by the allies, and passed control of the American army into the hands of *Généralissime* Ferdinand Foch as Supreme Commander.

The German army made its thrust towards the allied lines in March 1917 and by June had opened up a gap between the British and the French. Although they continued to make ground, the Germans failed to break the British lines. The main thrust then moved towards the French lines along the River Aisne, but the French had failed to destroy some of the bridges and the Germans were able to cross virtually unopposed. On 29 May they captured Soissons and a week later had reached the River Marne. Then for some inexplicable reason the Germans halted their advance, apart from a number of brief but intense battles along the allied lines. The lull enabled the allies to regroup and re-arm and when the next push came, it came from the allies at Château-Thierry and was, to some, the turning-point of the war.

Slowly but surely the number of aircraft increased, as did the availability of spares and tools, until it reached an almost acceptable level. Most of the observers who had graduated from the school at Amanty and had been 'farmed out' to the various French Escadrilles and other squadrons returned to form the nucleus of the 1st Observation Group. The group consisted of the 1st, 12th and 88th Observation Squadrons and was based at Francheville, 25 miles from the front line.

The 88th Observation Squadron, together with the 90th and 91st, had arrived in Liverpool in November 1917 from Texas aboard the Cunard liner RMS *Orduna* together with 9,000 other troops. Their journey then continued via a cross-Channel steamer from England and then across France aboard a rattling, decrepit French train packed with twenty-four men to a carriage to Barisey-la-Côte and then by means of a 5-kilometre march to Colombey-les-Belles. The cramped conditions aboard the liner and the train were alleviated somewhat by the less cramped conditions of Colombey-les-Belles finest hotel/livery stable. The 88th's commanding officer Lieutenant Mahan immediately embarked the squadron on building their own barracks, forming the basis of what was to become the 1st Air Depot. The 91st Observation Squadron then moved on to Amanty to equip itself with aircraft, then on to its base at Gondreville to take up the task of an Army Observation Squadron. Although not as glamorous as the image of the fighter pilots, it was nevertheless one of the most dangerous aspects of flying during the war. Their task was to observe troop movements and gun positions far behind the enemy lines, up to 20 miles in some cases and at a height of around 15,000ft. It required some of the best pilots and observers in the USAS and by the end of the war the squadron had lost eight pilots and eleven observers, but had accounted for twenty-one enemy aircraft; not bad for an observation squadron.

Chapter Seven

On 1 April 1918, fifteen pilots who had been regarded as some of 'Issoudun's best' had been assembled at Le Bourget airfield to defend Paris from the German bombers. Known as Escadrille de Chasse N.471 and consisting of American pilots with French ground crews, they were equipped with Nieuport 27s. Under the command of Lieutenant Le Comte Sanche de Gramont, French Air Service (FAS) and Lieutenant Walter L. Avery, USAS, their role was that of a night-fighter squadron, and even though the mechanics fitted landing flares on the lower wings, it soon became obvious that the whole experiment was a total disaster. Inadequate landing lights on the airfield combined with virtually no instrument lighting in the cockpit and not being able to see the enemy bombers in the dark ensured the cancellation of the project. The Germans by this time were rapidly approaching Paris, so it was decided to deploy the squadron on ground-strafing duties.

There was another unit assembled on similar lines: the British 2nd Army Corps, designated the 183rd Flight Detachment. The squadron had started life as one of ten squadrons trained by the RFC in Canada and collectively known as the 'Toronto Group'. After extensive training both in Canada and in Texas, they were sent to France for advanced combat flying instruction. On completion of their training, ten of the American pilots were assigned to become a 'flight detachment' of the British 2nd Army Corps based at Luxeuil-les-Bains.

The airfield was already a legendary place; it had been the original home of the Lafayette Escadrille and the base from which the Zeppelin sheds at Friedrichshafen were bombed. Equipped with obsolete Sopwith 1½ Strutters, the 183rd was no match for the German fighters, so were only able to operate as observation aircraft when there were no German aircraft in the area. This, of course, was not always possible and there were the inevitable casualties. The pilots became impatient for new aircraft, but the

183rd Flight Detachment was just a memory in the minds of the hierarchy until just before the St Mihiel offensive when, under the command of Lieutenant Hughes, they were merged with the 258th Observation Squadron. Within two months twenty-four new Salmson 2-A2s arrived.

Also arriving in late July from England, where they had been with the repair and maintenance section at the Central Flying School, was the 104th Observation Squadron. They arrived at St Maixent where Lieutenant Clearton Reynolds took charge. Their name was 'squadron', but they only had one aircraft and one pilot, Reynolds. The remainder of the squadron was made up of mechanics. Lieutenant Reynolds and Sergeant Dube ferried the Salmson to their new base at Luxeuil-les-Bains, while the rest of the squadron went by motor transport. At the end of August, 99th Observation Squadron pilots, who themselves had only just arrived in France, ferried in eighteen Salmson 2-A2 aircraft, but still no pilots for the 104th. Time was spent checking out each aircraft, after which Reynolds carried out test flights. The biggest problem that faced the squadron then was that not only did they did not have sufficient pilots, but the aircraft had arrived far too late and the war was rapidly coming to a conclusion.

The squadron did see some action when they, together with the 24th Army Observation Squadron, who like the 104th had been in England

Souilly airfield, home of the 88th, 99th and 104th Observation Squadrons, USAS.

in the servicing and maintenance sections, were moved up to the front at Souilly. The two squadrons were there when the push in the St Mihiel sector came, and a number of the new and very inexperienced pilots, who had only just arrived at the squadrons, were lost. However, after the initial surge, the observation flights turned into what can only be described as pleasure flights, which ended with the signing of the Armistice. The 99th Observation Squadron, after having delivered the 104th's Salmsons, had to wait for the delivery of their own aircraft and by the time they had arrived, so had the bad weather. The result was that they never saw any action.

Both the 43rd and the 69th Balloon Companies were involved in the action at St Mihiel. The 43rd initially took a terrible pounding when the Germans found an allied ammunition dump and rained shells down upon them for a number of hours. When the push started and the Germans retreated, it was so rapid that the Balloon Company only managed to make two ascents during the battle. Their one claim to fame was that they heard the last shell from either side pass overhead on 11 November 1918. The 69th, on the other hand, supported the 42nd Infantry Division and during the battle lost two balloons but no men. This was a similar story for all the balloon companies and although they did not get the recognition that they thoroughly deserved, they, like many others, played a significant part in the war.

The 1st Day Bombardment Group, under the command of Major James L. Dunsworth, made its appearance just prior to the St Mihiel offensive, and consisted of two squadrons, the 11th and 20th. The formation of the two squadrons came about after it was realized that they could aid the offensive by 'softening up' the opposition by bombing their supply and movement depots. The two squadrons were assembled and sent to collect their DH.4s from the 1st Air Depot at Colombey-les-Belles and fly them to Amanty to join up with their respective ground crews. The DH.4 was not an aircraft wanted by the squadron pilots and mechanics. They were satisfied with the French Bréguets that they had been using since they had arrived and had no desire to change. The intention was to join the two squadrons with the 96th Bombardment Squadron, but the 96th, known as the 'Red Devils', was recovering from a disastrous raid on Conflans on 10 July 1918 when the squadron was virtually wiped out.

On arriving at Colombey-les-Belles to collect their aircraft, the pilots discovered that the DH.4s had been sitting outside and subjected to all the weather conditions that had been going through the area in the past weeks. Fortunately they had taken some of the ground crews with them and

Bréguet of the 96th Bombardment Squadron, USAS.

after many, many hours of checking the rigging, the control surfaces and test-flying the aircraft, they were ready to fly them to Amanty in preparation for the St Mihiel offensive. During the preparations it was discovered that none of the aircraft had been equipped for bombing duties, and on arrival at Amanty, were told by their new commanding officer that the aircraft were to be prepared for a bombing raid the following morning. Throughout the night the crews worked relentlessly, only to find out by 2100 hours that day that after making the bomb racks and starting to fit them, they had no bombs to put in them. Two hours later a convoy of trucks sped off towards Colombey-les-Belles to collect the bombs and by noon the next day the aircraft had been fuelled and bombed up ready. At 0720 hours the following morning they took off on their first bombing raid, their target being Buxières.

On 25 June 1918, another veteran of the Lafayette Escadrille, Captain David McKelvey Peterson, had replaced Captain Davenport Johnson as commanding officer of the 95th Pursuit Squadron. He stayed with the squadron for four months before going home, when his replacement was Captain John Mitchell who had served as flight commander with the 95th Pursuit Squadron.

Another squadron arrived in late June: the 9th Night Observation Squadron commanded by Lieutenant Thomas Box. When Box arrived at Amanty, he brought with him some of the pilots who had served with him in the 88th Observation Squadron: Gardiner Daily, Harold Merrill, Willard Thomas, Leslie Thompson, Harry Grainger and Philip West. Box's first communication with headquarters was 'It will be impossible for us to do much until we are assigned some hangar space.'

Space was offered to them in the 96th Bombardment Squadron hangars and six Bréguets were ferried in, three from Colombey and three from the 90th Observation Squadron. At the end of August 1918, the squadron moved to Vavincourt and by this time they had scrounged an additional six aircraft, bringing the total to twelve. Lieutenant Box had managed to acquire the aircraft, but he had only three pilots and four observers, so he spent time going around other airfields, only managing to acquire a few more pilots. The ground crews worked countless miracles in preparing the aircraft for the armada that was to support the St Mihiel offensive and when it happened, the 9th had eighteen aircraft in the air.

Two other observation squadrons arrived and the three of them were formed into the 1st Corps Observation Group under the command of Lieutenant Colonel Lewis H. Brereton, who later became a general during the Second World War. Within two months all were in action and the glamorous facade of the fighter pilot created by the media back in the United States was suddenly stripped away to reveal the brutal, unglamorous reality of war and death.

Lieutenant Quentin Roosevelt, son of US President Theodore Roosevelt.

The Toul Sector, however, was the ideal place for the squadrons to gain combat experience, because although there was action, there were not the frantic air battles going on that were being experienced in other sectors. Yet this was not to say it wasn't hazardous as there were casualties, among them Lieutenant Quentin Roosevelt, the son of former US President Teddy Roosevelt. Quentin Roosevelt was one of those rare characters who, although coming from distinguished parents, possessed great charm and never lived on his name. His name, however, was to cause him some problems when his superiors tried to keep him away from the front until he insisted that he be treated the same as his fellow pilots. Such was his determination to get involved in the war that he dropped out of Harvard University. Despite having defective eyesight (he memorized the eye chart), he passed the physical and was sent for training at Mineola Airfield at Garden City, Long Island, New York.

The relatively short period of time Quentin Roosevelt spent in France was uneventful. However, he died on 14 July 1918 while on a reconnaissance mission when he and several other pilots from the 95th Pursuit Squadron were attacked by a force of German fighter aircraft. During the fight his aircraft received numerous hits from a Fokker D.VII flown by *Unteroffizier* Carl Gräper of Jasta 50, although many reports said that it was *Feldwebel* Karl Thom (later to be awarded the coveted Pour le Mérite) who had shot Roosevelt down; also *Leutnant* Donhauser of Jasta 17 claimed the 'kill'. (There was always some debate about this as neither Donhauser nor Thom scored on that day.) It was established later from German records that it was indeed *Unteroffizier* Carl Gräper of Jasta 50. According to German reports at the time, Lieutenant Roosevelt suffered two bullet wounds to the head and then his aircraft caught fire and crashed. The Germans later dropped a note saying that they had 'buried him with full military honours after he had showed conspicuous bravery against highly experienced adversaries'. In the

The body of Lieutenant Quentin Roosevelt lying beside the wreckage of his aircraft.

Fokker D.VII of Jagdstaffel 65 flown by *Leutnant* Heinz von Beaulieu after being forced down by aircraft of the 95th Pursuit Squadron.

same engagement a Fokker D.VII U10 of Jagdstaffel 65 flown by *Leutnant* Heinz von Beaulieu-Marconnay was forced down. Captain Hamilton Coolidge and a team of engineers from the 303rd Engineer Battalion discovered Roosevelt's grave three weeks later, when the allies' front lines had moved forward towards the River Vesle.

Lieutenant Colonel Brereton took advantage of the relatively quiet Toul Sector and organized a training scheme that enabled his aircrews to train with the infantry divisions that were located in the area. Conversely, the infantry divisions trained with the aircrews in accumulating intelligence information and passing it back to the Branch Intelligence Officer and his team of four. The chief of the air staff had integrated them into the 1st Observation Group because he dreamed of a time when the whole sector would be under the control of the Americans and would have to rely on nobody but themselves. In the meantime, the USAS was entering into an area of warfare they had never experienced before, so the 1st Observation Group came under the tactical control of the French XXXVII Corps.

Major Ralph Royce, as the group operations officer and also commander of the 1st Aero Squadron, organized the first assignments for the squadrons. They flew long-range photographic missions, long-range reconnaissance flights and 'spotted' for the heavy artillery units, the first mission being with the 26th Yankee Division. However, quiet as the Toul Sector was, these missions were not without their moments of danger as there were reports of the aircraft being fired upon by their own side. This rude awakening to the realities of war not only served to highlight the need for co-operation and training between the various sections of the army, but of the dangers of flying reconnaissance missions.

At the beginning of January 1918, Colonel Billy Mitchell had become Chief of the Air Service, 1st Corps. There existed a strained relationship between Mitchell and Brereton at the time, which General Pershing knew about, but although strained, Mitchell's appointment seemed, if anything, to heighten their professionalism and their respect for each other. The 88th Squadron, in the meantime, had moved to Amanty under the command of Major Harry B. Anderson to begin their observers' course. As was the problem with nearly all the squadrons at this time, the lack of aircraft was causing great discontent.

Major Ralph Royce continued to prepare the missions for the group's three squadrons – the 1st, 12th and 88th – dividing each squadron into three flights of six aircraft each and keeping at least six aircraft on alert at all times. Even at this stage, Royce had the pilots and ground crews for the squadrons but hardly any aircraft. The only aircraft available at this time were French Dorands and they were fast becoming obsolete. After planning the first mission over enemy lines, Royce volunteered to do it himself and on 15 April 1918, he carried out the first reconnaissance mission over German lines.

The use of aerial photography, although in its infancy, was regarded as being of great importance and because the 1st Aero Squadron were the only ones with any sort of experience, they were given the initial task of coordinating with the 51st Artillery Brigade Headquarters. The 12th Observation Squadron was used for infantry liaison in the quiet sector east of Lunéville with the 42nd Division, an unenviable role. It meant that pilots and observers had to fly their aircraft close to the ground, leaving themselves targets for everything that could fire a bullet or a shell. It was also a time when the use of display panels, correction of artillery ranging and aircraft recognition were practised.

In May 1918, the first of two obsolete Sopwith 1½ Strutters were assigned to the squadron and flown in by two delivery pilots. The first one landed without incident, but the second misjudged his landing and careered into Major Anderson's Cadillac staff car. Anderson was not best pleased. Aircraft, in his eyes, were deemed to be an expendable item but staff cars were not, especially his!

The Sopwith repaired, the squadron moved to Ourches and started reconnaissance flights over the sector, giving support to the artillery of the 26th and 77th Divisions and taking photographs of the Toul Sector. The area was relatively quiet, giving the squadron pilots time to get accustomed to flying over combat areas and practising manoeuvres. An attack on one of the Sopwiths on 5 July, when it was attacked by two Albatros Scouts but driven off after suffering only minor damage, heralded the end to the inactivity in the sector.

The allies counterattacked at Château-Thierry on 18 July 1918, and all the observation squadrons, now equipped with a variety of aircraft, came into their own. Their almost hourly reports of enemy movements and positions to the American 4th Division and the Sixth French Army were instrumental in playing a major part in this turning-point of the war. All along the front, British, French and American divisions made their push supported by the RAF, and the USAS started to drive the Germans back. The bitter fighting made slow progress at first, but then it gathered momentum and as one observer put it: 'The sky was black with Sops [Sopwiths].'

The 1st and 12th Squadrons moved to Coincy, while the newly-blooded members of the 88th Squadron came face to face with the horrors of war when their squadron moved up to Ferme des Greves. The whole area had been turned into a wasteland pitted with craters and shell-holes, and was littered with the bodies and remains of soldiers and their equipment. With the move to Ferme des Greves, the 88th Squadron became part of the 3rd Corps Observation Group.

The 94th also had its share of losses and among them was Lieutenant Chalmers who, after being shot down, was captured and held as a prisoner of war. The report on his capture and eventual escape can be seen at the end of this book, together with other escape reports. Formed at Kelly Field on 20 August 1917, the same time as the 95th Pursuit Squadron, was the 94th commanded almost from the word go by Major Jean Huffer, who had been born in France of American parents. A fluent French-speaker, he had served with the Lafayette Flying Corps with distinction and was given command of the 94th Pursuit Squadron while the pilots were in their final days of training at Issoudun. Among the pilots at Issoudun were Eddie Rickenbacker, Oscar Gude, Joe Eastman and Douglas Campbell who, on completion of their course, were sent to Cazeaux for gunnery instruction while the remainder of the squadron moved to Villeneuve. Prior to the arrival of the squadron at Villeneuve, Huffer arranged for a number of former Lafayette Escadrille pilots to be assigned to him. They included Hall, Lufbery, Marr, Peterson, Chapman, Cunningham, Davis, Loomis and Winslow. The addition of these

Captain Douglas Campbell of the 94th 'Hat in the Ring' Squadron, USAS.

highly-experienced pilots to his squadron gave a tremendous boost to the new members which showed in their confidence while on patrol.

The squadrons' arrival at Villeneuve was not without problems, the main one being that there were no aircraft for them. They were told that the pilots would have to go to Colombey and Villacoublay to collect Nieuport 28s, but fortunately the 95th Squadron was pulled out to go to Cazeaux and seven of the aircraft were taken over by the 94th. Yet even then the aircraft were not ready for combat and ground crews worked around the clock to prepare them. The first observation flight on 19 March had to be carried out with French escort fighters from the Groupement Ménard because the American aircraft had no machine guns, but it wasn't long before this had been rectified and the squadron was fully operational.

On 21 March the Germans opened up a massive offensive along the front from the English Channel to Reims, with the result that every British and French squadron along the front was on full defensive alert. The 94th Squadron was moved from Villeneuve to Épiez as a back-up, and within two days of the move they were in action. Then suddenly on 7 June, without reason and much to the chagrin of the squadron members, Huffer was replaced by Major Kenneth Marr and given command of the

Lieutenant Campbell standing where his lower port wing used to be.

93rd Pursuit Squadron. It was rumoured that he had somehow upset the Air Service hierarchy, but no reason was ever given.

The 94th suffered its first loss on 3 May 1918 when, while on patrol over Autrepierre, Lieutenant Charles Chapman, a former member of the Lafayette Flying Corps, attacked five German aircraft, bringing down one before he himself was shot down in flames. For this he was awarded a posthumous DSC (Distinguished Service Cross).

Raoul Lufbery continued to increase his score but on 19 May 1918, a lone German Rumpler[4] flown by Stabsunteroffizier Kirschbaum with his observer *Leutnant* Schibe had got past the French anti-aircraft batteries and prowled over the airfield. Lieutenant Oscar Gude, who had exhausted his ammunition from six very long-range passes, had engaged the Rumpler briefly. Lufbery, who was in the squadron office at the time, jumped into his Nieuport and gave chase. After a brief skirmish, Lufbery's aircraft was seen to career all over the sky, then flip onto its back. As the aircraft rolled on its back, a figure and a cushion were seen to fall from the cockpit and

---

4. The two Germans in the Rumpler were shot down later that day by French fighters and the crew captured. They spent the remainder of the war in a prison camp.

crash into the garden of a nearby cottage. The aircraft then caught fire and crashed into a nearby field. By the time the first of the squadron members arrived, the peasants had reverently laid out the body of Lufbery. The only external mark on his body was of a bullet-hole through his left hand. It was decided after a great deal of investigation that Lufbery had climbed into the cockpit of his aircraft and not fastened his seat belt. During the skirmish that followed, it is thought that the control wires in his aircraft were severed, with the result that he lost control. As the aircraft rolled onto its back, Lufbery fell out and he plunged several hundred feet to the ground. He was given a large military funeral attended by some of the highest-ranking officers of the French and American air services. His coffin was borne by Huffer, Peterson and Marr, together with three French pilots.

After the funeral, a report regarding Lieutenant Gude's part in the incident was sent to Colonel John Mitchell, who said: 'For his performance I sent the pilot to the rear.' Oscar Gude was transferred from the 94th on 11 July and posted to the 93rd Pursuit Squadron.

Chapter Eight

The sometimes forgotten side of First World War aviation started to make its presence felt when, on 3 July 1918, the United States Navy raised the American flag over the RAF base at Killingholme, Lincolnshire, making NAS Killingholme the largest US naval air station in Europe. Just prior to taking over the station, a Zeppelin was reported heading for the area and two of the American pilots, Ensign Ashton 'Tex' W. Hawkins and Lieutenant (junior grade) G. Francklyn Lawrence, took off in their H-16 flying boat to intercept. After flying through heavy rain and strong winds, Tex Hawkins climbed the aircraft through the clouds to 10,000ft. There was no moon that night and the two Americans scoured the star-filled skies for a sign of the Zeppelin, but to no avail. After several hours of chasing shadows, they brought their aircraft down through the heavy overcast and into heavy fog. Hopelessly lost, they cruised at wave-top height until they spotted a line of trawlers heading out to sea. Assuming that the trawlers were going to sea, they reversed the course the trawlers were taking and headed towards the coast. When a rock breakwater loomed in front of them, they hopped over and landed in a harbour. As they taxied towards the shoreline, a seaplane ramp loomed up in front of them with a black cavernous hangar situated at the end of it. An amazed RNAS ground crew hauled the H-16 up the ramp, whereupon a Royal Navy officer asked how the devil they had managed to find the base in such filthy weather. Tex Hawkins glanced at his co-pilot and with a wink replied, 'The one thing they taught us to do in flight training was to navigate', grinning with obvious relief.

On 5 June 1917, the first contingent of United States naval aviators had arrived at Pauillac, France aboard the converted collier USS *Jupiter* (AC-3). Three days later a second contingent aboard a converted collier, USS *Neptune* (AC-8), landed at St Nazaire, France. The two groups were under the command of Lieutenant Kenneth Whiting and consisted of 7 officers and 122 enlisted men, none of whom had any aviation training or experience.

CHAPTER EIGHT

Whiting immediately negotiated with the French for accommodation and training for one of the groups, as it was his intention to get his aviators into the fray as quickly as possible.

With agreements reached, he headed for London with the other group and a meeting with Admiral William S. Sims, Commander US Naval Forces Europe, to tell him what he had done. Lieutenant Whiting arranged with the Royal Navy that the US naval pilots would be sent to various RNAS stations for training after finishing their introductory course at Calshot. On arrival at the RNAS stations, the strict regime once again came as a bit of a shock to the Americans, who were used to a rather relaxed form of discipline. The expression 'running a tight ship' took on a whole new meaning to them when they came up against the rigid discipline of the British navy. Two ensigns, John Vorys and Albert Sturtevant, were posted to RNAS Felixstowe under the command of Lieutenant Commander O.H.K. Maguire. Sturtevant's large red moustache was the first thing to go, as in the Royal Navy men were only allowed to be either clean-shaven or have a full beard. The two ensigns immediately addressed themselves to fitting in with the regime and were soon part of the complement of sixty RNAS officers and ratings that manned the station.

Back in London, Admiral Sims immediately took to Lieutenant Whiting's eagerness and sent him back to the United States with a request that Washington establish a training station at Mount-Lacanau near Bordeaux. This was granted and the training establishment was set up, together with operational stations at St Trojan, Dunkirk and Le Croisic. Promoted to lieutenant commander, Whiting was replaced by a more senior officer, Captain Hutchinson Cone, USN, and returned to the United States in January 1918 after having organized the setting-up of US Naval Air Stations throughout Europe in conjunction with the Royal Air Force. Through Whiting, the US Navy now had in place the makings of a very respectable aviation force.

One American sailor, who remembered his first introduction to flying in the navy, was Ensign Joe C. Cline. He had enlisted in the United States Navy on 3 April 1917 as a Landsman for Quartermaster (Aviation). He was sent to NAS Pensacola with a number of other eager student aviators for flight training, but unfortunately there was no provision for such a large contingent of students at ground school or otherwise. For three weeks the group was drilled and indoctrinated into the naval way of life. This in itself was no hardship for Joe Cline, as he had spent four years in the Illinois Naval Militia prior to joining the navy, then quite suddenly the group was posted overseas to France. They boarded the SS *Neptune* at Baltimore and with the destroyers USS *Perkins* and USS *Jarvis* as escorts, headed across the Atlantic towards France.

Two days after reaching France the group headed for the then small fishing village of Brest and took over what were once the barracks of Napoleon's soldiers. In the meantime, Lieutenant Whiting had returned from Paris with an agreement that the French would train them as pilots and supply them with aircraft, engines, fuel, armament and bombs. The group was loaded into trucks and driven to Tours, the home of L'École d'Aviation Militaire de Tours. They were arranged into groups of eight and each group was assigned to one instructor. One leather flying coat, one pair of goggles and one crash helmet was given to each group, and these were passed from one student to another as and when they came to fly in the school's Caudron G.3.

There was one minor problem, however; the French instructors did not speak any English and the American students did not speak any French. It was resolved by having paste cards with a line drawn down the middle, with English on one side and French on the other. After each flight the instructor would point out the mistakes on the paste cards, while giving the student a verbal berating in French. Two-thirds of the group managed to solo after only five hours of instruction, so it said something for the ability of the French instructors and the ingenuity of the American students. On completion of the course, the students were sent to L'École d'Aviation Maritime de Hourtin based on a small lake outside Bordeaux. It was here that the Americans received their preliminary seaplane training on FBAs. After one month, the students were sent to L'École d'Aviation de St Raphael in the south of France. Here the students were taught to fly a variety of seaplanes, carry out bombing and gunnery courses and carry out a number of landings on the sea. Just four months after arriving in France and with thirty-one hours and fifty-two minutes of flying time behind him, Joe Cline received his French brevet. He was later posted to Le Croisic to join pilots of the First Aeronautic Detachment.

At the small village of Le Croisic by the River Loire, the small US naval air station based there had been operational since October 1917. The building of the station had commenced back on 26 July 1917 and had been built using nineteen German prisoners of war, but it wasn't until 29 October that the base was activated, with the arrival from the United States of three ensigns (two of whom were pilots), thirteen enlisted men and eleven observers. The first flight from the base was made on 18 November, and the US Navy had their first taste of action. They were called to investigate the sighting of a German submarine off the coast, and Ensign Kenneth Smith (the pilot), Ensign Frank Brady (observer) and Machinist W.M. Wilkinson clambered aboard their newly-arrived Tellier flying boat and with a bomb under each wing, took off. Dawn had only just broken, but by the end of the day they still hadn't returned. As soon as it was light the following day, the other flight crews were scrambled to look for them. They had no luck and it wasn't until late afternoon the following day that the aircraft and its crew were spotted by a French torpedo boat tossing about on the rough seas some 50 miles from land. They had run out of fuel after misjudging the length of time they had been in the air and had to touch down on the water and ride out the bad weather. The following report is now part of US naval history:

Thursday, Nov. 22, 1917.

Weather conditions were not ideal for flying, clouds being very low and quite a sea running.

After leaving Le Croisic, we started south steering course 195. On reaching Ile d'Yeu, found our drift to be considerably to the East. After picking up Point Breton on Ile d'Yeu, we sighted a four-masted barque, in ballast with auxiliary engine, to the N.E. We circled over her a number of times, increasing our radius on each turn until we were nearly out of sight of Ile d'Yeu. We then left the barque and headed for Ile d'Yeu. After searching the shore for mines and submarines, returned to Point Breton.

From Pt. Breton we steered course 29 for 45 minutes. We then headed due East for 30 minutes at altitude 50 metres. Motor died and we were forced to make a tail-to-wind landing. We found it possible to land the Tellier in rough water. Dispatched at 2:30 P.M. pigeon with the following message:

'Left Ile d'Yeu at 1:10 P.M., headed 29 for 41 minutes. Then direct East 30 min. had to come down, big sea running. Send all aid....'

Could not tell for certain our location. We took watches during the night. One bailed while the other two slept. As we could not get motor started, we thought over all possible things that could happen to it. Wilkinson had found that left gas tank had not been feeding; but too late to fix it, as we could not see. Passed a very uncertain night. We knew they would do all possible things to help us.

STRIKE FROM THE AIR

Friday, Nov. 23, 1917.

Sent pigeon at 7:40 A.M. and message as follows:

'Sighted last night two lighthouses on starboard bow which we considered Ile d'Yeu. Send torpedo boats and aeroplanes. Have no food. We are taking in water. We are not positive of our location, but are going to sea. Send help. If you do not find us, say we died game to the end.'

Put in new spark plug, cleaned magneto, shifted gasoline from left to right tank. We were all so seasick that we could not work to best advantage. Bailed water out of boat. Wilkinson finally got motor started at 11:40 A.M. Saw hydroplane and blimp to the North of us. Did not give up hope. Beautiful day. Got motor going and started to taxi toward Ile d'Yeu. We were not making much headway on account of the sea. Our left pontoon had filled with water.

Finally decided our only hope was to try and get machine off water. As a result of trying, I broke left wing and got ourselves into a hell of a shape. Things began to look black. There was no founding fault with anyone. Couldn't help marvelling at the morale of the men. It was a case of heroic bravery on their part to see their only hope smashed.

We took part during the night, first lying on wing, then bailing, then sleeping. Wilkinson turned to and got all ready to cast adrift the left wing. We all decided to die game to the end...

Wing began to crumble. We all decided to let it stay on as long as possible. Sea began to grow bitter toward evening, and the water began to come in. We all hoped that we would be able to ride out the night. Very uncomfortable night and we were all growing very weak. Very long night. Our hopes were beginning to go very low, but no one showed it.

Saturday Nov. 24, 1917.

Day finally came. Wing getting near to boat as it crumpled. It was heart-rending. We had to bail and stay out on wing-tip. As waves came over, we began to feel lower and lower. It was finally decided to cast off wing, and let what might come. We tried to get other wing ready to cast off, but we could not get off nuts as we were so weak and tools were inadequate.

> We were going over gradually on starboard side. We were
> all on port side trying to keep her righted. We then saw that
> there was no way of us staying up much longer unless we could
> get the wing off. We had just about given up everything when
> Wilkinson let out a yell that something was in sight. We were
> not able to believe our eyes. We thought it was a submarine,
> but we did not care. If it was a submarine, we hoped it would
> blow us up and end it all.

As luck would have it, the vessel was a French torpedo boat, which pulled alongside the battered wreck of the aircraft and hauled the three crew members aboard to safety. The torpedo boat sank the battered Tellier flying boat with gunfire and took the American sailors back to hospital in La Pallice. Their first taste of wartime action nearly turned out to be their last, but what it had highlighted was that all aircraft had to be equipped for every emergency and signalling devices, rations and sea anchors were of paramount importance.

Another incident at NAS Le Croisic on 4 March 1918 was nearly the last for two US Navy aviators, Joseph Cline and Frederick Lovejoy. As Joseph Cline lifted the flying boat off the water at Le Croisic, the bomb under the port wing fell off and exploded on contact with the water. The explosion almost simultaneously set off the other bomb under the starboard wing, the blast cutting the flying boat in half just behind the cockpit. The rear of the aircraft crashed in pieces back onto the water, while the front section fortunately remained almost intact and slid back onto the water. Neither man was hurt. Joseph Cline was later posted to NAS Brest, where he served with distinction until the Armistice.

The first attack on a German submarine by a US naval aircraft took place on 25 March 1918, when Ensign John F. McNamara flying from NAS Portland, Dorset attacked the submarine while it was on the surface. It had disappeared below the surface by the time McNamara had turned for another attack and he was given a 'probably damaged' evaluation. Later in October McNamara was posted to NAS Wexford, southern Ireland, where he again attacked a German submarine, this time causing severe damage but still not confirmed as a 'kill'.

Early in February 1918, the US Navy lost its first airman in action, Ensign Albert Dillon Sturtevant. He was the epitome of the young, eager aviator. He had been educated at Yale University and had joined the navy to see action. He had finalized his training at RNAS Felixstowe the previous year and had gone on patrol on 15 February 1918 at 0900 hours with his co-pilot Flight Lieutenant Purdy, RNAS in their Curtiss H.12 together with another H.12 flown by Flight Lieutenant Faux. As they approached the Dutch coast, they were jumped by nine German seaplanes, four of which attacked Ensign Sturtevant's aircraft. The following report was sent to Ensign Sturtevant's father when he was told of his son's death:

> On sighting Dutch traffic at 9:55 a.m., 55 miles S. by E. of Felixstowe, machine 4338 and the accompanying 4339 were attacked by a formation of nine hostile German seaplanes. Four hostile machines were seen to attack and surround Ens. Sturtevant's machine.... The last seen of Ens. Sturtevant's machine was 1 and 1/2 miles to the S.W. of the accompanying machine (4339).... From a German report several days later this machine was brought down in flames in the South Downs.

Sturtevant's body and those of his crew were never recovered, and he was awarded the Navy Cross posthumously with the following citation:

> For distinguished and heroic service as an aviator attached to the Royal Air Force Station at Felixstowe, making a great many patrol flights over the North Sea (he) was shot down when engaged gallantly in combat with a number of enemy planes.
>
> For the President.

On 27 April 1918, one of the navy's first major successes of the war took place. Ensign Kenneth Smith and his observer Quarter Master First Class C.E. Williams were on patrol from NAS Ile Tudy, near Brest, with another flying boat flown by Ensign Robert H. Harrell and Quarter Master First Class(A) H.W. Struder when they spotted the periscope of a German submarine cruising just below the surface of the sea some distance from an incoming convoy. Calling for back-up from a couple of French torpedo boats, Ensign Smith attacked the submarine with his bombs, scoring a direct hit. The French torpedo boats also opened fire and between them they sank the submarine with all hands. For their part in the operation, the two American aviators were awarded the Croix de Guerre with Palm.

The Naval Air Station at Ile Tudy was one of the most active seaplane bases in the war in terms of action. In another incident on 5 July 1918 concerning a submarine, Ensign Harold Rowen and Quarter Master First Class C.J. Bolan were alerted to the possible sighting of a German submarine and were scrambled to investigate. After searching the area for over an hour, they spotted something in the water and unloaded their bombs. A violent explosion erupted from the water and oil was seen to spread over the surface but no debris. It was deemed a 'possible', but that was all. Two months later Ensign Edwin Pou attacked and sank two German submarines, for which he was awarded the Navy Cross and Croix de Guerre.

Surprisingly, it was during this period that the Argentinian Navy decided to send a number of their officers to the United States for flight training. One of them, Ensign Ceferino M. Pouchan, later to become admiral, was sent to Le Croisic at the beginning

Lieutenant Albert Dillon Sturtivant.

of 1918 for seaplane training. He was the only one of the Argentinians to be sent to an active war zone flying station. After completing his training at Le Croisic, he was sent to Lake Bolsena for further training and from there on to Malpensa for training on Caproni bombers. He was to end up as the No. 2 aviator in the Argentinian Navy.

By the middle of 1918, the US Navy had a number of patrol aircraft operating from various French bases around the coast; they were at Le Croisic, Brest, L'Aber Wrac'h and Paimboeuf. In addition to these they had four seaplane patrol bases and one kite balloon base in southern Ireland at Queenstown, Wexford, Whiddy Island, Lough Foyle and Berehaven. The station at Berehaven on the southern tip of Ireland was the base for kite balloons, thus enabling the convoys arriving from across the Atlantic to be afforded some degree of protection. With command of NAS Killingholme in their hands, the US Navy together with their allies virtually controlled the area of sea between the North Sea and the Channel Islands. The Lighter-Than-Air (LTA) operations of the First World War were overshadowed by the fighter and bomber exploits, but they played an important part in the patrols over the Atlantic approaches.

The Admiralty in England had chosen the sites for the US naval bases and construction work on these bases started by T.J. Moran & Co., the British Admiralty contractors. With the arrival of the US Navy and the subsequent handing over of the bases to them, the US Navy then completed the construction. The need for a supply base close to the port of Dublin

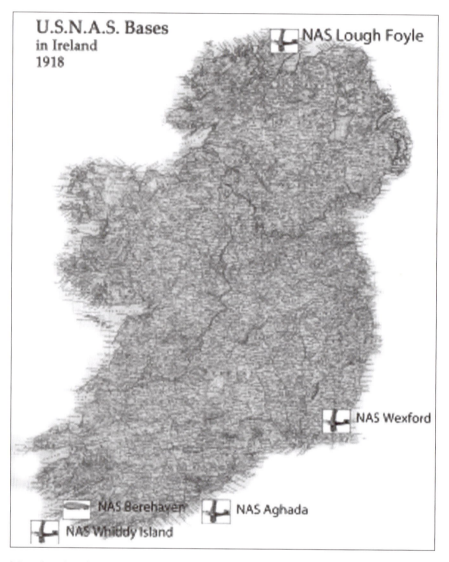

Map showing the USN bases in Ireland in 1918.

gave rise to the urgent selection of a site. The one chosen was a dilapidated warehouse with no roof or floor, 100ft wide and 390ft long, at 76 Sir John Rogerson's Quay in Dublin. It became known as the United States Naval Aviation Supply Base and stored its first materials there in March 1918.

Queenstown became the first NAS (Naval Air Station) in Ireland and was located close to the village of Aghada. On 14 February 1918, it became the headquarters of Commander F. McCrary, USN, Commander US Naval Air

Stations Ireland, although the naval air station itself was under the command of Lieutenant Commander Paul J. Peyton. All aircraft that arrived in Dublin in crates were shipped to Queenstown by road for assembly and testing before delivery to their respective air stations. It was also an ideal training base for aircrews, as they would be close enough to the war zone without actually being in it. They could be trained to carry out patrols over the Western Approaches without the risk of being attacked by enemy aircraft.

The construction of the base was a source of concern for the navy, who employed their own labour force from the local inhabitants, only to find that the necessary equipment was not available. A large, very old and dilapidated steam shovel was found in an abandoned quarry and after much bargaining with its owner, it was dismantled, loaded on to lorries and transported to the site of the base. After a great deal of repair work it was ready, and managed to complete all its excavation tasks before finally giving up the ghost. After what must have seemed like an eternity, the base was ready to receive its first aircraft. The first eight seaplanes arrived at Queenstown harbour aboard the USS *Cuyama* on 27 June 1918. From the ship they were placed aboard 'lighters' (flat barges used for moving large objects from ships in the harbour to shore) and ferried to NAS Queenstown. It is said that it took longer to ferry the aircraft from the ship to the naval air station than it did to bring them from the United States to Queenstown harbour. A further ten aircraft arrived on 24 July aboard the USS *Kanawha*, and by the end of the war this number had risen to thirty-eight.

It wasn't until the end of August that the first of the seaplanes took to the air to carry out any kind of patrol and it wasn't until October that the first contact with the enemy was made. During this month, more than 40 patrols were flown, accounting for more than 130 hours' flying time.

As the size of the US naval force grew in Ireland, an additional US naval air station was set up at Ferrybank on the Wexford Harbour and was known as NAS Wexford. Construction work by the British Admiralty had started back in December 1917 and it was formally handed over to the US Navy on 2 May 1918. It was commanded by Lieutenant Commander Herbster USN, and consisted of two hangars and a variety of other buildings and amenities. Accommodation, unlike the other US naval bases in Ireland, was quite luxurious. Two mansion houses, Bann Aboo and Ely House, were taken over and renovated and then, after the enlisted men's quarters had been built, turned into the officers' mess.

From NAS Wexford, patrols covered the southern entrance to the Irish Sea, east of Queenstown and just 12 miles from Tuskar Rock lighthouse.

It was the busiest area for shipping traffic as most of the shipping in and out of the United Kingdom passed through its waters. Consequently it also became the hunting ground of German submarines, and air patrols had to be extremely vigilant when convoys were due in the area. At the same time as NAS Wexford was being activated, another naval air station, NAS Lough Foyle, this time on the remote northern tip of Ireland, was being constructed. Its location, although ideally placed for a patrol squadron, caused numerous problems for the construction gangs. All materials had to be shipped by sea up to Londonderry and then by road to the site. It wasn't until 31 July 1918 that the naval air station was completed and ready for operational use. The purchase of a 24ft whaleboat and two dinghies so that the crews and supplies could be ferried out to the moored seaplanes completed the itinerary for the base. All they wanted now were the seaplanes.

Just prior to the opening of the base, a ship from the United States carrying five seaplanes destined for the base actually sailed past, to the cheers and waves of the air and ground crews who were waiting for the aircraft to arrive. So remote was the base that the aircraft had to be taken to Londonderry and unloaded on to trucks before making the round trip back to NAS Lough Foyle. Later, aircraft destined for Lough Foyle were assembled at NAS Queenstown and flown around the coast to the base and used NAS Wexford as a transient base.

Curtiss H-16 flying boat at its base in Aghada, Nr. Cork.

Curtiss H-16 flying boat being manhandled after its first flight over Cork.

Although the seaplanes based in Ireland never had any success in real terms, their presence caused the German naval high command to become extremely wary of them. It is an accepted fact that the waters around these patrol areas became among the safest for Allied shipping and not a safe place for the 'Kaiser's tin fish', as one American war correspondent put it.

* * *

The first of the US Navy's aircraft to arrive in France from the United States were Curtiss HS-1 seaplanes with Liberty engines. They were assembled at Brest, and then delivered to other American stations along the French coast. At first all the aircrews were excited at the prospect of getting into the air and joining in the fight, but then it was discovered that when they had built the aircraft, the manufacturers had not taken into consideration all the additional equipment that would be necessary to turn the aircraft into a war machine. By the time bombs, machine guns, radios, Aldis lamps, fire extinguishers, pigeons and enough fuel for a four-hour patrol were installed, the aircraft could not get off the water. Another 6ft had to be added to the wingspan and the aircraft was redesignated the HS-2. Even then, three strands of salmson cord had to be installed on the right rudder to offset the torque in order to fly the aircraft normally.

The US Navy had also established a base in Italy, at Porto Corsini some 50 miles south of Venice on the shores of the Adriatic Sea. It was under the command of Lieutenant Willis B. Havilland, but under the direct control of the Italian Director of Marine Aviation. The site of the base at Porto Corsini

Above: NAS Porto Corsini from the air, showing the Adriatic Sea in the background.

Left: Lieutenant Commander Willis Haviland standing by his Macchi M.5 at Porto Corsini.

Macchi M.5 negotiating the 70ft-wide channel at USNAS Porto Corsini.

was at the V-junction of two canals that opened out into the Adriatic Sea, and had been determined because of its location in relation to the Austrian naval base of Pola situated on the other side of the Adriatic Sea about 70 miles away. The battleships and cruisers of the Austro-Hungarian High Seas Fleet were anchored at Pola and it was one of the main bases for the German and Austro-Hungarian submarines that hunted in the Mediterranean.

Macchi L.2 on the slipway of USNAS Porto Corsini.

Hauling a Macchi flying boat out of the canal at USNAS Porto Corsini.

Among the Austro-Hungarian submarines based in Pola was SM *U-5* commanded by the now legendary *Korvettenkapitän* Georg von Trapp. Over the past few years von Trapp had sunk more than fifteen ships, including the French armoured cruiser *Leon Gambetta* and the Italian submarine *Nereide*. At the beginning of the Second World War von Trapp refused to join the German navy because of his dislike of the Nazi regime. Von Trapp and his family were later the basis of the famous film and play *The Sound of Music*.

The US Navy's arrival at Porto Corsini was immediately recognized by the Austrians by their carrying out an attack on the base, but fortunately they were unable to inflict any damage or casualties. Initially it was thought that there might be a problem with the language, but the US Navy had realized this and with Lieutenant Havilland they had sent naval aviator Bosun(T) Giochini Varini. Varini had been born in Venice and had emigrated to San Francisco as a young man. The fact that he spoke both English and Italian fluently and was fully versed in the local customs and ways made the transition and integration of the 300 American navy men into the community a relatively smooth one.

Initially there were problems in getting the Italians to actually fight the Austro-Hungarians; they seemed to be content to just carry out observation flights and drop leaflets. Because the US Navy was directly under the control of the Italian Director of Marine Aviation, they had to go along with it, but as time progressed they explored the enemy coastline in greater depth and eventually were able to persuade the Director to allow them to carry out bombing raids on the Austro-Hungarian bases. At first it was decided to operate HS-2Ls and Macchi M.5s from the base, but the wingspan of the HS-2L was far too wide for the canals and the Macchis were only just manageable with great caution. It was decided to use the M.8 seaplane whose wingspan was just under the width of the canal, but there were problems in

Macchi M.5 seaplane taking off from the canal.

the very limited bomb loads that could be carried. Training was carried out on Lake Bolsena on an area, marked off by buoys, which equalled the width of the Porto Corsini canals. Within a few weeks the pilots had mastered the take-offs and landings sufficiently to enable the Macchi M.5s to be re-introduced.

A large number of the American pilots had originally been in the American Ambulance Corps and had transferred to the US Navy. Their initial training had been at the ground school at Moutchie followed by a flying course at Lake Bolsena. Upon graduation they were posted to NAS Porto Corsini where they carried out combined operations with the Italians.

One of the first contacts with the enemy was on the night of 21 August 1918 when a force of Austro-Hungarian fighters attacked a flight of bombers (Macchi M.8) and fighters (Macchi M.5) from NAS Porto Corsini en route to attack the Austrian base at Pola on the other side of the Adriatic Sea for the purpose of dropping propaganda leaflets on Pola. So regular had this mission become on the Italian Front at this time that the Austro-Hungarians had announced that anyone caught engaged in this activity would be regarded as a spy and executed. After the seven-plane group had been under way for about fifteen minutes, one of the bombers and one of the fighters had to return on account of motor trouble. The remaining bomber, piloted by Ensign Walter White with his observer Ensign Albert Taliaferro, and the four fighters flown by Ensigns George H. Ludlow, E.H. (Pete) Parker, Dudley A. Vorhees and Landsman for Quartermaster Charles Hammann continued on, approaching Pola from the south in order to avoid fire from AA batteries at the harbour entrance.

At 1120, the fighters arrived over the city at 12,000ft, but the bomber was only able to get up to 8,000ft. The leaflets were thrown down and the Austrians sent up anti-aircraft fire. Five Austro-Hungarian Phönix D.I fighters, led by *Fregattenleutnant* Friedrich Lang, immediately took off with two seaplanes following them. The latter were soon lost to sight, but the enemy fighters climbed rapidly and in five minutes neared the navy's Macchi M.5 fighters. The enemy had created a new fighter unit to protect Pola from such attacks and they attacked in two sections. The first section was made up of three planes, while the remaining two gave covering fire. Ensign Ludlow gave the signal to attack the oncoming fighters in an effort to protect the bombing plane. Followed by Parker, Voorhees and Hammann, Ensign Ludlow went into a dive towards the three Austrian-Hungarian fighter aircraft and the dogfight was on at 8,000ft.

Ludlow attacked the lead plane with a quick burst of fire, and then swung over to engage the plane to his left. Parker then took on the leader who tried to escape by diving. Parker followed him down. His right gun jammed, so he pulled out, firing from his one good gun on another Austrian which swept into view, and broke out of the fight.

Vorhees no sooner got into action than his guns jammed and he was forced to leave. The bomber also departed. This left Ludlow and Hammann to carry on the fight. While Hammann took on the two planes of the second section, Ludlow was in a fight with three. He drove one down, its engine smoking, and in the next instant he himself was shot down. He took hits in his propeller and engine; oil streamed out and broke into flames. He went into a spin but managed to pull out of it and make a landing 5 miles west of the harbour entrance. Although Hammann's aircraft was also damaged, he was still flying. Looking down, Hammann saw Ludlow's wrecked plane in the water and determined to try rescuing him; an extremely daring decision to make since the wind was blowing at the rate of about 20 mph and the

Ensign Ludlow in the cockpit of his Macchi M.5.

Left: Ensign Hamman MoH with an Italian airman at Porto Corsini.

Below: Charles Hammann with his Macchi M.8 flying boat in the hangar at USNAS Porto Corsini.

sea was choppy. To land his plane in such a sea was bad enough, but worse still was the fact that Hammann's flying boat was damaged and he might not be able to take off. Furthermore, he was near the harbour and enemy planes were still in the vicinity. It seemed unlikely in these circumstances that Hammann could rescue Ludlow and make a getaway, for the enemy might easily capture them and they would be considered spies and executed.

Without a moment's hesitation, Hammann spiralled down and drew up beside Ludlow's crippled plane. Ludlow opened the port in the bottom of the hull and kicked holes in the wings to make the Macchi sink faster. He then jumped onto Hammann's plane, climbed up behind the pilot's seat and sat under the motor, holding the struts to keep from being swept into the propeller or into the sea. The tiny Macchi M.5, however, was only built to carry one man and Hammann had no idea how he was going to get into the air. The bow of the plane, already damaged by machine-gun fire, was smashed in as the craft gathered speed, but finally the little seaplane lifted off the water. After becoming airborne, Hammann fired his remaining ammunition into the wrecked plane and watched it sink; he was not going to leave the enemy that trophy. He began his 60-mile flight back to Porto Corsini, expecting to be attacked at any moment.

For reasons never discovered, the Austrians made no attempt to follow the damaged plane, a pursuit they could have undertaken with no hazard to themselves. At Porto Corsini, Hammann made a good landing in the canal, but because of the damage to his aircraft, the water poured through the holes in the bow and turned the Macchi over, a complete wreck. Both men were rescued with just minor injuries. For this heroic rescue, Hammann received the Medal of Honor and the Italian Silver Medal of Valour, while Ludlow received the Navy Cross and the Italian Bronze Medal of Valour. (Less than a year later, Ensign Hammann lost his life in a crash in a Macchi M.5 seaplane.)

Porto Corsini was becoming the target for frequent bombing attacks mainly because it was easily located, as was Pola. These tit-for-tat exchanges became more and more frequent, but it was the Austrians that were coming off the worst. On 17 July 1918 two squadrons from Porto Corsini and Venice carried out a bombing raid on Pola. Four Austrian hangars and one German hangar were destroyed and the Austrian battleship *Babenberg* was hit a number of times by bombs, forcing her to be put into dry dock for major repairs.

Just before the end of October 1918, Italy and Austria-Hungary signed an armistice, which meant an immediate cessation of hostilities. This in effect meant that the US Navy, still under the control of the Italian Director of Marine Aviation, although technically still at war with Austro-Hungary, could not carry out any more attacks.

The US Navy in Italy actually achieved very little with regard to the war effort in this part of the world, but this was not of their making; more of the Italian high command's unwillingness to fight. The only other American casualty of the air war concerning Porto Corsini was when Ensign Louie J. Bergen crashed while landing his Macchi M.5 on the canal. He died from his resulting injuries.

In France, four sites were selected for the combined US Navy and Marine bomber squadrons: the US Navy squadrons 1, 2, 3 and 4 would use the bases at St Inglevert and Campagne, and the US Marine squadrons A, B, C and D, commanded by Lieutenants Geiger, McIlvain, Captain Douglas Roben and First Lieutenant Russell A. Presley respectively would use Oye and La Fresne. The only aircraft available at the time were a few DH.9s and 4s that had come from the RAF. In America, production of the DH.4 bomber was still only trickling through and it acted as a reception base for these aircraft prior to being sent to the navy and Marine Corps' bases in France. One of the bases set up by Lieutenant Commander Kenneth Whiting, USN was at Dunkirk in June 1918, which combined squadrons of the US Marine Corps and navy. They were collectively known as the Northern Bombing Group and first flew under the command of Captain David C. Hanrahan, USN in February 1918 with Caproni aircraft supplied by the army. The group was originally planned to operate a day wing and a night wing from the Calais-Dunkirk area, and consisted of six squadrons in each wing. Within the vicinity of this group was an assembly, repair and supply unit known as Base B. The operational project of the group initially was to continuously bomb German submarine bases at Ostend, Zeebrugge and Bruges.

On 31 May 1918, a cable was received from the Department of the Navy stating that the group be reduced to four squadrons in each wing. One month later another cable cast doubts about having such a base in northern France because of the military situation at the time. It was decided to secure a site in southern England and the British Air Ministry was approached. Late in July 1918, it was decided to turn over the existing base at Eastleigh, near Southampton over to the US Navy under the command of Lieutenant Geoffrey de C. Chevalier, USN. The flying time from Eastleigh was only one and a half hours, and enabled all materials transported across the Atlantic to be unloaded at the major port of Southampton, which was only a few miles away from Eastleigh.

CHAPTER EIGHT

The new location of Base B caused the airfields of the bomber squadrons in France to be moved correspondingly. Night Squadrons 1 and 2 moved to St Inglevert; 3 and 4 to Campagne; Day Squadrons 7 and 8 to Oye; and 9 and 10 to La Fresne. The headquarters of the group was also moved to Autingues, just outside Ardres.

At the end of July 1918, the first United States Marine Corps pilots together with their ground crews and equipment arrived at Brest, France, en route to their base at Calais. Earlier in the year, Marine Corps Aviator No.1, Major Arthur Cunningham, had visited France to inspect the French and Italian bomber bases. His primary job was to select bases for the combined Northern Bomber Group pilots who were to follow him from the United States. His main problem was that he had more than enough pilots to fill the squadrons but no aircraft. Cunningham had had earlier problems with the US Army, who had told him quite bluntly that they wanted nothing to do with him or his pilots: 'If the [Marine] squadron ever got to France it would be used to furnish personnel to run one of the [Army] training fields, but that this was as far to the front as it would ever get.'

Cunningham immediately turned to the navy and offered them the services of his Marine Corps' pilots in hunting and attacking the German submarines that operated from the Belgian coast. After consultation with senior navy officers, Cunningham returned to the United States and presented his plan to the General Board of the Navy, stating that his Marine pilots could also bomb the German submarine bases, therefore releasing the US Navy aircraft to carry out other duties. The Navy Board had approved the setting-up of a group called the Northern Bombing Group and Cunningham went down to Miami, Florida to set about joining up all the other Marine units into the 1st Marine Aviation Force. It was originally planned that the group was to operate as one day wing and one night wing, consisting of six squadrons each. The whole group would be under the command of a group commander, the two wings under the command of wing commanders and the six squadrons under the command of squadron commanders. Each of the squadrons was divided into three flights under the command of flight commanders, but because of the difficulties in obtaining aircraft, the group was reduced to four day and four night squadrons.

The aircraft Cunningham had been offered was the Italian Caproni 600, but he had wanted the Caproni 450 with the Isotta Fraschini engine. The Caproni 600 had the Italian Fiat engines and had been proved to be most unreliable and in some cases downright dangerous. Hundreds of the Caproni 600 were ordered by the United States, but only a handful were ever delivered and the ones that did arrive were plagued with problems of poor-quality workmanship and engine malfunctions. It was said that the Caproni 600 with the Fiat engine killed more allied crews than the Germans and Austrians combined.

It has to be remembered that nearly all the American aviators were still in the learning stage of combat and that a large number of them had been assigned to battle-hardened allied units. As one Marine pilot succinctly put it:

> We had flown nothing but Jennies [JN-4s]. We got one DH.4, and all of us got one flight in the first DH.4 – one flight! Our gunnery training had consisted of getting into the rear seat and using a Lewis gun, shooting targets on the ground. None of us had ever fired a fixed gun, or dropped a bomb in our lives.

Nevertheless, these pilots were to become a major asset to the main force of the USAS and USNAS when they finally arrived, and before the war was over the American pilots and their squadrons would leave their mark on the world of military aviation.

At the beginning of June 1918, a number of US Navy pilots and observers were assigned to No. 214 Squadron, RAF at St Inglevert for combat training on Handley Page bombers after their base at Coudekerque had been bombed. By the middle of July the US Navy crews had enough training and experience to go on raids in aircraft manned entirely by American crews. The first of the long-awaited Caproni bombers arrived on 11 August 1918. Four days later, flown by Ensigns Leslie Taber and Charles Fahy with D.C. Hale as gunner/observer, it made a successful night raid on the submarine pens in Ostend, but this was marred by two more missions that had to be aborted because of engine trouble. More time was spent in repairing and trying, most of the time unsuccessfully, to keep these aircraft serviceable. The only combat time the American crews were able to get was with No. 214 Squadron on their Handley Page bombers.

After a couple of months of trying to make the Caproni an acceptable bomber, an arrangement was made between the US Army and British authorities to procure British Handley Page bombers in exchange for Liberty engines; these were to be mounted in the Handley Page aircraft. Unfortunately, the agreement was reached and the night-bombers tested just as hostilities ceased.

One pilot, Lieutenant (junior grade) McCormick, USNRF had carried out a number of these flights at night and was assigned to 214 Squadron RAF to fly bombing missions in the Handley Page. Returning from a bombing mission in the middle of the night and having suffered flak damage, the aircraft crashed in a forced landing. McCormick managed to extricate himself from the wreckage and then ran forward to aid the RAF members of the crew. In the darkness he ran into one of the large propellers that was still turning and was killed.

On 18 July 1918, the 1st Aviation Force sailed from New York for France aboard the USS *DeKalb*, arriving in Brest, France on 30 July. It was here that their problems began. There were no arrangements made to move the squadron 400 miles to Calais; in fact, no one knew what to do with them. Cunningham requisitioned a train and set about moving his entire force, lock, stock and barrel to Calais. On arrival, the 1st Aviation Force was billeted temporarily in a British rest camp before they set to work building their own landing fields. The force had been split into four squadrons, A, B, C and D. A and B Squadrons were located at a small town by the name of Oye, while C and D Squadrons (D Squadron at the time was still in the United States) were located at La Fresne, just south of Calais. The headquarters for the group was set up in the town of Bois en Ardres.

The 1st Marine Aviation Force, as it was now known, was brought up to strength with 149 officers and 842 enlisted men. The original plan of Major Cunningham of bombing the German submarine pens was shelved because the retreating Germans had evacuated them all. This enabled the Marine squadrons, now renumbered 7, 8, 9 and 10, to operate alongside their RAF counterparts in support of the British and Belgian ground forces who were gathering momentum in the final push.

The US Marines flew the day wing of the NBG, now under the command of Captain David Hanrahan, USN, but like their navy counterparts were lacking in combat experience. Three crews were assigned to No. 218 Squadron, RAF for 'hands-on' combat training and after qualifying they returned to their own units. This system proved to be extremely successful, so the American crews were rotated so that at any one time there was a pool of US Navy and Marine pilots and observers being trained by the RAF.

The Marine/Navy day bomber squadrons, however, had more success when they were given DH.4 bombers with Liberty engines. Four of the aircraft were shipped over from the United States and assembled at Pauillac. After being assembled they were inspected by American and British engineers, and after a number of modifications were put into active service. More of the aircraft were expected from the United States, but after a number of delays, the Commander, US Naval Aviation Forces and Foreign

A new DH.4 arrives for the 278th Observation Squadron, USAS.

Service, obtained by concession of the British government fifty-four DH.9 aircraft in exchange for Liberty engines. These aircraft were assembled at Eastleigh and flown across the English Channel to Pauillac before being assigned to their various squadrons. The first aircraft arrived on 2 October 1918, just too late to make any significant impact in the war.

The Marine crews, however, did manage to get involved in operations. Because of a shortage of pilots, the RAF, who had taken a battering over the war years, had more aircraft than crews. An arrangement was made with two RAF squadrons, Nos 217 and 218, for the US Marines to fly three bombing missions with them; it was one that gained approval from both sides. On 28 September 1918 while flying with 218 Squadron, RAF the US Marines scored their first victory when First Lieutenant E.S. Brewster and Gunnery Sergeant H.B. Wersheiner, although both wounded when attacked by fighters while over Belgium, shot down a German Albatros. One week later, three Marine crews, again operating with 218 Squadron, RAF were involved in a dramatic relief operation. The crews, consisting of Lieutenant Frank Nelms and Gunnery Sergeant Archie Pascal, Captain R.S. Lytle and Gunnery Sergeant A. Winman, and Captain F.P. Mulcahy and Gunnery Sergeant T.L. McCullough, dropped over 2,600lb of food and supplies to a beleaguered French regiment that was cut off from the main supply lines. For carrying out this dangerous mercy mission, the pilots were awarded the Distinguished Service Cross (DSC), while the gunnery sergeants were awarded the Navy Cross.

At the end of the war, the US Marine Day Wing in France was credited with shooting down six German aircraft and another eight possibles. The crews were awarded two Medals of Honor, four Distinguished Service Medals and thirty Navy Crosses.

* * *

On 13 August 1918, American and British squadrons combined to carry out a raid on the German airfield at Varssenaere, Belgium. The Germans had been carrying out patrols with their Fokkers and bombing raids on Dunkirk with Gotha bombers from the airfield, causing a great deal of damage. The planning of the raid had been masterminded by Lieutenant Colonel J.A. Cunningham of the RAF and Major Harold Fowler of the USAAS. One week previously a rehearsal for the raid had been carried out on the British airfield at Audembert, near Calais, watched by Cunningham and Fowler. On the day of the raid all went according to plan and when all the aircraft had returned safely, the RAF issued the following communiqué:

> A raid was carried out by No.17 American Squadron on the Varssenaere Aerodrome, in conjunction with squadrons of the 5th Group. After the first two squadrons had dropped their bombs from a low height, machines of 17 American Squadron dived to within 200 feet of the ground and released their bombs, then proceeded to shoot at hangars and huts on the aerodrome, and a chateau on the N.E. corner of the aerodrome was also attacked with machine-gun fire. The following damage was observed to be caused by this combined operation: A dump of petrol and oil was set on fire, which appeared to set fire to an ammunition dump; six Fokker biplanes were set on fire on the ground, and two destroyed by direct hits from bombs; one large Gotha hangar was set on fire and another half demolished; a living hut was set on fire and several hangars were seen to be smouldering as the result of phosphorus bombs having fallen on them. In spite of most of the machines taking part being hit at one time or another, all returned safely, favourable ground targets being attacked on the way home. No.211 Squadron bombed the aerodrome after the low-flying attack was over, and demolished the chateau previously referred to.

In France, the German army had driven a wedge through the French lines at Château-Thierry and a First Brigade was created under the control of General Mitchell in an attempt to support the army. The American 1st Pursuit Group and 1st Observation Squadron, together with some French squadrons, made up the First Brigade and were soon in action against the Germans. It was to become a 'baptism under fire' for nearly all the American pilots, as they came up against a hard core of experienced German pilots whose machines were far superior to theirs. In the weeks that followed before the German push was halted, American pilots became hard-bitten and experienced and aged about five years in as many weeks. They were subjected to discipline levels they had never experienced before, but necessary ones that were designed to keep them alive. There were a few that rebelled and became mavericks, but they were few and far between. The AEF suffered terrible losses both in the air and on the ground, but the tide had turned.

On the other hand there were the 'All-American Boys' who fought in the war and adhered strictly to the rules, and none more so than Captain Eddie Rickenbacker. Rickenbacker was to become America's top ace with a score of twenty-six 'kills', the vast majority of these being shot down in a two-month period. He had come into flying late in life, having been a sergeant driver for General Pershing for a period of time before applying for flying duties. His background as a racing driver was to help him master the complexities of flying an aircraft. He was not a natural pilot, but one who had to work at all the problems flying in combat brought with it.

Rickenbacker had soon tired of being General Pershing's chauffeur and looked around for a position that would move him closer to the world of aviation. Then by luck he met General Billy Mitchell, whose 'official' car was a fast sports car and who wanted nothing better than a noted racing driver as his chauffeur. Despite his lack of college education, he persuaded General Mitchell to put him forward for pilot training and was assigned to an aviation unit. On completion of an engineering course, he was given a commission and assigned to Issoudun initially as the engineering officer. Frustrated with his position and the length of time it was taking to be accepted into flying training, he managed to persuade the instructors to give him some lessons in their spare time. After some weeks his orders to flight school came through and after only five and a half hours of dual-control flying, he went solo. His experience as a racing driver stood him in good stead, as did his skill as a mechanic. He was posted to Issoudun, the base for replacement aircraft and where all the major repair work was done.

Rickenbacker's job was to test the aircraft after they had been repaired, a job that soon bored him. He was then posted to the aerial gunnery school at Cazaux where, after two weeks of intense practice, he passed out with flying colours. Then followed a posting on 3 March 1918 to a new squadron, No. 94 Pursuit Squadron at Villeneuve under the command of Major John Huffer. It was to be a month before their aircraft arrived and Rickenbacker made his first flight over the lines with Major Raoul Lufbery (Lufbery was killed the following month). It didn't take him long to realize that flying training was one thing, but flying in combat was something totally different. Rickenbacker was not a natural pilot, so everything he did had to be thought out prior to doing it. Combat, he realized, was going to consist of loops, rolls, tight turns and all done in a split second because that could mean the difference between life and death. He developed his own training programme of various manoeuvres and soon became adept at them. The slow build-up to his squadron becoming fully operational was to his advantage and when the first of the action arrived, he was somewhere near ready.

On 29 April, six weeks after arriving at the squadron, Rickenbacker scored his first victory: a Pfalz. He had been flying with James Hall over Pont-à-Mousson when they encountered a German aircraft on a reconnaissance mission. After the experienced Hall had climbed into the sun and attacked, forcing the German aircraft to turn into Rickenbacker's path, Rickenbacker shot the Pfalz fighter down in flames. The following month the intrepid pair were flying patrol when they encountered a patrol of German aircraft. Rickenbacker shot down his second, an Albatros D.III, but Hall's aircraft was hit by what fortunately later turned out to be a dud shell. Fighting the controls of the badly-damaged aircraft, Hall managed to crash-land just inside the German lines. The aircraft smashed into the ground with such force that Hall's face was smashed violently into the butts of his guns. Badly injured, he was extricated from the wreckage by his German captors and taken to a field hospital. There doctors treated him, but his war was over.

One month later Rickenbacker chalked up his fifth 'kill' and with it came promotion to flight commander, although he retained his rank of captain and was not given the rank of major which usually went with the position. Maybe it was his background and lack of college education that was holding him back, because it has to be remembered that it was not only the RFC who nurtured class distinction among flyers. His fellow pilots admired Rickenbacker because he would not ask them to do anything that he would not do himself. He stressed teamwork all the time, both to the ground crews

The heavily-bandaged James Hall in the back of a German staff car after being shot down.

and the pilots. His knowledge of engines surpassed even the best of flight mechanics and he was not averse to getting his hands dirty when the need arose. He communicated with everyone all the time, developing a team spirit second to none. He was not a 'death and glory' pilot either, but one who was methodical and assessed situations before embarking upon them. This was not say that he would shy away from a fight; on the contrary, he could scrap with the best of them, but he was mature enough to know that discretion was the better part of valour. It was this attitude that was to lead him to become America's top fighter ace with the 94th Pursuit Squadron and be awarded his country's highest accolade, the Medal of Honor, albeit some eight years after the war had ended.

Chapter Nine

The 2nd Pursuit Group, which consisted of the 13th, 22nd, 49th and 139th Pursuit Squadrons, also operated out of the Toul area. When the squadrons first arrived, the majority of the pilots were fresh from training, but the 139th Squadron, commanded by Major Angstrom, that had spearheaded the group was joined by three of the USAS's most experienced pilots, Captain David Putnam from the Lafayette Flying Corps and Captains Ray Bridgman and Dudley Hill from the Lafayette Escadrille. The day the group moved to Toul was also the day that the 139th Squadron opened its account when on 30 June while on their first patrol, Captain David Putnam shot down a Rumpler C, adding to his already impressive list of 'kills'.

However, it wasn't the quality of the pilots that concerned the Americans, but the lack of aircraft. Fortunately the French aircraft manufacturers had been stirred into increasing their production of SPADs, Bréguets and Salmson 2-A2s. Unfortunately, the pilots and mechanics had all been trained on rotary-engined aircraft and not the water-cooled ones like the Hispano-Suiza V8s. Not only did the water-cooled-engined aircraft have their own flying idiosyncrasies, but tuning the aircraft engines with virtually no spares also caused its own problems. A complete retraining programme had to be thought out, and this in the middle of the final push of the war. The commanding officer Major Angstrom decided that as far as the mechanics were concerned it would be quicker to send the best of them to the French Air Service acceptance park at Étampes and have them given a crash course in maintenance on the new types of aircraft. After numerous problems, the main one being the language barrier, the mechanics returned to Vaucouleurs and immediately spread themselves around to give instruction to the remainder of the ground crews. The engineering officer used the handbooks extensively and in doing so realized that the Hispano engine, although excellent, had to be handled with meticulous care and tuned like a racing engine. The pilots, on the other hand, trained themselves through a system of trial and error. Fortunately for all concerned, the American Sector at that time was quiet, but it was to be the calm before the storm.

Then on 11 September came Battle Order No.1 from General Mitchell: 'Our Air Service will take the offensive at all points, with the objective of destroying the enemy's air service, attacking his troops on the ground, and protecting our own air and ground troops.'

Lieutenant Colonel Atkinson, who had been recently promoted from major, issued his order from the headquarters of the 1st Pursuit Squadron the same day: 'The entire 3rd Pursuit Group will be on alert after 0900 hrs,

Lieutenant Colonel Bert Atkinson, USAS.

subject to the call of the Chief of Air Service. It will be prepared to carry out missions of bombardment and to attack designated objectives on the ground.'

Captain Robert Rockwell, who only days earlier had replaced Major Thaw as commander of the 103rd Pursuit Squadron, issued an order in the name of Major Thaw: 'All available planes, including those with bomb racks installed, will be held on alert from 8:00 o'clock, ready to leave within ten minutes after receiving a call from this office.'

The tactics of low-level strafing were completely new to the majority of the pilots of the 3rd Pursuit Group and one that left the aircraft extremely vulnerable to ground fire. Yet the big push by the American infantry at St Mihiel needed all the support it could get and General Mitchell was determined not to be found wanting when the time came. All the SPADs of the 103rd Squadron were equipped with bomb racks capable of taking 20-pounder bombs. Their round trip route would take them from Vaucouleurs-Mars la Tour-Chambley-Arnaville-Chambley-Vaucouleurs at heights that ranged from ground level to 500ft.

On the evening of 11 September 1918, Colonel Davenport Johnson called his squadron leaders to a briefing: the St Mihiel offensive would start at 0500 the following morning. Captain David Putnam, who was standing in for his commanding officer Major Angstrom, looked at the wet, misty weather and wondered what part they would be able to play in the forthcoming battle. By dawn the whole camp was alive with anticipation and as daylight broke through the driving mist, the mechanics wheeled the aircraft out and started the engines. After ten minutes the engines were shut down and the vital parts of the aircraft covered with tarpaulins against the increasingly inclement weather. Colonel Johnson issued an order: 'Pilots and ground crews will mess in rotation by Flights until further notice. Return to alert positions as soon as possible.'

Throughout the morning the squadron commanders waded back and forth in the ever-thickening mud between the hangars and the offices. It was to be lunchtime before the first of the aircraft was ordered to fly a patrol. The airfield by this time resembled a muddy ploughed field and the inevitable accident occurred. Lieutenant Joe Carr of the 139th Pursuit Squadron was taxiing to take off when his propeller hit a large clump of mud and disintegrated. His ground crew spent the rest of the morning manhandling his aircraft through the mud on a tail dolly back to its hangar for repair. Finally six of the pilots managed to get their aircraft into the air, but in less than an hour they were on their way back, or at least some of them were. The pilots had not seen anything of the enemy; indeed they had seen very little at all and had great difficulty in finding their way back. Two of them had to force-land due to engine problems and mechanics had to be sent to repair the aircraft.

By mid-afternoon the weather had eased enough for a two-man patrol to be sent out. Led by Captain David Putnam and accompanied by Lieutenant Wendell Robertson, the two set off for a reconnaissance of the front lines. They met up with an enemy patrol and in the ensuing melee they were separated. Robertson returned to the airfield alone, and the following morning Putnam's body was found in the wreckage of his aircraft inside the American lines.

In the Toul sector, No.1 Observation Squadron was carrying out reconnaissance flights over the enemy lines. They were joined by the 96th Bombardment Squadron ('Red Devils'), who were to be the first day-bombardment squadron to see action, flying French Bréguet 14Bs. The creation of the 1st Day Bombardment Group on 10 September 1918, under the command of Major James Dunsworth, had also meant the addition of two more bomber squadrons, the 11th and 20th. These two squadrons were armed with American-built DH.4s, but when they tried to replace the ageing Bréguet 14Bs of the 96th, the move was strongly resisted. The pilots and ground crews had mastered all the idiosyncrasies of the French aircraft

DH.4 of the 1st Day Bombardment Group.

and could see no point in learning about a new aircraft at this late stage of the war.

The 11th and 20th Bombardment Squadrons were sent to Colombey-les-Belles to collect their DH.4s, only to find that the aircraft had been parked, exposed to the elements without cover for a number of weeks. The ground crews set to immediately in drying out the aircraft, re-tensioning the flying wires, checking the rigging and engines to bring them up to operational standard. On 10 September orders came from Group Headquarters to convert all the 11th and 20th Squadron aircraft to bombers and prepare them for the St Mihiel offensive. The problem was that the squadrons had neither bombs nor bomb racks, but by the next morning, after numerous heated telephone calls, all the equipment arrived and by midday on 11 September twelve DH.4s with tarpaulins over the engines and cockpits were fuelled, bombed and armed, ready to go.

At one minute past midnight on 12 September 1918, the St Mihiel offensive began with a barrage from 3,000 guns that was to be constant until dawn, when the 550,000 American and 110,000 French troops on the ground would make their push forward. However, in the air, the weather had closed in and all aircraft were grounded. The previous night, all along the front, US and French balloon companies had been preparing their observation balloons for the assault. Some 10 miles to the north of St Mihiel, the 2nd Balloon Company, one of fourteen balloon companies in the US Army, had spent most of the night preparing its balloon and as dawn broke, so did the weather. With winds gusting up to 50 mph, while the men on the ground paid out the cable, the observers in the basket held on for their lives. At 400ft the observers peered through the driving rain as the basket, hanging precariously below the inflated gasbag, rocked violently backwards and forwards, and watched as American infantrymen moved forward. The forward movement at first was relatively slow because of the adverse weather conditions, but as the morning progressed it gained momentum. By noon the positions of the balloon companies had to be reassessed as they could no longer see the front line of troops.

One of the crews of the 20th Bombardment Squadron's St Mihiel offensive was Lieutenant Guy Wiser (pilot) and Lieutenant Richardson (observer) who were shot down by *Leutnant* Albert Greven of Jagdgeschwader II and taken prisoner. After being entertained by their captors, they were sent to Transchutz Castle as prisoners of war. In 1963, Guy Wiser visited Transchutz Castle and his old adversary *Leutnant* Albert Greven.

By midday the weather had cleared enough for nine of the DH.4s from the 96th Bombardment Squadron to take off to bomb Buxières.

Lieutenant Guy Wiser (pilot) and Lieutenant Richardson (observer) of the 20th Bombardment Squadron, together with their German captors after being shot down by *Leutnant* Alfred Greven of Jagdgeschwader II. Behind the two Americans are *Leutnant* Stolting, *Flieger* Wilke, *Leutnant* Koch and *Leutnant* Greven.

Guy Wiser in 1963 visiting Transchutz Castle where he was held as a prisoner of war after his DH.4 aircraft was shot down by *Leutnant* Greven. While in Germany, Guy Wiser visited Greven.

By mid-afternoon seven of the nine aircraft had returned, two having been shot down by an enemy patrol that jumped the bombers while on their way back. Another eight Bréguets left later in the afternoon, again to bomb Buxières; all returned safely. Later the same afternoon another raid on Buxières resulted in three aircraft crashing in the darkness on their return. At the end of the day the 96th Bombardment Squadron had lost three pilots and eight aircraft and had a number of other aircraft with minor damage.

Among the other casualties on the first raids was First Lieutenant Codman of the 96th Bombardment Squadron who, together with his observer, was shot down. His report describes the incident and capture of both men, culminating in the escape of Lieutenant Codman; this can be seen with others at the end of the book.

The 96th Bombardment Squadron was carrying out a bombing raid on Conflans during the St Mihiel offensive at the time of Lieutenant Codman's incident, when he and three other crews flying Bréguet bombers were attacked. Because of their inexperience, they had broken the cardinal rule of all bombing squadrons: never fly without fighter cover if the squadron is flying well below operational strength. All four of the bombers were shot down and only Lieutenant Codman and his observer Lieutenant Stewart A. McDowell survived. The squadron may well in this case have thought that because it was only a relatively short flight to Conflans they could do without the cover, but it was an expensive lesson to learn and it was not the first time it was to happen and most certainly not the last.

On the morning that the St Mihiel offensive began, the 103rd began opportunity bombing of the trenches and roads. The 1st and 3rd Pursuit Groups caught a heavy concentration of enemy troops on the road between Creuse and Vigneulles late in the morning of 12 September, and attacked them with machine-gun fire and bombs, causing considerable damage and confusion. The 1st Day Bombardment Group also carried out a number of very successful missions on the first day of the offensive despite the ferocious anti-aircraft fire ('Archie'), and dropped in excess of 13,120kg of bombs on railroads, troop concentrations and dumps. Although the rewards were high, so was the price. The first week of the St Mihiel offensive cost the 1st Bombardment Group dearly, as they lost thirty-five officers and men during raids over the lines. Reconnaissance missions on the first day of the offensive were many and enabled the air and ground commanders to deploy their forces where they would inflict the greatest damage and confusion.

By 15 September the offensive had pushed the Germans back significantly and the tide had turned. The line was firmly established from Haudiomont, through Fresnes-en-Woëvre, Doncourt, Jaulny to Vandières, north of Pont-à-Mousson. However, after the initial surge the drive forward was slowing noticeably due to three German observation balloons that were spotting for the artillery with unerring accuracy. Major Harold Hartney, commander of the 27th Pursuit Squadron, called Lieutenant Frank Luke into his office and explained the problem.

Second Lieutenant Frank Luke was not the epitome of the 'All-American Boy'; he was a maverick, but a well-respected member of No.27 Pursuit Squadron. Luke's family background was pure German. His father was born in Prussia and his mother was descended from the first German settlers on Long Island, but that is where the connection ended. The Luke family was as patriotic as any natural-born Americans.

Frank Luke's career started at Rockwell Field Flying School, San Diego, where he passed the course without difficulty and obtained his wings. In February 1918 he was posted to France and assigned to the 27th Pursuit Squadron under the command of a Canadian, Major Harold E. Hartney,

Lieutenant Frank Luke with his ground crew.

Lieutenant Frank Luke practising with a heavy machine gun.

Members of the 27th Aero Squadron with Lieutenant Frank Luke.

Lieutenant Frank Luke with his SPAD XIII.

Lieutenant Joseph 'Fritz' Wehner, Frank Luke's balloon-busting partner.

RCFC. It was soon discovered that, despite his ancestry, Lieutenant Frank Luke had not inherited the German trait of discipline. Major Hartney was a much-respected commander; a former volunteer in the Saskatoon Fusiliers, he had transferred to the RFC and served with No.20 Squadron RFC during the period of 'Bloody April' in 1917. A highly-experienced combat pilot, he was slowly getting through to Frank Luke that the day of the 'lone gunfighter' was over and survival now depended on teamwork.

This was never more apparent than when he teamed up with Lieutenant Joseph Wehner and started the formidable 'balloon-busting' team. At the beginning of September 1918 Luke and Wehner were sent to attack a German observation balloon near Buzy. While Luke took care of the balloon, Wehner found himself mixing it with eight Fokker triplanes. Luke joined his wingman and between them shot down two of the German aircraft. Over the next few days Frank Luke and Joseph Wehner accounted for six balloons.

At 6.45 pm on 15 September, together with his wingman Lieutenant Joe Wehner, Frank Luke took off and sped towards where the balloons were thought to be. At 7.10 pm the sky in the north-east beyond Verdun suddenly flared red. Eleven minutes later the sky flared red again and fifteen minutes later the last of the balloons flared red against the black sky. Hartney had

Lieutenant Frank Luke standing amid the wreckage of one of his victims, a Halberstadt.

Above: Rare photograph of a German observation balloon falling from the sky after being attacked by an American fighter aircraft, possibly Lieutenant Frank Luke's plane. The observer can just be seen on a parachute in the bottom right-hand side of the photograph.

Left: Two German observation balloons plunging to earth after being shot down by Lieutenant Frank Luke, USAS.

flares lit on the airfield for the returning pilots, delighted that they had accomplished what was at first thought would be a suicidal and almost impossible mission. With the balloons down, the rumble of trucks and the sound of soldiers' boots pounding on the roads increased and the drive forward carried on in earnest.

The following are the incident reports of Frank Luke and Joe Wehner:

> Lt. Frank Luke reports: Patrolled to observe enemy activity. Left a little after the formation, expecting to find it on the lines. On arriving there I could not find formation, but saw artillery firing on both sides, also saw light at about 500 meters. At first I thought it was an observation machine, but on nearing it I saw that it was a Hun balloon, so I attacked and destroyed it. I was archied with white fire and machine guns were very active. Returned very low. Saw thousands of lights in woods north of Verdun. On account of darkness coming on I lost my way and landed in a wheat field at Agers at about 21h30. Balloon went down in flames at 19h50. A true copy.
>
> Lt. J.F. Wehner reports: Left airdrome after formation expecting to pick them up at the Front. I was instructed to attack enemy balloons with Lt. Luke, so I stayed at a low altitude. Saw formation coming north so flew towards the Hun lines to pick up a balloon. Attacked a balloon N.E. of Verdun and S.W. of Spincourt at about 17h10 bringing it down. I was forced to pull off immediately as a formation of five Hun planes were trying to cut me off, and my guns were empty. Hun planes were both Fokker and Albatross [*sic*]. I manoeuvred down towards Chambley where the Huns left me, after seeing a formation of French SPADs approaching. I fired approximately 100 rounds into the balloon.

The potentially dangerous game of 'balloon-busting' was one that had attracted Frank Luke and his close friend Lieutenant Joseph Wehner (also from a German family and, because of his name, constantly under the unfounded suspicion of over-zealous intelligence officers), and together they became one of the best such teams in the USAS. They would watch each other's tails while one or the other was attacking a balloon. That was until one mission, when Frank Luke attacked two balloons over Labeuville while his friend patrolled above to protect him. As he climbed away after

German reconnaissance balloon under attack from an American aircraft.

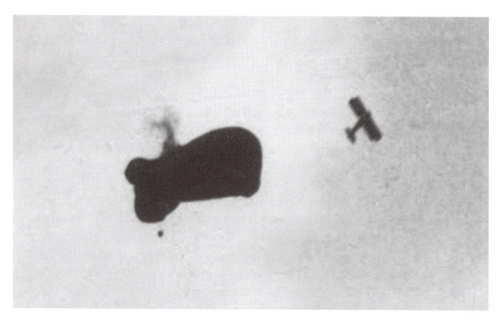

Lieutenant Frank Luke attacking a German observation balloon.

that attack he saw his friend engaged in a fight with six Fokker triplanes. Frank Luke immediately went to the aid of his friend and managed to shoot down two of them, but in the melee lost sight of Wehner. Frank Luke was returning to his base when, just south-east of Verdun, he saw a patrolling German Halberstadt and finding himself in a good firing position, he shot it down, making his score for the day two balloons and three aircraft. On returning to base he discovered that his friend Joseph Wehner had been shot down and killed during the incident with the six Fokkers. From that moment on Luke's hatred of the Germans filled his mind to the exclusion of everything else; a potentially dangerous frame of mind for a combat pilot, and one that would eventually be his downfall.

Then Major Hartney was promoted to commander of the 1st Pursuit Group and Captain Alfred Grant took over. Frank Luke and Alfred Grant took an instant dislike to each other, with the result that Luke lapsed back into his old ways of indiscipline. Grant was a military martinet and demanded discipline, something that had always eluded Frank Luke. Despite their animosity towards each other, Grant could not help but have a grudging respect for the skill and bravery of Frank Luke. Luke had already shot down a number of German aircraft, and shown a propensity for attacking and destroying enemy observation balloons.

On 26 September 1918, Frank Luke and his new chosen wingman, Lieutenant Ivan Roberts from Massachusetts, took off to attack a German observation balloon operating between Consenvoye and Sivry. Frank Luke's report of the mission described the incident from which only he returned:

> On patrol to strafe balloons in vicinity of Consenvoye and Sivry, I attacked with two others a formation of five Fokkers. After firing several short bursts, observed the Hun go down out of control. While at 100 meters I was attacked by two e.a. [enemy aircraft], so I did not see the first e.a crash. I turned on the other two who were on my tail, getting on the tail of one.... One confirmation requested. The last I saw of Lt. Roberts, who was on this patrol with me, was in combat with several Fokkers in the vicinity of Consenvoye and Sivry.

No trace was ever found of Lieutenant Ivan Roberts or his aircraft, and one can only assume that he crashed and was burned beyond all recognition.

Frank Luke claimed another balloon on the 27th when, observed by Lieutenant Joseph N. Fox, he attacked a balloon near Marieulles. He made three passes at the balloon as it was being winched down, and it was on the third pass when the balloon was near the ground that it burst into flames, falling on top of the winch and the German crew. Luke tried to land in a field nearby to confirm the 'kill', but his engine was giving him trouble so he returned to his field and rode back to the site on his motorcycle. On his return he was told that he was grounded from further flying until he could conform to the requirements of military discipline. Angered by this and in defiance, he took off in his SPAD to hunt for more balloons, while in his absence an order had gone out for his arrest. Just before sunset he approached the Meuse area and saw the first of three German observation balloons at Dun-sur-Meuse and shot it down. As he approached the second he came under fire from the ground and was wounded, but managed to shoot it down before crash-landing his aircraft near the village of Murvaux 5 miles east of Dun-sur-Meuse, but not before he had shot up the main street full of Germans. Badly wounded, he dragged himself towards a stream nearby. The German soldiers called for him to surrender; his reply was to open fire with his Colt .45 pistol, but he then collapsed with a bullet through his lungs.

It was later ascertained that he had received the fatal wound while making his strafing run and died as he had lived, a 'lone gunfighter'. His body was stripped of all identification by the Germans, thrown onto a handcart, then taken to the local graveyard where it was left to the French villagers to bury. They buried Second Lieutenant Frank Luke, USAS, with all the dignity they could. He was later identified by his Elgin wristwatch No.20225566 that had been overlooked by the Germans. After the war *Leutnant* Mangels, who had commanded one of the balloon companies attacked by Frank Luke on that day, said that he had gone to Murvaux after being told that the American who had shot down two of his balloons had himself been shot down. He saw Frank Luke's body in the churchyard and confirmed everything that the French villagers had said about the incident. His grave was later found by Merian C. Cooper, who was tasked to find the graves of fallen American airmen.

In a meteoric career that lasted no more than a few months at the front, Frank Luke was awarded the Medal of Honor (the first to be awarded to the USAS), the Distinguished Service Cross with clusters, the Croix de Guerre and the Italian Cross of War, but never lived long enough to wear any of them. His flying career consisted of only thirty hours of combat flying, but during this brief period of time, he downed nineteen enemy aircraft (the nineteenth was not confirmed by the army but was by

French civilians) and fifteen observation balloons, becoming the second-highest-scoring 'ace' in the USAS.

In his recommendation for Frank Luke's Medal of Honor, Lieutenant Colonel O.C. Aleshire wrote:

> On Sept. 29th, 1918 Lieut. Luke, after having dropped from his plane a note to the 7th U.S. Balloon Company reading: 'Watch for burning balloons', Luke attacked and shot down in flames three enemy balloons despite extremely heavy fire from the ground and from a formation of eight enemy planes protecting the balloons. Although mortally wounded in this combat, and although more than ten kilometers within enemy territory, Lieut. Luke descended to within fifty meters of the town of Murvaux and opened fire with his machine guns, killing six enemy soldiers and wounding many more. He then landed, stood by his plane, and when surrounded and called upon to surrender, drew his automatic and held off the enemy until he died from the effects of his wound.

Lieutenant Frank Luke broke virtually every rule in the book, objected to military discipline, and had he returned from his last flight would undoubtedly have been charged for going absent without leave and court-martialled for actually going on the flight without permission. The 'Balloon-Buster' from Arizona was just 20 years old at the time of his death.

The continuing bad weather was making General Mitchell – not famed for his patience – extremely irritable, as he had hoped to prove that his air force was a necessary part of the offensive in supporting the ground troops. He had visions for the future and wanted the world to see what a properly-equipped and trained air force could contribute to a military situation.

Of the sixteen squadrons General Mitchell had at his disposal, only six were at full strength; the remainder for a variety of reasons were well under strength. His aim of letting the ground front-line troops see the support they were getting from his airborne squadrons was excellent in theory, but in reality a non-starter. The main problems were that the bombers would be attacking targets well beyond their own lines, and the escort fighters accompanying them would be flying at medium to high altitudes. Consequently, the only aircraft that the front-line troops would ever see would be the reconnaissance ones. Added to this was that the majority of the troops could not distinguish one aircraft from another, so they would have no idea of the nationality or type of any of the aircraft.

On the second day of the St Mihiel offensive, with the threat of the German observation balloons now removed, the weather eased and patrols were increased. The French and US Balloon Companies moved forward and consolidated new positions. Contact with enemy was still sparse, but over the next couple of days the Germans lost a few more of their aircraft. In the meantime the front had moved away from Toul and on 24 September 1918, it was decided that the 2nd Pursuit Group should be moved to Belrain, about 8 miles west of Verdun. The move also prompted a change of tactics. Bomb racks were fitted to the SPADs, the ground staff labouring through the night of 25/26 September to ensure all the aircraft were ready for the low-level ground strafing and bombing to which they were about to be subjected.

Ground strafing was one of the most dangerous aspects of military warfare. Usually flown at heights between 50ft and 200ft, the object was to attack columns of ground troops, their artillery, horses and vehicles and troop and supply trains, inflicting the heaviest of casualties possible on both men and equipment. The first passes by the aircraft were often the safest, due in the main to the element of surprise. By the time the aircraft made its second pass, the ground troops would have recovered from the surprise attack and would sometimes reply with devastating ground fire. Many an aircraft returned with the fabric covering the wings and fuselage in tatters.

The weather in the area continued to cause problems for the squadrons. Strong, gusty winds accompanied by rain hampered the observation

Colonel William 'Billy' Mitchell in a SPAD XIII about to take off on an observation flight.

aircraft and attack, especially those flown by pilots on their first missions. Yet despite this, the squadrons continued to take their toll on the enemy and the St Mihiel offensive petered out in favour of the allies. On the ground, the maintenance crews were performing nothing short of miracles: changing and repairing engines, replacing propellers and patching up tattered airframe fabric, some of which looked like patchwork quilts, all carried out under the most appalling conditions.

With the German army still reeling from the St Mihiel offensive, the order came for a concerted attack by the allies on the front between the Meuse and Suippe rivers. The place for the attack, the Meuse River and Argonne Forest area, had been General Pershing's choice. The First Corps was to attack on the front between Verignois and La Harazée, with the 35th, 28th and 77th Divisions in line from left to right. Attached to the 28th Division was the 12th Observation Squadron for all required aviation duties. The 12th had been chosen for this duty as it was now one of the most experienced of all the American squadrons, and this was hopefully to be the last major battle of the war. Orders from General Mitchell were that all flights over the Meuse-Argonne area were to be made in French aircraft, so as not to make the Germans aware of the huge build-up of American troops. He ordered that the 1st Day Bombing Group carry out raids on the city of Metz and its surrounding railway yards, so as to make the enemy think that the point of any offensive by the allies might be there.

The group suffered heavy casualties both in men and machines during this period. All American aircraft to be used in the offensive were brought into position over the preceding days, so that on the afternoon of the 25th they were all in position and ready, while the balloon regiments near the front itself remained inactive until late in the afternoon of the 25th, when they started to inflate their balloons. Mitchell then quietly moved his headquarters to Souilly, so as to be close to the front when the offensive began.

The reason for the secrecy was because the day before, 24 September, a German reconnaissance aircraft had been shot down and undamaged photographic plates were found in the wreckage. When developed, they showed General Pershing's headquarters and a very large area surrounding it, highlighting the build-up of troops and their weapons. Whether or not the Germans had wind of something Pershing was not sure, but one thing was certain: a complete security cordon had to be thrown around the whole area.

The Meuse-Argonne offensive, as it was to become known, started just after midnight on 26 September 1918 when 2,700 allied guns, just behind the infantry's jumping-off point, opened up on the enemy's positions. After five hours of continuous bombardment, 600,000 men, predominantly Americans, went over the top and into the final major battle of the war. The weather could not have been worse: torrential rain, thick mist and acres of mud. The intention was to drive wedges through the Hindenburg Line for about the first 16 kilometres, then a second push for a further 16 kilometres with the Americans heading for Sedan to capture the major railway centre there, thus preventing any reserves being brought up. The British were to attack from the Western Front and the French to push through the Champagne area.

The balloon companies raised their observation balloons all along the front, attracting Fokker D.VIIs like moths to a flame. The 8th Balloon Company raised and lowered their balloon time and time again as it was attacked, then late in the afternoon of the 26th at a height of 1,200 metres it was attacked again, only this time it was set on fire. The two observers in the basket, Lieutenants C.J. Ross and H.E. Hudnut, jumped for their lives. Hudnut jumped first, his parachute opening very soon after leaving the basket. Ross, on the other hand, waited until Hudnut was clear before he too jumped. Unfortunately, burning remnants of the balloon fell upon his parachute as it deployed and collapsed it. Ross plunged to the ground and was killed; the first balloon observer to be killed in the action. That particular Fokker D.VII accounted for a further three American balloons that afternoon.

The 9th Balloon Company lost its first balloon on 28 August 1918 when a Fokker D.VII flown by *Leutnant* Otto Weisshaar appeared from nowhere and riddled the balloon with machine-gun fire. Fortunately Lieutenant Sheldon Clarke and Corporal Lionel Bailey managed to jump to safety and were able to watch with some satisfaction as their own machine-gunners brought the enemy aircraft down. On 12 September they raised their second balloon, only to see it destroyed by enemy artillery fire. Ten days later the incident was repeated, only this time they were in the process of inflating the balloon when it was hit. In the following weeks as they were to follow the advancing troops, they were to lose two more balloons, but the war was over before there were any more casualties.

The initial advance was slowed significantly as it approached the River Meuse. The Germans still held the high ground above the River Meuse and the Bois d'Apremont and were able to get six divisions into the area. No man's land was a quagmire, and it took General Pershing five days to get his heavy artillery into position to pound the German positions.

On 7 October 1918, the American army launched a major assault on the German positions and gradually clawed their way onto the high ground and secured it. As the exhausted German army fell back, their resistance crumbled and soon they were in full retreat. The initial early successes gave rise to speculation that it was to be a short-lived offensive in favour of the allies, and that all resistance would soon peter out. This was to prove very wrong indeed and the Germans counter-attacked on 8 October 1918. To protect their troops, the German high command marshalled more and more aircraft into the sector as the American 1st Army counter-attacked almost immediately. The result was that aerial fighting became a daily occurrence and within weeks, novice pilots either became battle-hardened or just didn't survive.

It was decided by the USAS high command that a night-fighter squadron might help to keep the pressure on the enemy and the momentum of the advance going. A collection of SPADs was put together with pilots who were between squadrons and placed under the command of Captain Seth Low. The squadron became known as the 185th Night Pursuit Squadron and became operational on 18 October 1918. No sooner had the SPAD aircraft been allocated to the 185th than it was decided that they were required as replacements for other squadron aircraft. Seth Low finally got the squadron up to the front at Érize-la-Petite, but with no aircraft. Five days later fourteen Sopwith Camels arrived powered by Gnome Monosoupape engines and the squadron was in business.

Members of the 85th Aero Squadron.

Sopwith Camel of the 41st Aero Squadron, USAS.

It was not the success that had been hoped for. None of the pilots had done any night-flying, the aircraft had no night-flying instruments and there were no landing lights on the aircraft or on the airfields. Casualties started to pile up and when Captain Jerry Vasconcells replaced Seth Low, the night-flying programme was unofficially put on hold and then slowly allowed to fade into obscurity.

The following week of the Meuse-Argonne offensive saw the USAS carrying out raids on the retreating German army and their lines of communication, but at a cost of more than twenty aircraft and thirty-six experienced air crew. The commanders were struggling desperately to keep up the morale of their respective squadrons, but the American airmen were having a hard time coming to terms with the sudden loss of their friends. The 50th Observation Squadron, which was attached to the 77th Infantry Division, just prior to carrying out reconnaissance missions over their area painted a large insignia of the Statue of Liberty on the sides of their aircraft. The squadron pilots and observers felt this was necessary because of previous problems with infantry divisions who had fired upon their aircraft due to poor or in some cases non-existent aircraft recognition instruction.

Lieutenant Daniel Morse, Commanding Officer of the 50th Observation Squadron, was having great difficulty in liaising with the 77th Infantry Division. On 2 October, after twelve hours of flying through rain, fog and the dense smoke drifting up from the battlefields below, the squadron had achieved virtually nothing. Meanwhile, on the ground, the 77th Infantry Division had been pushing on into the Argonne Forest, oblivious to the fact that they had lost almost all contact with the 50th Observation Squadron. The 2nd Battalion, 308th Infantry Division, commanded by Major Charles Whittlesey, had in fact lost all contact with the Air Service.

The 2nd Battalion was in the process of a combined attack with the French 1st Dismounted Cavalry Division, on a hill aptly named Moulin de l'Homme Mort (Dead Man's Mill), with the express purpose of pushing the Germans off the surrounding hills and ridges. The Americans made good progress and fought their way past the hill, pushing the Germans back. The French, on the other hand, did not sustain their attack and were halted. They then retreated to regroup and resupply without letting their American counterparts know what was going on. The Americans, oblivious to all this, pushed forward, creating a gap in the offensive line. The Germans, on seeing the gap, pushed their troops forward and behind the American lines, cutting them off. With no contact with their headquarters or the French, the 2nd Battalion was in trouble: unfortunately because of the circumstances surrounding the attack, no one knew where they were and they became known as the 'Lost Battalion'.

Major Whittlesey and his troops were trapped in a ravine, surrounded by Germans and being subjected to heavy fire from rifles and mortars. Whittlesey sent their coordinates out by carrier pigeon, but they were woefully wrong and at one point even found themselves under 'friendly' fire from an American battery. The battalion found themselves short of food and ammunition after days of continuous combat and was reduced to looking for rations on the dead members of their number. Somehow reports filtered back of their predicament and on 4 October the 77th Division was ordered into the area to try to relieve them, but was driven back by the Germans. Aircraft then tried to deliver food and ammunition by air-drop, but this failed miserably, mainly because the exact location of the battalion was not known. Three aircraft from the 50th Observation Squadron searched for the battalion, two of which were shot down. Both crews survived and managed to return to their base. The third crew, Lieutenants Harold Goettler (pilot) and Irwin Bleckley (observer), thought that they had seen the battalion and went back for a second sortie. They did not return, and their crashed aircraft and bodies were found near Binarville by American ground troops. They were later posthumously awarded the Medal of Honor for their heroic efforts.

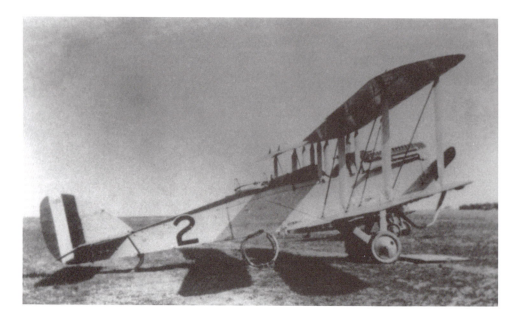

Above: Lieutenants Goettler and Bleckley's DH.4 aircraft.

Left: Lieutenant Harry Goettler, MoH of 50th Observation Squadron, USAS.

On the morning of 7 October 1918, three more aircraft from the 50th Observation Squadron went out in a search pattern to try to locate the missing battalion. This time, after repeatedly diving and making low-level runs through heavy 'Archie' and small-arms fire in the suspected area, one of the aircraft, flown by Lieutenants Maurice Graham and James McCurdy, saw a marker set out on the ground. The pilots immediately rushed the location back to the Division P.C. and at 1800 hours, the 82nd and 28th Divisions fought their way through the German lines to rescue the 308th. Of the 463 men in the 308th, 69 were killed and 159 wounded, and all the survivors were completely exhausted after five days of being subjected to relentless rifle and mortar fire by the Germans.

With the gradual retreat of the German army gathering momentum, the opposite was happening in the air. The German Air Service became more concentrated and began to offer greater resistance against the allied aircraft. The Fokker D.VII was far superior to the SPAD and, together with

Lieutenant Irwin Bleckley, MoH of 50th Observation Squadron, USAS.

Ground markers being laid out to signal to observation aircraft.

Ground markers being used to signal aircraft.

hardened veteran pilots from the various Jastas, began to take their toll of the allied aircraft flown by less experienced pilots of the 2nd Pursuit Group. No.22 Squadron alone lost nine pilots in the following two months, while the 2nd Pursuit Group as a whole lost forty pilots: thirty-one killed and nine taken as prisoners of war. Although the war on the ground was rapidly changing in favour of the allies, the war in the air was becoming more and more intensified, neither side giving an inch. The only bit of light in this period of darkness was that from the end of September to the middle of October, the USAS had shot down more than 100 enemy aircraft and more than 20 observation balloons.

As the Americans pushed forward, other problems manifested themselves. The heated battles on the ground were taking their toll on men and supplies; consequently infantry units within the divisions, because of losses, were being amalgamated with other depleted units. Among these various infantry units had been Air Liaison officers who had kept in constant touch with their counterparts in the Aero Squadrons. They also had a good working knowledge of the divisions' strengths, weaknesses and tactics, and also understood the need for communication with each other. When some of these officers were killed or moved to another sector and a new unit formed, there was always the possibility that the new unit would have no one who had had previous contact with an aero squadron or air liaison experience.

When the third phase of the Meuse-Argonne offensive got under way, this problem was highlighted when the 50th Observation Squadron was assigned not only to support the 77th Infantry Division but also the 1st and 12th Observation Squadrons who were flying photographic missions. The 77th had no one with any knowledge of air liaison, and had to rapidly assign one of their officers to the task. This, as one can imagine, caused numerous problems, but fortunately none that were insurmountable. Even the balloon units did not find themselves immune to this problem. They too found themselves being shifted along the front as the offensive gathered momentum, only theirs was a slightly different problem. Their trained observers and telephone operators were hard to replace when they were either killed in action, suffering from influenza (an epidemic that was at the time sweeping across the country) or dysentery, leaving the tasks for those left to be increased, and their services spread increasingly thinly over a larger area. Infantry units could be relieved and given respite, but the balloon units had no such luxury available to them. In fact, when the weather prevented them from launching their balloons, instead of resting, they were split into teams of stretcher-bearers and sent into the wood and no man's land to find wounded soldiers and take them back to clearings where ambulances would be waiting.

Despite the advance by the allies things didn't get any better, and in the middle of October, General Pershing became General of the Armies when the 2nd US Army was formed under the command of General Robert Bullard, while the 1st US Army was commanded by General Hunter Liggett. Colonel Milling became Chief of the Air Service for 1st Army, while Colonel Lahm assumed command of the 2nd Army's Air Service and General Billy Mitchell became Chief of the Air Service for both armies. Now came the problem of dividing the air units between the two armies and General Mitchell issued the following directive to all concerned:

> The duties of the Chiefs of the Air Service of the armies are, primarily, to see that the aviation assigned to the armies works in the closest possible liaison with the troops on the ground. Every effort will be made to make this a success, particularly with the staffs, infantry and artillery.

The 2nd US Army was assigned the 85th, 168th and 258th Observation Squadrons together with the 8th and 354th Observation Squadrons.

After some debate, the 135th Pursuit Squadron was reassigned to the 2nd Army and attached to the 4th Corps. To increase the number of squadrons to be assigned to the 2nd Army, the AEF (American Expeditionary Force) requested that the 17th and 148th Pursuit Squadrons be released from duties with the RFC. The British agreed to the request, but refused to allow the Sopwith Camels used by the squadrons to return with them. This was not out of a fit of pique, but simply that they themselves had suffered a number of losses of both men and aircraft and could not afford to lose the latter. Both American squadrons arrived at Toul without aircraft and joined up with the 25th Pursuit Squadron, who had recently arrived at the front but also had no aircraft.

The French were pressurized into providing aircraft for the three squadrons and agreed to provide SPADs. This, of course, meant that the pilots had to go through transitional training, which was not completed until the first week in November. Colonel Lahm was angry about the delay, because it meant that the only protection for the 2nd Army's Observation Squadrons lay with the 141st Pursuit Squadron and they could only provide limited cover because they were carrying out patrols and strafing missions in addition to their protection flights.

The 3rd Pursuit Group, consisting of the 93rd, 213th and 28th Pursuit Squadrons, had been a plan of General Pershing's for some time. While the 93rd and 213th Pursuit Squadrons were already stationed at Vaucouleurs,

Members of C Flight, 148th Aero Squadron, USAS.

Members of A Flight, 148th Aero Squadron, USAS.

Oscar Gude (L) with Eddie Rickenbacker, Alan Winslow and Raoul Lufbery.

the 103rd had been prepared to move since 29 July. Major Thaw, who had headed up the 103rd Pursuit Squadron ever since the Lafayette Escadrille had been absorbed into the squadron, was relieved of his command and replaced by Captain Robert Rockwell, a former member of the Lafayette Flying Corps. The 103rd had fought under the command of four different French army commands up to this point and was temporarily assigned to the 2nd Pursuit Group, but later assigned to the 3rd Pursuit Group. Major Thaw, in the meantime, had moved to Vaucouleurs to take charge of the 3rd Pursuit Group. With all the moves came a lull in activity which was to last the month of August. The 3rd Pursuit Group was moved north to Lisle-en-Barrois and some of the fiercest air activity they had ever encountered. The Germans' backs were now against the wall and they were fighting for every inch of ground and air space.

Among the members of the 93rd Pursuit Squadron was Lieutenant Oscar Gude, who was the squadron's flight commander. He had been the subject of a great deal of scepticism and criticism over the previous months regarding his moral fibre. This arose from an incident on 19 May when, after exhausting his ammunition on long-range passes, his engine allegedly 'ran rough' (this wasn't the first time he had claimed this problem), causing him to return to base just before his patrol encountered an overwhelming hostile enemy fighter patrol. His aircraft, SPAD No.15219, always seemed to be out of commission whenever missions were needed, causing a great deal of discontent among the other pilots. On 22 October 1918, Major Huffer, commanding officer of the squadron, ordered Gude on an offensive patrol and when Gude said that his aircraft was again out of commission, Huffer ordered him to take his aircraft, SPAD No.7662. The following report gave rise to a great deal of speculation:

> On the 22nd a patrol of eight planes, under the command of Lt. Wright, set out on a patrol (over) the east bank of the Meuse in the region of Fontains [*sic*]. The leader observed an enemy biplane coming from Germany. With Lts. Follmer and Hartman, Lt. Wright engaged the enemy in combat. The fight took place in a teeming rainstorm and they arrived back at the airdrome wet and happy. Lt. Gude failed to return from this patrol. When last seen he was flying toward Germany.

A few days after the Armistice, a number of USAS pilots visited a German fighter unit near Metz. One of the pilots, Lieutenant Jeffers, was shown a photograph by one of the German pilots of Major Huffer's SPAD with

Close-up of Major Huffer's SPAD from the 95th Pursuit Squadron flown by Lieutenant Oscar Gude after it had landed on a German airfield with him claiming it was out of fuel.

Members of a German squadron in front of Lieutenant Oscar Gude's SPAD after it had landed on their airfield, Gude claiming to have run out of fuel.

several German flyers around it. They said that an American pilot had landed the aircraft on the field and told his captors that he had run out of fuel. The German pilot told Jeffers that when they checked the aircraft there had been plenty of fuel in the tanks. What happened to Lieutenant Oscar Gude after the war is not known, but his actions seem to endorse the suspicions long held by many of his fellow American pilots.

In the middle of all this Major Marr was relieved of command of the 94th Pursuit Squadron and replaced by Captain Eddie Rickenbacker. This was a popular move as his fellow pilots did not like Major Marr, but Rickenbacker was liked and he set about raising the morale of the squadron immediately. Within days the whole squadron was moved to Rembercourt only 21 miles from the front line. As the allied armies pushed forward, so did the lines and a forward base was set up near Verdun with the 27th Pursuit Squadron under the command of Captain Jerry Vasconcells. The 94th's role was mainly as protection for the advancing allied troops, but on days when there was very little aerial activity they were assigned to ground-strafing the retreating German army.

The 4th Pursuit Group was formed under the command of Major Charles Biddle and consisted of the 17th, 25th, 141st and 148th Pursuit Squadrons. The 17th and 148th had recently returned from operating with the RFC, where they had been flying combat missions since August 1918 and were probably the most experienced squadrons in the USAS. The 1st Day Bombardment Group, now supplemented by the addition of the 166th Bombardment Squadron, faced its hardest battle on 4 November 1918. On a mission to bomb Cheveney-le-Château, fifteen Fokker fighters intercepted the 96th Bombardment Squadron and during the skirmish two of the enemy aircraft were shot down. The same day, thirty aircraft from the 11th, 20th and 166th Bombardment Squadrons joined together in an attack on the same target. They were attacked by eighteen enemy aircraft and lost three bombers. The number of enemy aircraft destroyed has never been recorded, but it is believed that the bombardment squadrons gave a good account of themselves. This was the last time the squadrons had contact with the enemy, as bad weather closed in and kept the aircraft grounded until after the Armistice had been signed.

One of the last two bombing squadrons to come to the front, the 100th Bombardment Squadron, arrived at Ourches on 1 November. They had had extensive training in England at various RFC airfields and by the time they reached the front, they were in their own words 'Ready to the last man to bomb the Boche', but their chance never came. The Armistice was signed before they could even take off in anger. They had had their share of the

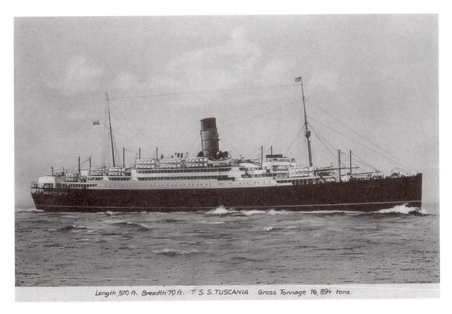

Length 570 ft. Breadth 70 ft. T. S. S. TUSCANIA Gross Tonnage 16,894 tons.

SS *Tuscania*.

war when they, the 155th Bombardment Squadron and the 213th Aero Squadron had embarked aboard the liner SS *Tuscania* in America back in the April. On 5 February, just off the Irish coast, the German submarine *U-77* commanded by *Kapitänleutnant* Wilhelm Meyer saw her and fired two torpedoes at the ship. The first one missed, but the second struck home amidships and she started to sink. More than 200 members of the three Aero Squadrons perished in the icy waters, along with a number of the ship's crew. The chance to avenge their comrades had eluded them, but it had not been for the want of trying.

A similar problem had faced the 155th Bombardment Squadron, except they had only five pilots assigned to the squadron just weeks before the Armistice was signed and there was no possible way that the men could be trained in such a short period of time.

The 27th Aero Squadron finally left New York on 28 February aboard the 833-ton liner RMS *Olympic*. She was one of the first ships to have black and white zigzags painted on her sides in an effort to confuse U-boats trying to calculate a firing distance. Her trip across the Atlantic was uneventful, zigzagging continually because of the threat of German U-boats. As she approached the Scilly Isles several Royal Navy destroyers and a number of cargo ships joined her. As they made their way slowly to the approaches to

Members of the 100th Aero Squadron examining a new mounted gun.

the English Channel, two U-boats spotted the convoy and prepared to attack. One of the submarines, the *U-103* under the command of *Kapitänleutnant* Rücker, made to attack the *Olympic* but had been spotted and instead of taking avoiding action, Captain Bertram Hayes ordered full speed and sent the *Olympic* on a collision course with the submarine. *U-103* was struck right behind the conning tower, almost slicing it in two. There were no survivors and RMS *Olympic* continued on her way.

The 163rd Bombardment Squadron was in a totally different position to the 155th and the 100th; they had probably the best-equipped squadron and most experienced pilots and observers of them all. Their commanding officer, Lieutenant Charles M. Kinsolving, had begun the war as a member of the legendary Lafayette Escadrille and had later joined Escadrille BR117 as a bomber pilot carrying out a number of bombing missions. Given command of the 163rd, he and his squadron were sent to Delouze to prepare for the final push. The airfield was nothing but an empty field when they arrived in October 1918 and no effort was spared to make an efficient operational station. The squadron took off on its first patrols on 5 November and scoured the trench areas, but the Germans had retreated, leaving the areas empty. An occasional enemy aircraft was spotted, but it did not want to engage the American aircraft and quickly hurried away out of sight.

By 5 November 1918, the German counter-offensive had fizzled out and their lines were in total disarray as they retreated. The 3rd Pursuit Group had moved up to Faucoucourt, known locally among the pilots as 'Fokker Bend' as the SPAD, although a very good aircraft for the role of bombing and strafing, was no match for the Fokker fighter. On 8 November, on one of the bombing runs on a German airfield at Gibeny, four pilots from the 93rd Pursuit Squadron dropped their bombs and were rewarded with one of the most dramatic explosions and pyrotechnic displays of the war as one of the largest of the German ammunition dumps exploded.

Also on 8 November orders came to bomb Metz, but as the squadron prepared for their first bombing mission, the weather closed in, preventing any flying. Three days later at 1100 hours on 11 November, the Armistice was signed and the war in Europe was effectively over. The aircraft had just been wheeled from their hangars when the news of the Armistice came through. The bomber aircraft were pushed back inside their hangars for the last time.

There were other squadrons that arrived too late for the war, such as the 41st, 138th and the 638th Pursuit Squadrons. The 638th became operational at the end of October 1918 and the 41st on 11 November and neither saw any action.

The 138th Pursuit Squadron had embarked for the front at the end of 1917, but was diverted to Fort Sill, Montrose, Scotland to take over the work of the RFC's flying maintenance work. As the final push against the Germans in November of 1918 increased, the squadron was sent to Lay St Remy to join up with the 41st and 638th Observation Squadrons, but like them they had arrived too late. The 138th Pursuit Squadron was then intended to go into the Army of Occupation, taking over the aircraft of those squadrons that had returned home. The counterattack on the ground soon fizzled out, but the battle in the air was still being fought, and it was to rage on right up until 1100 hours on 11 November 1918, when Germany capitulated and the Armistice was signed.

At the end of the war, General Mitchell had forty-five combat squadrons under his command, two of which, the 148th Pursuit Squadron and the 17th Pursuit Squadron, had spent most of the war serving with the RFC on the British front. In just over two years the United States Air Service, although its experience in war had been limited and brief, had risen from relative obscurity into a force to be reckoned with and left an indelible mark on the world of military aviation. The USAS was to be the forerunner of what was to become the most powerful air force in the world.

Chapter Ten

The Polish-Soviet War 1919–1921

Although the war in Europe had officially ended, another war between Poland and Russia had started. Eight American pilots – Carl Clark, Merian C. Cooper (20th Bombardment Squadron), Edward Corsi (96th Bombardment Squadron), George Crawford (20th Bombardment Squadron), Cedric Fauntleroy (94th Pursuit Squadron), Arthur Kelly (96th Bombardment Squadron), Edwin Noble and Kenneth Shrewsbury – decided to volunteer to fight on the side of the Polish people. The pilots were to fly combat and reconnaissance missions in support of the Polish ground troops. Their squadron was to be given the name Kosciuszko Squadron after Tadeusz Kościuszko, the Polish patriot who went to America to fight for the Americans against the British in their War of Independence.

The Polish-Soviet War had started on 14 February 1919 when sixty-two Polish soldiers encountered a roaming band of Bolsheviks encamped on a remote Lithuanian site. In October 1917 the Bolsheviks, together with others, had revolted in Russia against the Tsar and had taken control. Remnants of the Bolshevik army were still scattered around and it was one of these groups that the Poles had encountered. A skirmish took place and, despite being outnumbered, the Poles captured the group together with eighty soldiers of the Red Army. This seemingly innocuous action was said to be the cause of the year-long war between Poland and Russia that followed. However, at the same time in the north-east of Poland in the Galician district, or Little Poland as it was sometimes called, Ukrainian nationalists had taken the opportunity to try to extend its boundaries to include the city of Lwów (also known as Lemberg), the cultural centre of Poland and home to Eastern Europe's oldest university.

The inhabitants of the city, after seeing the Ukrainian flag flying over the town hall, took up what arms they could find in an effort to drive the Ukrainians out. With very few men of fighting age, theirs was a hopeless cause and soon they were blockaded in and starving. It was then that President Herbert Hoover's American Relief Program came to the rescue and Captain Merian C. Cooper USAS, who had flown with the 20th Bombardment Squadron in the First World War, was tasked with taking supplies to the beleaguered inhabitants of Lwów. Together with a battalion of Poznań Poles, they loaded up a train with food supplies and fought their way through to the starving inhabitants. Over the coming weeks Captain Cooper was to make a number of trips until the invaders were finally driven out.

Captain Cooper was frustrated by being limited to just running supplies, so he made a request to be reassigned to the Air Service at Archangel to join up with allied units or be allowed to resign his commission with the USAS and join the Polish Air Force. His request to resign was accepted and he returned to Paris to be demobilized. While there he ran into Major Cedric Fauntleroy, who had flown with the 94th Pursuit Squadron, and explained that he was putting together a volunteer squadron to fight alongside the

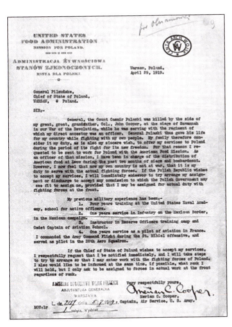

Above left: Document from Merian C. Cooper offering his services to the Polish government in their fight against the Russians.

Above right: Colonel Cedric Fauntleroy.

Poles in their war against Russia. After a great deal of discussion, Major Fauntleroy agreed to join him and the two of them approached the head of the Polish Military Mission in France, General Tadeusz Rozwadowski with their proposal. At first he thought they were just mercenaries, but after a long discussion General Rozwadowski endorsed their proposal and gave them a letter stating that they had been enlisted into the Polish Aviation Service with their existing ranks.

The task now was to recruit more pilots and observers to join their cause, so they started to haunt all the establishments in Paris frequented by American officers of the USAS. Within a matter of days they had recruited a further five airmen. The first to join their ranks was Lieutenant George Marter Crawford from Bristol, Pennsylvania who had enlisted in the USAS in May 1917. After his initial flight training where he earned his wings, he was posted to Issoudun and from there on 1 September 1918 to the 20th Bombardment Squadron. Lieutenant Crawford flew a number of missions before being shot down ten days later and becoming a prisoner of war.

One week later, wearing their new Polish uniforms including its unique four-cornered cap, they were summoned to the Ritz Hotel to meet the premier of Poland, Jan Paderewski. He expressed his heartfelt gratitude for

Polish Paderewski bidding the American members of the Kościuszko Squadron 'god speed'.

their commitment to a courageous undertaking. In reply Major Fauntleroy, the senior-ranking officer of the new squadron, said that he and his men were all Americans who had no Polish ancestry but were willing to fight against the enemies of America's friend in defence of Poland. After a wonderful dinner and reception that went on into the early hours of the morning, daylight brought reality. With all the speeches and backslapping done, it was time to turn theory into practice and dispatch the squadron to Warsaw.

The following morning the seven members of the Kościuszko Squadron, as they were now called, boarded a goods train to Coblenz where they transferred to an American Typhus Relief Train dressed as enlisted men. Throughout the journey the officers took turns working on the train as kitchen police as the train made its way through the battle-torn German countryside towards Warsaw. Arriving in Warsaw, the seven members of the squadron changed into their Polish Air Force officers' uniforms, much to the astonishment of the other enlisted men. Once they had disembarked, the seven members of the Kościuszko Squadron made their way across the war-torn city to Mokotów airfield where the Polish Air Force had their headquarters. There they faced a completely disorganized jumble of men and equipment, the latter consisting almost entirely of captured German material including aircraft.

The Kościuszko Squadron commander, Major Fauntleroy, had travelled to Warsaw ahead of them and was waiting for them when they arrived at their assigned billet, the Hotel Bristol. The hotel was located almost in the centre of Warsaw, giving the men the ideal location to relax and sight-see before going to the front. For the next few weeks they relaxed and enjoyed themselves, partying with other Americans who were either with the Red Cross or the Diplomatic Corps.

Major Cedric Fauntleroy was the ideal person to command the Kościuszko Squadron; he had served in the French Foreign Legion before transferring to the USAS, or Air Section of the American Expeditionary Force (AEF) as it was also known. He was no stranger to discipline and combat and understood men and how to handle them. With the American pilots that joined the squadron came Poles Lieutenant Rayski, who had been taught to fly with the Turkish Air Force by German officers during the First World War, Lieutenants Wladyslaw Konopka and Alexander Senkowski who had fought on the side of the Austro-Hungarians, and Lieutenants Jerzy Weber and Ludwik Idzikowski who had learned to fly with the Russian Imperial Air Service. Major Fauntleroy soon realized that their combat experience was very limited and he initiated a training programme.

One of the major stumbling blocks was the language barrier. The Polish language is difficult to learn and with a mixture of French, German, Russian, Polish and English being thrown into the melting-pot, getting the ground crews to understand what was needed became a priority. Another difficulty was getting the Poles to accept the American relaxed ideas of discipline and their direct way of solving problems by cutting out red tape and bureaucracy.

The major problem facing the Polish government at the time was the fact that there was a drastic shortage of food and medical supplies for a nation whose citizens were on the point of starvation. Disease was rampant because the existing sanitation system had broken down and the hospitals were desperately short of doctors and nurses, so any monies that were available had to be given to those most in need. This, of course, placed the Polish Air Force way down the list. The one saving grace was that all the pilots who returned to join the air force had been trained in Germany, Austria or Russia. In addition, there was an abundance of captured equipment acquired from abandoned airfields. This, however, limited the pilots and ground crews to a choice of what was available. The biggest haul was from the German airfield at Lawica near Poznań where more than 250 Fokker, Brandenburg and Albatros aircraft were discovered in an old Zeppelin hangar, together with a huge haul of various makes of engines and air frames. Although a large number of the aircraft were deemed to be flyable, almost all needed attention.

There were a few White Russian pilots whose experience was limited to flying obsolete Russian aircraft, so they had no experience of flying the German- and Austro-Hungarian-built aircraft. However, their enthusiasm could not be faulted and through a series of trial and error they quickly learned to fly the aircraft. From this assortment of material and men emerged the Polish Air Service. Twenty combat squadrons of fifteen aircraft each were envisaged. Two were already in existence, the 7th Fighter Squadron and the 3rd Combat Squadron, which was re-created after the defence of Lwów.

Major Fauntleroy had divided the Kościuszko Squadron into two flights, 'Pulaski' and 'Kościuszko'. The first flight was commanded by Captain Merian Cooper and the second by Captain Edward Corsi. To identify the two flights, the noses of the aircraft under the command of Captain Cooper were painted bright red and those of Captain Corsi bright blue.

Albatros D.IIIs of the Kościuszko Squadron at Lewandoka airfield in the winter of 1919.

The first airfield was the Lewandówka airfield just on the outskirts of Lwów, and was ideally situated with the main railway line passing just outside the perimeter of the camp. The field itself was made of soft white sand, which provided a level take-off and landing surface but could cause problems if the pilot made any errors with his landing. The rest of the facilities at the camp were very basic but adequate and the squadron soon got to grips with getting all the aircraft and pilots ready.

The aircraft were captured German and Austro-Hungarian Fokker E.Vs, Albatros D.IIIs and Brandenburg C.Is. The next month was taken up with the pilots familiarizing themselves with the various aircraft, carefully carrying out familiarization flights and determined not to be the first to wreck one of the squadron's serviceable aircraft. One pilot who seemed to ignore this was Lieutenant Edmund Graves, an American who had been trained as a pilot by the Royal Flying Corps in Canada and from there posted back to the United States as an instructor. He was one of the finest test and aerobatic pilots around at the time and was seen to throw the aircraft around in the sky without fear. That was to be his undoing. During an exhibition on 21 November to celebrate a festival at which Chief of State Marshal Józef Piłsudski would be present, Graves produced some stunt flying that left everyone watching breathless

Polish President Józef Piłsudski.

with excitement. As he reached the end of his display he entered into a series of 'snap' rolls, but suddenly the upper wing buckled and crashed down onto the lower wing, tearing it off. The aircraft spun violently out of control and plunged into the top of the Potocki Palace, killing Lieutenant Graves instantly. The squadron had its first casualty and they hadn't even gone into action. Many dignitaries attended the funeral and almost the whole population of Lwów lined the streets to pay their respects.

The loss of Lieutenant Graves was a bitter blow to the squadron, but a replacement soon turned up in the shape of Lieutenant Harmon Rorison from North Carolina. Rorison had been a fighter pilot with the 22nd Pursuit Squadron and had been awarded the Distinguished Service Cross after shooting down three Fokker aircraft while on a bombing mission during the First World War. Five USAS aircraft had been attacked by eighteen Fokker E.Vs during which three of the five USAS aircraft were shot down and the fourth badly damaged. Lieutenant Rorison had fought ferociously, shooting down three Fokker E.Vs before being wounded. With his aircraft badly damaged, he managed to shake off his attackers and return to his own lines. Harmon Rorison had been discharged from the USAS at the end of the war and had immediately decided to join up with the Kościuszko Squadron at his own expense. The combat experience of such an experienced pilot could not be refused and he was immediately accepted into the squadron.

As winter approached and the weather started to deteriorate, the number of training flights became limited and the canvas hangars in which the aircraft were repaired and serviced were becoming more like refrigerators by the day. The lack of action was creating problems of morale accompanied by long periods of boredom. In an effort to keep his fliers busy, Major Fauntleroy had them make supply runs by both air and rail. One of the pilots, Lieutenant Elliott Chess, spent a great deal of his time trying to modify the synchronizing gear of the machine guns. This turned out to be a great success as he managed to modify the mechanism, enabling the guns to fire at twice their previous speed, something they would all be thankful for in the coming months. He also designed the Kościuszko Squadron insignia, which consisted of a circle with thirteen stars around the inside together with thirteen stripes representing the thirteen original colonies of the United States, and a four-cornered Tadeusz Kościuszko cap in the centre superimposed over crossed scythes.

On 28 January the squadron was called upon to deliver an important message to the Polish army's advance base at Tarnopol over 80 miles from Lwów. Lieutenant Chess was given the mission and readied himself for the flight in the sub-zero temperatures. The pilots prepared themselves by donning heavy warm clothes and covering their faces with either grease or Vaseline to protect them against the bitter winds they would experience in the open cockpits. Despite crashing on landing because of ice, the mission was a great success with the message being dropped with great accuracy.

It wasn't until 5 March 1920 that the first real taste of action was experienced by the squadron. Lieutenant Rorison was on a training flight when he saw a large contingent of Bolshevik forces together with three panzer trains near Bar. Returning to the airfield, he quickly refuelled and armed his twin machine guns, then had a 12kg bomb mounted beneath his aircraft. Taking off again, he then attacked the unsuspecting Bolshevik camp, causing a great deal of damage and many casualties. Surprisingly the Poles played down the raid, but one Polish pilot from another squadron said that he saw the devastation created by the raid and that it had given his fellow squadron members a tremendous boost.

One month later on 3 April 1920, the squadron was moved to a new air base in Polonne and incorporated into the Polish Air Force Second Group. Just one week after settling in, the squadron was given its first official mission: they were to bomb the Bolshevik headquarters at Chudów just 50km from Polonne. Once again it was Lieutenant Rorison that led the raid, mainly because his was the only aircraft equipped with bomb-carrying equipment. With Rorison were Major Fauntleroy, Captain Cooper, Lieutenant Clark, Lieutenant Crawford and three Polish pilots. The raid took the Bolsheviks by surprise, the bomb almost destroying their headquarters. The Bolshevik troops also suffered a large number of casualties after the remaining aircraft strafed the area with more than 1,000 bullets. On returning, Major Fauntleroy decided that the aircraft should be refuelled and re-armed and another attack be made while the Bolsheviks were trying to recover. The second attack was equally successful, only this time they met with some anti-aircraft fire, giving the pilots a strong indication that it wasn't always going to be one-sided.

That evening while they were celebrating word came through that several new Italian Ansaldo Balilla aircraft were waiting for them at Mokotów. Major Fauntleroy decided that he and Lieutenants Alexander Senkowski, Crawford, Chess and Rorison should go and collect the aircraft and test them before returning to the squadron. Captain Merian Cooper was left in command and over the next few days he sent out a number of observation

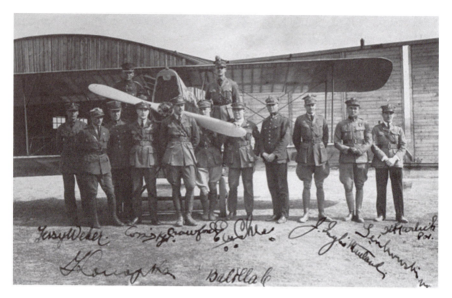

The 7th Escadrille Kościuszko, signed by all.

and bombing missions, dropping large numbers of propaganda leaflets at the same time. The leaflets invited Russian soldiers to defect to the Polish army with promises of good treatment and a regular food ration, something the Russian soldiers often lacked.

While all this was going on, negotiations between the Polish and Ukrainian diplomats in Warsaw reached a mutual political understanding and agreement that both their armies were to merge but under Polish command, with the intention of forcing the Bolshevik army to leave the Ukraine. The inhabitants of the Ukraine were told that the Polish army, when entering their country, would only remain there until a legitimate Ukrainian government was formed and Ukrainian troops were capable of defending their frontiers. Then and only then would Polish troops withdraw. It was against this background that the Polish army launched a major offensive against the Red Army on 25 April 1920.

The problem for the Kościuszko Squadron was that they had virtually no fuel, their aircraft were in very poor shape and they were almost out of ammunition. Captain Cooper sent Lieutenant Jerzy Weber, with a couple of ground crew and the squadron horses and cart, to Nowogród Wołyński to fetch fuel, ammunition and spare parts with the instruction to travel night and day in order to get back with the supplies within forty-eight hours, even if it meant killing the horses. In just under forty-eight hours the crew returned with everything they had been asked to get. Within a couple of days the squadron was back in readiness.

Within hours of declaring the squadron ready, Lieutenant Shrewsbury was airborne making a long reconnaissance flight over the terrain that was to become the area of the Polish offensive. He came back with reports on Bolshevik troop movements, their dug-in positions, railways and the position of the trains and which bridges were secure. He also spotted a likely airfield site, which would be of great help once the Polish troops had taken control of the surrounding areas and the squadron could move up to support them. It would also reduce the flying time towards the front line, thereby preserving valuable fuel.

The Kościuszko Squadron was assigned to the southern sector to give air support to the Polish Second and Third armies under the command of Generals Antoni Listowski and Edward Rydz-Śmigły respectively. The offensive was to be a three-pronged attack: General Listowski's objective was to capture Berdichev, a cattle and grain marketing centre; General Rydz-Śmigły was to take his armoured division and take Zhitomir; while General Jan Romer was to take a cavalry division between the two attacks and take control of the railway leading to Kiev. The Kościuszko Squadron was short of five pilots as they were away testing the new aircraft, but as the morning of the offensive started the sky was clear and perfect for reconnaissance missions. As dawn broke, the engines of Captain Cooper, Lieutenant Clark, Lieutenant Konopka and Lieutenant Shrewsbury burst into life and the four flimsy bomb-carrying aircraft raced into the sky. In a gesture of moral support to the advancing ground troops, the four aircraft raced at head-height over them and then climbed away to begin their reconnaissance missions. Eager to make contact with the enemy, the four aircraft scoured the sky and terrain for two hours but saw nothing. Disappointed and running low on fuel, the four aircraft headed back, jettisoning their bombs in a forest.

Later the same morning Captain Cooper and Lieutenant Noble took off on another observation flight to try to make contact with the enemy ahead of General Listowski's rapidly-moving units. After being airborne for about an hour and seeing nothing, they were delighted to come across a Bolshevik cavalry patrol out in the open. Immediately the two aircraft dived and strafed the patrol, scattering them and forcing them to take refuge in a forest. Having had their first taste of combat and with the adrenaline running high, the two fliers turned towards Berdichev ahead of General Listowski's army and the railway station there. As they approached, they saw a large tent next to the station and then men scattering as they dived in. The two aircraft made two passes, emptying their machine guns into the tent and the station. On the second pass they encountered some return fire but neither aircraft was hit.

Lieutenants Konopka and Clark also took off on the first day of the offensive and shot up an armoured train near the town of Chudnov. This attack was followed by another from Lieutenants Noble and Shrewsbury on the railway station at Zhitomir. The Polish Third Army continued its advance using information being given to them by the squadron's reconnaissance missions. An advance motorized section of the army took control of the town of Zhitomir, without firing a single shot and not seeing a single enemy soldier.

The small aircraft squadron was proving its worth and throughout the day they made raids on targets well ahead of the advancing armies. It was becoming increasingly obvious that there was little or no resistance, just the odd encounter with small groups of Bolsheviks, mostly cavalry units. This became a source of concern for the Polish generals: were the Bolsheviks not prepared to face them or was there another reason why the Russian commanders were reluctant to become involved? It was discovered some months later that in the southern sector of the Ukraine there had been an uprising, and large numbers of Bolshevik troops had revolted against the Red Army, throwing the Russian military hierarchy into confusion and disarray.

The day after the offensive the squadron lost another of their pilots, Lieutenant Shrewsbury, who had been assigned to protect the headquarters of Marshal Piłsudski at Novograd-Volynskiy from possible Russian air attack. This reduced the squadron to just four pilots, so Captain Cooper decided that they would fly individual reconnaissance missions while at the same time carrying out strikes against the Bolshevik forces where they could. On one occasion Lieutenant Clark, after carrying out his initial reconnaissance flight, attacked a cavalry company, a troop train and a train of more than 100 horse-drawn supply wagons. The enemy was now getting used to the attacks from the air and was setting anti-aircraft sections to which Lieutenant Clark's Albatros D.III could lay testament when it returned and was found to have nine bullet-holes in the fuselage and right wing. In fact, the right wing was so badly damaged it had to be replaced.

Lieutenant Noble was carrying out an observation flight over Berdichev in his Albatros D.III when he was suddenly attacked by anti-aircraft fire. Pretending to be hit, he switched off the engine and slowly spiralled towards the ground as if out of control. Below, the Bolshevik gunners danced with glee at their success; that was until Noble restarted his Austro-Daimler engine and raked the gun emplacement with machine-gun fire, sending the survivors running for cover. On his return, the squadron was informed that they were to carry out a combined attack on the Bolshevik positions at Berdichev in preparation for an all-out assault by the Polish infantry on the town itself.

The four exhausted pilots snatched a couple of hours' rest while the ground crews readied their aircraft with bombs, ammunition and fuel. The importance of the mission was made clear to the pilots and they needed no other motivation. They were to make the first attack in formation and then each pilot was assigned an individual target. Polish pilots from Polonne would join in the air attack and their objectives were to take care of the machine-gun positions on the western edge of the town. As the four-man Kościuszko Squadron flew over the town it soon became obvious that the Bolsheviks were retreating towards the railway, leaving the town almost undefended. Lieutenant Noble was the first to attack when he spotted an armoured train about to get under way at the station. Diving in at hedge height he strafed the embarking troops, sending them all diving for cover. Machine guns on the train opened fire as he pulled up and started to climb away. Suddenly he felt a sharp pain as a bullet smashed through the fabric-covered fuselage and shattered his elbow. Realizing he was in trouble after looking at the blood running down his now useless right arm, he headed back to base with all the speed he could get out of his bullet-ridden aircraft. Frantically trying to stay conscious, he approached the airfield, barely managing to control the aircraft. As Noble touched down he felt he was slipping into unconsciousness, but managed to bring the aircraft to a halt. The ground crews rushed to his aid and gently pulled him from the cockpit. After a week in a Polish hospital at Kovel he was transferred to the American Red Cross hospital in Warsaw where he spent several weeks before being discharged. His flying days were over but his exploits were not forgotten by the Polish military and he was awarded Poland's highest military honour, the Virtuti Militari.

The remaining three aircraft of the Kościuszko Squadron continued to support the Polish ground troops that had advanced more than 50 miles, capturing all the primary objectives without meeting any serious opposition. Marshal Piłsudski, although delighted with the progress his army was making, was concerned knowing that he had to meet the Soviet army before his troops had time to reorganize. If he could defeat the Soviet army it would create an independent buffer state between Poland and Russia.

None of this concerned the members of the Kościuszko Squadron, who were more preoccupied with day-to-day matters and how they were to keep their aircraft flying to meet the needs of the infantry on the ground.

Marshal Piłsudski was becoming concerned about the rapid advance his ground troops were making and the need to supply them with supplies and air support. Captain Cooper was instructed to try to find another airfield closer to the front line and so at the end of April he, together with Lieutenant Weber and some of the ground crew, took the squadron truck to search for a likely field. After driving for some hours they came across a large flat field close to Berdichev. Nearby was another field that the locals said had been used by Bolshevik pilots, but the ground was too rocky for Captain Cooper to consider. Leaving a couple of the ground crew to start preparations, he returned to Polonne and had all the aircraft taken to the first field. Within a few days the squadron was airborne and carrying out reconnaissance missions. On the ground the infantry commanders were starting to realize what an asset these flimsy aircraft were and what a difference their pilots were making to the army's efforts.

In Warsaw Major Fauntleroy was having a few problems with the Ansaldo A.1 aircraft that the Poles had purchased. In the words of one of the pilots, 'It was like flying a tank.' It was faster than and could outclimb the Albatros D.III, but had very limited manoeuvrability mainly because of the short wingspan (22ft 5in) and very heavy 220hp SPA engine. The Italians had never used it as a front-line aircraft because of this and it was relegated to home defence duties. There were also some concerns over the reliability of the engines that apparently suffered from carburettor problems. This was partially overcome by modifying the carburettor jets, but there were still some concerns.

On 23 April Major Fauntleroy and the remaining members of the squadron took off in the Ansaldo A.1s, but within an hour problems with the engines and adverse weather conditions forced them to return to Warsaw. Further work was done on the engines but there were problems delaying the flight once again. Finally on 1 May all the aircraft returned to the airfield at Polonne, although a large number of the squadron were already at the advance airfield just outside Berdichev. The Kościuszko Squadron was at full strength.

The offensive was now a week old, and Bolshevik resistance that was at best just a rearguard action had not checked the momentum. As the Polish army swept towards Kiev, Warsaw announced to the world that the army had taken 15,000 of the Red Army prisoner, together with a mountain of weapons and supplies, including seventy locomotives. The role of the Kościuszko Squadron was now of reconnaissance missions for the advancing troops and also to search for another airfield from which to operate. The latter was the most important because the advance was so rapid and covering so much territory. The moving of the airfield became a priority when, on 5 May, Major Fauntleroy made the decision not to fly because the advancing army was now well out of range of his aircraft. One place suggested was a small field outside the town of Belaya Tserkov just 30 miles from Kiev. Lieutenant Shrewsbury, together with a couple of ground crew, was sent using the squadron truck to take a closer look at the field. Travelling with the Polish infantry, he found the field and decided that it would be suitable for their needs.

Bad weather in the shape of heavy rain was hampering efforts to clear the ground, so Lieutenant Shrewsbury took the opportunity to look for help and found it in the form of fifty Jewish labourers. Five days later the airfield was ready for the arrival of the entire squadron and, on 8 May, Major Fauntleroy flew in with the first aircraft to assess the suitability of the field and pronounced it acceptable. The use of the portable Bessonneau timber and canvas hangars provided a good measure of protection against the elements for the ground crews and within a matter of hours they had been assembled. Two days later the whole squadron arrived, and within twenty-four hours the aircraft were in a state of readiness.

As the squadron waited for orders, word came through that Kiev had fallen with virtually no resistance. Apparently a forward patrol had entered the town, boarded a tram and actually captured a Russian officer who happened to be waiting for the tram. The patrol returned to the main force with their bewildered prisoner. Two days later the main force moved into the town only to find that the Bolsheviks had retreated across the River Dnieper. Although there was great celebration, Marshal Piłsudski realized that the Bolshevik forces had escaped intact, and to continue the advance would stretch their supply lines almost to breaking-point.

The Kościuszko Squadron was restricted to flying observation and search missions along the banks of the heavily-swollen river. The break in the conflict gave the Bolsheviks a chance to re-arm and re-supply their troops and gave their senior Russian commanders the chance to reassess the situation. A couple of days after the fall of Kiev, Lieutenants Crawford and Senkowski were on patrol when they spotted seven riverboats: four carrying supplies and the remaining three jammed full of troops. Lieutenant Senkowski had to withdraw because of sickness, leaving Crawford to attack on his own. Although he wasn't carrying a bomb, his machine guns were armed with tracer bullets, so swooping in to attack he made his approach. The Bolsheviks, realizing that they were about to be attacked, opened up with all the firepower they had. They were supported by even more gunfire coming from the banks of the river. Despite this, Lieutenant Crawford threw his Ansaldo Balilla into a low zigzagging attack and opened fire, sending tracer bullets into the riverboats. Climbing away after the first attack, he looked back to see Bolshevik troops leaping into the swollen river in an attempt to escape. He took his aircraft round again, only this time making a steep dive towards the lead boat, pouring everything he had into it. As he pulled up and climbed away, he saw a ball of flame belch from the boat as one of the tracer bullets had obviously found its mark on some explosives. Reports later told of numerous casualties from both the bullets and from drowning in the river as the soldiers tried to escape. One report said that the pilot had actually dropped a bomb down the funnel of the lead boat, causing it to blow up. On his return Lieutenant Crawford examined his aircraft, looking at the bullet-holes through the wings, rudder and fuselage with a rueful smile.

In lighter moments the members of the Kościuszko Squadron were enjoying the delights of Kiev. Their accommodation was far better than they had envisaged and the company of the beautiful Ukrainian girls more than made up for the dangers they faced on a daily basis. On one occasion the interrupter mechanism malfunctioned on Lieutenant Senkowski's guns as he attacked a Bolshevik battery. The result was that the timing was put out of synch and he put two bullets through his propeller, almost shattering it. He hurriedly returned to base, thankful that his guns had also jammed at that moment.

Depending on the weather, the daily routine was to make reconnaissance flights along the banks of the River Dnieper, occasionally attacking a Bolshevik patrol. As the days rolled by, the chance of an offensive by the Bolsheviks seemed to diminish by the day and an air of complacency started to set in. Then early in the morning of 25 May, Lieutenant Crawford was on a routine patrol at around 500ft heading towards the banks of the Dnieper. In the distance he saw a massive dust cloud rising from the ground and advancing towards Kiev over the Ukrainian plains. Intrigued, he dropped down to about 100ft and found himself flying over what appeared to be an endless heaving mass of horsemen. He quickly recognized Cossacks and immediately tried to get an estimate of how many. Banking his aircraft round, he swooped in for a low-level attack and emptied his guns into the

Russian Cossacks attacking.

lead riders. Not waiting to see what casualties there were, he headed back to the airfield to tell them of the threat coming towards them. What they didn't know at the time was that this was the Konarmiya, the feared Cossack army of the legendary General Semyon Budyonny. Every Russian army had its own political commissar, and the Konarmiya's was Ioseb Besarionis dze Jughashvili, better known as Joseph Stalin.

The Cossack army, which consisted of approximately 20,000 horsemen, was an illiterate rabble of partisans, misfits and bandits who rode into battle wearing their astrakhan hats and waving their sabres for the sheer pleasure of fighting and nothing else. The charismatic, hard-line General Budyonny, who ruled his troops with a rod of iron, had licked them into shape. When they had defeated Ukrainian General Denikin and his counter-revolutionary army earlier that year, General Budyonny gave his Cossacks five weeks' leave, allowing them to rape, pillage and plunder whatever they needed.

The news Lieutenant Crawford had brought sent shudders through the Polish generals as they thought that the Russians had not brought the Cossacks into the war at that time. They were also concerned that the Polish advance had been so rapid that their lines of supply and communication were stretched almost to breaking-point. If the Cossack hordes with their

Members of the 2nd Gorsko-Mozdoksky Cossacks.

large numbers of horsemen hit the front line, they would break through, throwing the Polish army into chaos. The only solution was to retreat to a point where they could re-form, and then stand and fight.

The Kościuszko Squadron was given the task of carrying out reconnaissance and harassing flights in an attempt to slow the force down. This meant that all the pilots were to carry out continuous flights, just returning to re-fuel and re-arm. The first two flights by Lieutenants Chess and Senkowski dropped bombs and strafed the oncoming horde. Both aircraft returned with numerous bullet-holes in their wings. These were quickly patched up and the aircraft readied to fly another mission. The next mission was to be a two-man one, with Lieutenants Chess and Weber. They found that the main Cossack force had split into groups, and they attacked an estimated 8,000 group with bombs and machine-gun fire. As they started to pull away, Chess and Weber realized they were running desperately short of fuel when their engines started to splutter and cough. They switched to their reserve tanks, knowing they had very limited flying time. Lieutenant Chess's engine spluttered into life but Weber's didn't and his aircraft spun into the swampy ground below. The fragile aircraft almost disintegrated on hitting the ground, but later Weber was rescued and found to have nothing more than a few cuts and bruises. However, the squadron had lost an aircraft, yet they continued to cover the Polish army's retreat, slowing the oncoming Cossack horsemen's advance by continuing to harass them.

The situation was becoming tense, so it was decided to abandon the airfield at Belaya Tserkov and move to another field at Fastov that Lieutenant Crawford and Major Fauntleroy had discovered earlier. This airfield was 30 miles to the north, and within hours withdrawal from the Belaya Tserkov airfield was well under way. Major Fauntleroy's problem was not only to keep the squadron operational, but also to try to keep one step ahead of the enemy.

The pressure was beginning to tell on the pilots. This was highlighted after the squadron had been sent to Kazatin to join up with the Ninth Polish Air Force in reconnaissance and bombing sorties. Lieutenant Rorison had returned from a particularly arduous mission and was so exhausted that his landing was over-heavy and he smashed the aircraft's undercarriage. Fortunately he was unhurt, but Major Fauntleroy ordered all the pilots and ground crews to rest, knowing that if they all continued under this pressure, the squadron was finished. Then an enemy aircraft, a lone Bolshevik bomber flying very high, dropped a bomb on the airfield causing no casualties or damage, but the American pilots were so tired they could only watch the bomber fleeing for home. They had been caught napping and were very disappointed that they could not give chase, but realized that by the time they got an aircraft off the ground the lone bomber would be long gone.

Captain Cooper, Lieutenants Corsi and Clark were fighting their own war from Kiev where they had been detached to fly Bréguet bombers. On one mission the bombers attacked the Bolshevik port of Cherkasy, where Lieutenant Clark dropped his bomb on a steamboat full of troops, sinking it almost instantly. The sudden attack caused chaos at the port, so much so that one troop-carrying barge ran aground in its effort to escape the raking machine-gun fire that followed the bombing. A Bolshevik radio report was intercepted later that day stating that the port had been attacked by thirty Polish aircraft consisting of bombers and fighters and had suffered a large number of casualties.

Vital to the whole campaign was the railway network, not only for the trains but because the telegraph system ran parallel to it. The bombing of the railway lines would cause a tactical dilemma for both sides if it were to be destroyed. When strafing the trains, particular attention was to be made not to damage the engines themselves as they could be captured and re-used. However, when bullets were flying through the fabric of their aircraft pilots really didn't take into consideration the usefulness of the engine and its carriages; self-preservation was the priority. Another target of the bombers were bridges, but then it was realized that although they were useful to the enemy, they were also useful to Polish troops, so only certain bridges were targeted.

In addition to the problem of Polish troops not being able to distinguish between Polish and Bolshevik aircraft, one of the continuing problems faced by the American pilots was the language barrier. This was highlighted in one incident when Lieutenant Shrewsbury made a forced landing after his engine failed just short of the airfield. After trudging across fields to get back to base, he met a truckload of soldiers and ground crew coming down the road towards him going 'to capture a crashed Bolshevik aeroplane'. He decided to join them, only to discover that it was his aircraft they were going to 'capture'. The aircraft was being guarded by some other Poles who, after a long argument through interpreters and the waving of arms, reluctantly released the aircraft to the ground crew after being convinced that the aircraft was in fact Polish. The aircraft was towed back to the airfield where the engine was removed and the remainder scrapped.

The usefulness of the aircraft in its reconnaissance role became even more apparent when Major Fauntleroy, while on such a mission, spotted some Bolshevik cavalry busy around the railway track. He realized that they were in the process of planting mines beneath the track itself. Looking around, he saw in the distance the smoke coming from an oncoming train and headed towards it. As he got closer he saw that it was packed with Polish troop reinforcements headed for Kazatin. Swooping down, he waggled the wings of his Ansaldo Balilla to attract their attention, but it wasn't until the third attempt that someone realized that something was wrong and the pilot was trying to attract their attention. The train was halted, and finding a level piece of ground close by, Major Fauntleroy touched down. Jumping out of his aircraft, he ran towards the train, shouting whether anyone could speak English. Fortunately a young officer, after examining Major Fauntleroy's papers, ordered all the soldiers off the train. They were instructed to prepare to attack the Bolshevik cavalrymen who were still blissfully unaware that their plan had been thwarted. Major Fauntleroy took off and after dropping a couple of bombs on the Bolsheviks and then attacking them with machine-gun fire, watched as they were then ambushed by the Poles as they tried to escape. For this act Major Fauntleroy was awarded Poland's highest honour, the Virtuti Militari.

Despite the renewed efforts of the Kościuszko Squadron, the Polish advance had been halted and breaches were beginning to appear in the front line. The Russian campaign had started in earnest and although being halted temporarily by the air units of the Kościuszko Squadron and the bomber unit from Kiev, the overwhelming Russian troop numbers finally broke through. Captain Cooper sent an urgent message to Major Fauntleroy asking for more pilots and aircraft. The reply simply stated that there weren't any to send.

The day of the Bolshevik assault, 5 June, the squadron flew virtually non-stop missions in an attempt to stem the flow of enemy troops. Constant reconnaissance flights to try to keep the Polish generals up to date with the situation on the ground were flown, eating up fuel and wearing out the already tired aircraft, pilots and ground crews. Then the weather changed in favour of the Bolshevik advance when heavy rain turned the airfield into a sea of mud, preventing the aircraft from taking off. Major Fauntleroy managed to get one of the aircraft off the ground for a reconnaissance flight and discovered that the Cossack horsemen were closer than at first thought and in danger of overrunning the Polish positions. On his return he raced to staff headquarters and explained in no uncertain terms the seriousness of the situation. The staff officers hurriedly collected all the maps and important paperwork and headed towards the railway. It was discovered later that as they were leaving the town the Cossacks were entering from the other end. Major Fauntleroy placed the squadron on immediate evacuation to Novograd-Volynskiy.

Within hours of setting up camp, word came that Zhitomir was now in the hands of the dreaded Konarmiya and that 5,000 Russian prisoners had been released. At the same time another section of the Konarmiya had taken Berdichev, leaving the inhabitants at the mercy of this marauding horde of Cossacks.

Reconnaissance flights were now the order of the day, but with the inclement weather dogging their every move the squadron was finding it increasingly difficult to get airborne. Despite this, messages between staff HQ and the army were still being sent by air and as the Bolshevik army continued to close around the main Polish army, cutting off the escape route of General Rydz-Śmigły's Third Army, the communication flights became increasingly important. The entire Polish army was in disarray and in full retreat, but then news came from Major Fauntleroy, who had flown a reconnaissance mission over the Zhitomir area, that the Cossack army had changed direction towards Kiev. This unexpected move by the Cossacks relieved the pressure on the Poles, enabling the remaining Polish troops to regroup in Warsaw.

Why the Cossack army never followed through after taking Zhitomir and Berdichev is not known, but what is known is that had they done so, then the Polish army, which was in full retreat, would not have been able to defend itself and would in all probability have been annihilated. General Semyon Budyonny had ordered his Cossacks to take control of the Kiev-Kazatin railway line and by doing so prevent the Polish army from escaping, or so he thought. General Rydz-Śmigły had anticipated this and sent his troops along the Kiev-Korosten line that was being controlled by a token force of Bolsheviks as it was considered to be just a secondary point. With the breakthrough made, the Third Army consolidated its position in the southern sector, enabling the rearguard resistance to fall back and join them. In the meantime, the Kościuszko Squadron was joined by the remnants of the Polish Fifth Air Force Group who had abandoned Kiev, destroying what they couldn't carry.

A change in the weather allowed what was left of the squadron to get airborne, searching out Bolshevik troops. Two of the squadron pilots, Captain Corsi and Lieutenant Weber, and four mechanics were reassigned to General Romer's cavalry command to carry out reconnaissance flights for a week. Such were the conditions that the six men were forced to live off the land, eating mainly fruit they found growing wild. Suddenly there was a lull in the fighting, enabling everyone to catch their breath, reassess their position and take stock. The ground crews got to work patching up the remaining aircraft by cannibalizing some of those not fit to fly. Preparations were made to move the entire air force back to Lwów.

The Bolshevik advance, which for a brief moment appeared to have been halted, suddenly gained momentum and all the Polish commands found themselves being driven back. Then on 4 July, as the Americans were celebrating Independence Day, the Red Army, under the command of 27-year-old Mikhail Tukhachevsky, launched a major offensive with the intention of driving the Polish army out of the Ukraine. Marshal Piłsudski called upon everyone to fight against the Bolsheviks, including the re-forming of the Polish women's battalion that had fought with such ferocity against the Ukrainians in the first siege of Lwów.

While preparations were being made for a counter-offensive, the Kościuszko Squadron was receiving twelve new Ansaldo Balilla aircraft. They had arrived in crates and were in the process of being assembled so that they could be test-flown before being put on the squadron strength. In an effort to bolster the squadron strength, Major Fauntleroy cabled a friend in America by the name of Colonel Benjamin Castle, asking if he knew any pilots, preferably scout/fighter pilots, who would be prepared to come to Poland at their own expense and fight against the Bolsheviks. All they would be offered was 2,000 Polish marks and a lieutenant's rank.

With all the new aircraft assembled and tested, orders came through for Captain Cooper to move the squadron once again, this time to Holoby, which was 90 miles to the north-east of Lwów. With all the ground crews and equipment safely stowed aboard a train, the pilots took off at intervals, using the trip to carry out reconnaissance flights along what they thought was the front line. They spotted a number of active Bolshevik units along the way, but no sign of any Cossacks or any other cavalry units being readied for a mass attack. This came as a surprise to Captain Cooper so he decided to carry out his own reconnaissance mission and flew out over the Brody area. Some hours later when he did not return, other members of the squadron took off to see if they could locate him or his aircraft, but nothing was found. He had last been seen in the direction of where General Semyon Budyonny's Cossack army had last been sighted and when he failed to appear the following morning it was feared that he had either been shot down and captured or killed. What, in fact, had happened was that he thought he had spotted enemy troops hiding in a forest and decided to carry out a low-level pass to make sure. As he did so, the hidden troops opened fire on his aircraft, hitting the engine. The engine seized, causing Merian Cooper to carry out a forced landing that resulted in his capture.

With Captain Cooper missing, Major Fauntleroy took over temporary command of the squadron. There was no more time to look for Captain Cooper as the Polish ground forces were in a desperate situation as the Bolsheviks continued their relentless advance and more information was required about their positions and strengths. The 21st Bomber Squadron, under the command of Lieutenant Rayski, joined up with Major Fauntleroy's Kościuszko Squadron. Almost all of the 21st's aircraft were tired, dilapidated German AEGs that had seen better days. At the beginning of July Captain Kelly was assigned to the 21st as an observer because of his experience in this role in the First World War. He and his Polish pilot flew more than a dozen reconnaissance missions over the next few days, reporting on troop positions and gun emplacements over the continually altering front line. It was on the last of these missions that Captain Kelly and his pilot were killed when their aircraft crashed. Some local peasants found their bodies in the wreckage and buried them nearby. The reason for the crash is not known; whether they were shot down or had engine or structural failure was never discovered.

Another incident concerning a Kościuszko Squadron pilot was when Lieutenant Buck Crawford was on an attack/reconnaissance mission over the front line. His aircraft was struck by a stray bullet that punctured his main fuel tank. Immediately he switched to his reserve tank, which was situated on top of the upper wing, but for some unknown reason the engine, which had just stopped, failed to re-start. Gliding down to carry out a dead-stick landing, he noticed in the distance a detachment of Cossacks galloping towards him. Putting the aircraft down in a rough field, he jumped out and headed for the safety of a large wooded area. Above him Lieutenant Edward Corsi had seen his friend's predicament, and dived to attack the oncoming Cossacks with both machine guns blazing in an effort to dissuade them. Buck Crawford turned to see what was happening and noticed that the engine of his aircraft had re-started on its own and was gently moving across the field. Without hesitation, he sprinted as fast as he could and clambered aboard. Opening the throttle, he roared into the air just seconds before the Cossacks reached the field. The undercarriage had been damaged and he was running on a fuel reserve, which meant his flying time was very limited. However, within minutes he was back over Polish lines and, despite the undercarriage collapsing on landing, he was able to walk away unscathed. Although the aircraft was recovered, like many others it was found to be beyond repair and was used as parts for the remaining aircraft to keep them flying.

The loss of another aircraft and with some of the American pilots returning home, the Polish Air Force was being stretched to the limit. The Kościuszko Squadron was operating from its railway base because of the need to be able to move at a moment's notice. Health problems started to cause serious concerns when an outbreak of typhus fever was discovered among the ground crews. All the while reports from the front told of continuing advances by the Red Army, and with the Polish troops retreating in general disarray, things did not look good. News filtered through of peace proposals, but nothing substantial.

In New York, Colonel Benjamin Castle, a former USAS airman, became the main contact for Major Fauntleroy in his search for more pilots. He had managed to persuade more than twenty American pilots to go to Poland at their own expense to join the Kościuszko Squadron, but when they requested permission from the State Department to go, they were told that passports would not be issued to them. This had come about after the allies in Europe had decided to give aid to the Poles, so the American War Department decided that they would not participate in this and would take on the role of an interested observer and nothing more. Major Fauntleroy then realized that he was going to have to work with what he had, and by the time any replacements did arrive it would probably be too late considering the way the war was going. Even Germany offered to send troops to fight the Bolsheviks, but General Erich Ludendorff demanded certain conditions that included the return of the Province of Posen to Prussia where he had been born and that a number of conditions in the Treaty of Versailles be removed.

When word arrived that the Bolsheviks had taken the town of Dubno, south-east of Luck, the squadron was forced to move once again. This time it was to the village of Ustilug just north of Lwów. This move came as a welcome respite to the battle-weary pilots and ground crews as the living conditions were a distinct improvement on their previous bases. The atmosphere throughout Poland was extremely tense as word filtered back of the Red Army advance. A meeting of all the top army generals was hurriedly called. Marshal Piłsudski, after consultation with his generals, came up with a strategy that he hoped would stem the tide of the Bolsheviks. Three combat zones were to be set up to replace the two existing fronts. The Northern Front, under the command of General Józef Haller, was to cover the area from Pułtusk, just north of Warsaw, to Deblin at the point where the Vistula and Wierprza Rivers merged. The Central Front, under the command of Marshal Piłsudski, covered the area from Deblin to Brody, taking control of the Lwów-Równe railway line. The Southern Front, commanded by General Waclaw Iwaszkiewicz, completed the front.

With all these fronts being mobilized, the Kościuszko Squadron was called upon to fly almost non-stop reconnaissance missions and message-dropping flights. The strain placed upon the pilots was enormous and was without doubt a contributing factor to one of the freakiest accidents of the war. Captain Konopka was returning from a reconnaissance flight in which he and Lieutenant Weber had been looking for an alternative airfield when he misjudged the distance on the field's short runway. Opening the throttle, he managed to get his Albatros airborne and just skim the top of the train that was a few yards away from the end of the runway. Going round for a second attempt, he made a steep approach and again he misjudged the distance, only this time as he flattened out, the aircraft bounced and then bounced again. Pouring on the power in an attempt to get the aircraft airborne once again, Konopka realized that he wasn't going to get airborne and seconds later ploughed through the open door of a railway carriage that was being used as the officers' kitchen. The impact sheared the wings off the Albatros as it went through the open door and the terrified cook, who was busy preparing lunch, was thrown across the carriage by the impact. The opposite door was closed

Left: Albatros aircraft buried into a railway wagon.

Below: Removing the wreckage of the aircraft.

and the remainder of the aircraft came to a shuddering halt. How the aircraft did not catch fire was a miracle because the fire in the stove never ignited the fuel spilling from the plane. The pilot was pulled from the wreckage with only facial injuries and bruises. The cook also survived, with only minor burns from the stove. Suffice to say lunch was a little late that day.

On 16 August a reconnaissance flight saw Russian troops close to Warsaw. Immediately the Poles reacted, and in a short, bitter fight defeated what turned out to be only a small section of the main Russian army.

This, however, left the left flank of the Russian army exposed and this was capitalized on by the Poles who immediately launched a counter-offensive. Budyonny's Cossacks, who were expected to join up with the Russian army, never appeared because of in-fighting within the Russian and Bolshevik high command. Orders came down from Moscow to Budyonny for his Cossacks to abandon their attack on Lwów and move towards Warsaw to join up with Tukachevsky's army. Then another set of orders from Stalin came for him to attack Lwów. By the time the confusing messages were sorted out it was too late; the counter-offensive had begun. The counter-offensive turned into a major offensive and within ten days the Russian army was in full retreat and the Bolshevik army in tatters.

Leon Trotsky, as Head of the Supreme Military Council, had initially proposed to make a peace settlement with Poland because he thought the Red Army was exhausted. His suggestion was ignored and when the Red Army was routed at the end of August 1920, he said: 'If Stalin and Voroshilov and the illiterate Budyonny had not had their own war in Galicia and the Red Army had been at Lubin in time, the Red Army would not have suffered the disaster.'

On 18 October 1920 the Polish-Soviet War was over when an armistice was signed and to all intents and purposes the need for the Kościuszko Squadron was at an end. Despite the armistice, the squadron continued to fly reconnaissance missions over what was the front line as there were still a few Bolshevik patrols causing trouble, but within weeks these too had disappeared. The feared Cossack cavalry, now decimated, retreated to the

Leon Trotsky at the Polish Front, 1919.

Crimea to try to recover. In Moscow Joseph Stalin was threatened with a court-martial for his part in the humiliating defeat of the Russian army, but it never materialized. Stalin never forgot the humiliation he suffered at the hands of the Poles and later exacted his revenge on the Polish people when in 1939, after forming an alliance with Hitler, he invaded Poland.

While the Poles celebrated their victory, word came through that Captain Merian C. Cooper was in a Russian prison camp. He had managed to get a note smuggled to a Red Cross worker by the name of Marguerite Harrison who was working in Moscow. The note was signed 'Frank Mosher'. The reason for this was that Cooper had adopted the name after being shot down by the Bolsheviks because he had been told that all enemy officers were to be shot on sight. He had acquired the name from a vest he was wearing that he had got some months earlier from the Red Cross. Fortunately he had no insignias of rank and had told his interrogators that he was a corporal. Cooper finally managed to escape while on a working party and, together with two Poles, made his way to Latvia and safety, the journey taking twenty-six nights as they could only travel at night. Once in Latvia, plans were made to get him to Warsaw where on his return he was awarded the Virtuti Militari by Józef Piłsudski himself.

The Kościuszko Squadron was disbanded in the spring of 1921 and all the surviving pilots who had fought in the conflict were awarded Poland's highest honour, the Virtuti Militari.

Merian C. Cooper's career after the war is a matter of record, when he became one of Hollywood's outstanding film producers with films such

as *King Kong* and *This is Cinerama*. During the Second World War he joined the USAAC, finishing the war with the rank of brigadier general.

Merian C. Cooper, together with two fellow escapers, wearing the clothes he wore when escaping from the Russian prisoner-of-war camp.

Chapter Eleven

The following are escape reports and reports of life as a PoW from American airmen who were either shot down or crash-landed behind enemy lines. All are verbatim reports.

The commandant of the new prison camp 'Schwarmstedt, Province of Hanover', a retired colonel of the Uhlans, introduced himself to allied prisoners of war when they arrived, saying:

> I know you do not like the look of this place. Neither do I. I do not like being here any more than you do. I know that it is your duty to try and escape. I know that it is my duty to see that you do not escape. Let us all do our duty to the best of our abilities.

(For the full signal that was issued to all American servicemen who were to fight in France regarding their probable treatment, see the end of Chapter 5.)

Reports from US Airmen

First Lieutenant George W. Puryear, USAS
95th Aero Squadron

Lieutenant Puryear, it is believed, was the first American officer to escape from captivity in Germany and a narrative of his experiences is one of vigour and youthful audacity. From the time of his capture, partly due to his own eagerness in a moment of success, he made it his aim to escape from the clutches of the Hun, and in the face of tremendous obstacles accomplished his purpose.

On 14 July, having completed his training in the United States, then at Issoudun and Cazaux and having served for two months as a ferry pilot, he was ordered to join the 95th Aero Squadron of the First Pursuit Group.

Lieutenant George Puryear's identity card issued by the Germans.

At that time the 95th was changing over from the Nieuport Type 28 machines to SPADs and on 18 July, from the Saints aerodrome, Lieutenant Puryear made his first flight over the Château-Thierry sector. With a week of patrol experience behind him, he went up on the 26th with four other SPAD Scouts to patrol the lines from Château-Thierry to Neuf-le-Château. It was a day of mist and rain, so thick that two of the machines turned back. The other three had an engagement with a German bi-plane machine, but Lieutenant Puryear ventured on alone in spite of the bad weather. The Hun observer was shot and the pilot forced into a landing. Puryear, in the enthusiasm of probable victory, followed the German plane down, shooting continuously and, thinking himself in allied territory, landed not far from the wrecked Hun.

The strange experience that was awaiting him had not even occurred to him before, but it happened that the combat had gradually carried him into German territory. As he taxied around the field in his plane, he suddenly realized that he might be behind the German lines so he headed his machine around to face the long way of the field and prepared to take off. As he was running up into the wind, the machine struck a ditch and nosed over. That gave him something to think about. In the distance behind him and around him, machine guns were snapping, and overhead he saw the white puffs from the bursts of other aircraft barrage, but still he was undecided as to his location. He jumped from the cockpit of his own machine and hunted around for the other planes. The German pilot, in the meantime, had pulled his dead observer out of his aircraft and taken him away. By a gradual process of assessment Puryear was convinced that he was behind the German lines and somewhere near machine-gun emplacements.

The first man he saw was an unarmed German who accosted him in a friendly manner. As the man spoke French and wore no helmet, Puryear was suddenly taken with the idea that the man was an Italian. The American asked where he was. The Hun told him civilly the thing that he feared, namely that he was within the German lines, and asked him if he were an American officer. Puryear replied that he was, whereupon the German saluted him at attention. A crowd of Germans began to gather about him from various sides (presumably a German observation balloon had telephoned warning of his descent), and he was taken captive.

He was conducted straight away to a house which was being used as an emergency hospital, where he was relieved of his flying suit, belt, goggles and other leather equipment except for his helmet, which was taken later, and searched for firearms. During the search he chatted in English with the officer in charge. From this point he was put through a series of quizzes by Intelligence officers who sought to enhance their knowledge of allied aviation by every sort of questions. Four different times he was quizzed and on each occasion in a separate office, but of all the questions the only one he considered to have any particular importance was the enquiry as to where his aerodrome was located.

After these inquisitions he was placed with 200 prisoners (including 2 French officers) in a temporary concentration camp, where he was given his first German meal. This consisted of old German bread, soddy and stiff like a piece of bacon and so unappetizing that he was unable to eat it, although it was then about noon and he had had nothing but a cup of coffee since the time he had tumbled out of bed in the morning and started from his aerodrome at 05.00 am. Thus he hungered until six o'clock in the evening when a German soldier in the guard house gave him some barley soup and some horsemeat which his fatigue from marching flavoured sufficiently for him to call it good. Here there was a private who was a German/American, quite familiar with Broadway and the Brooklyn Bridge. The Hun treated him quite well, but food was scarce and unappetizing. That night as he looked outside he estimated his chances of getting away and though he did nothing at that time, he first began to make his plans for escape which culminated in the bold venture of 6 October that opened the way to freedom.

The next morning he was taken along for an all-day march on a meal of so-called coffee made from brown barley and some unappetizing bread. Upon reaching another town he was engaged by a third in the series of German Intelligence officers who, after questioning him, told him in English that he would now be conducted to his 'room and bath'. The 'room and bath' were found to be an old barn with an insufficient layer of straw gathered in one corner. Here he seated himself and fed himself jam and bread, potato-type bread which Puryear characteristically referred to as a 'clod of dirt', and finally went to sleep with a chill creeping up his back.

The following day he joined a large detachment of prisoners, which included 400 French and 80 British, mostly Hospital Corps men, and 28 Americans who had been captured from the 26th and 42nd divisions during the Château-Thierry fight. The march to Laon that followed was one fraught with discomfort and suffering for many of the men. Puryear, although still possessing his officer's suit with insignia, was lightly clad and during the night of the 28th would have suffered much but for the generosity of a British Hospital Corps soldier who gave him food and a blanket. To add to his difficulties his shoes wore through during the long tramp and his feet became sore. It was during this trip he first made the acquaintance of Adjutant André Conneau, a French pilot with whom he was to make his first attempt to escape. The next day, which was the third on starvation rations of soup and bread, they took a train into Germany, starting at 05.00 am and arriving next day at 11.00 pm at Rastatt, Baden-Württemberg, where they were quartered in an old fortress overnight and then introduced at the Friedrichsfeste camp.

The treatment of the prisoners on this long trip was intended to aggravate them and wear down their morale. On the way Lieutenant Puryear kept company with First Lieutenant Zenos Miller, who had been a pilot in the 27th Aero Squadron of his own group, and with the following lieutenants: Willard Bushey, Crawford J. Ferguson, H.W. Shea and Oats. Between them the men continually complained, 'kicked', swore and precipitated arguments with the more conservative members of the group about the philosophy of accepting the hardships of war with equanimity. About them the men saw German wounded lying without care, as if they were so many dead horses, a country savagely devastated by the wastes of war, British captive soldiers, starved, pale and unshaven, toiling for the Huns behind their lines, brutally discriminated against, and a few solemn-looking French civilians. The atmosphere was anything but encouraging.

At the camp at Rastatt they first received passable food, which came through the British Red Cross. This food was distributed, after being inspected and checked by the Germans, by an American prisoner designated to issue it according to his own methods. At this point they discovered that they were only 160 kilometres from the Swiss border and, already strongly urged by the desire for freedom, Lieutenant Puryear made a mental calculation of the number of days' travel that would be necessary to carry him to the border in case he should escape. He estimated that he could do it in seven to thirteen days. On the following day he discovered an easy way to get out of the camp. The method, so far as the writer knows, still remains a secret in the minds of those who employed it. As Lieutenant Puryear gave this story to the interviewer prior to the Armistice, he desired to keep secret the means of escape in order that he might do nothing that would reveal to the Germans how a number of Americans found their way out of Rastatt prison camp. Puryear decided to couple his chances with those of Conneau the Frenchman who, he said, looked mean, hard and game enough to do anything, and together they planned their escape. Lieutenant Puryear depended upon Conneau, who appeared to have considerable knowledge of the country over which they were about to travel, and the only preparations which he personally made were to borrow a substantial pair of shoes from a British captain to replace his own which were in a very dilapidated condition. On 5 August at 11.30 pm, Lieutenant Puryear succeeded in making his escape unnoticed. He proceeded to a prearranged spot where he waited for an hour and a half until after the next change of guard, when Conneau appeared. Together they started on their journey. The Frenchman had a map and compass that they used to guide them, and a heavy French leather and fur coat, which he loaned to Puryear from time to time to warm him. After a few hours they entered the Black Forest. About two o'clock it had begun to rain, and from that moment it seemed that the heavens never ceased to cast a deluge upon the fugitives. During three nights of travel there were about three hours when it was not raining hard. During the daytime they hid in the forest, resting on the Frenchman's coat, trying to snatch moments of sleep, but no sooner had they fallen asleep than it would start to rain again, and they would have to take the coat from under them and crouch beneath it, using it as shelter from the rain. The Frenchman was a true comrade, and gave Lieutenant Puryear a full share of what he had. Under such circumstances they finally invented a method of thatching themselves in for the day with branches leaned against a tree, a method that succeeded in turning the rain. After resting by day, they would start again at 10.30 pm when darkness had fallen, and travel onward.

Conneau, however, was mistaken in his direction and bore too much to the west, with the result that they found themselves on the second day still at the edge of the forest with peasants working quite near them in the fields. Again on the next night they erred and at 03.00 am on 8 August they came out on the banks of the Rhine. Realizing that they were off course, they took a small road southward and just as they were intending to stop for the day at 04.00 am, they walked into a German sentry on duty. They knew the Rhine was well-guarded and the troop concentrations thick, and they were so fatigued and discouraged that they made no attempt to run from the guard. The Hun turned them into the guardhouse, where they were equipped with blankets and passed a good night's rest. They found that they had been captured 50 kilometres from Rastatt and now, after being rudely thrust into cells for a night's rest at Kehl, they were sent straight to Rastatt. Without any quiz or trial they were sent into confinement for five nights and transferred to Rastatt. Puryear was searched and relieved of his helmet. This left him without a hat. The commanding officer of the camp questioned him closely as to his escape and Lieutenant Puryear disclosed everything except the means he had used to get out. Within a short time he was sent with fifteen other American officers to Landshut, Bavaria, where he was assigned to the old castle on the hill north-east of the town which had been set aside as a concentration prison for American aviation officers. There were eighteen of them there, ten of whom were Major Harry M. Brown and his pilots and observers of the 96th Aero Squadron, who had been captured on 10 July after an unsuccessful bombing expedition in thick weather. The newly-arrived captives were quarantined and inoculated for cholera, typhoid and smallpox.

Bréguet 14B2 of the 96th Aero Squadron, USAS over the front lines.

The food here was good but scarce. They received meat once a day and white flour twice a week, occasionally pancakes, and although the Red Cross food was excellent they found it scarce. There were no special facilities for entertainment and the days dragged. Under such conditions the minds of the officers were often turned towards the chance of escape, but it was 240 kilometres to the Swiss border, and this combined with the approach of fall and its cold nights, were strong persuasion against attempts to escape.

It was a congenial group, however. Among the officers who were there were First Lieutenant Carlisle ('Dusty') Rhodes, also of the 95th Aero Squadron, who had been reported dead but had come down in a vrille [tailspin] in Germany, unhurt; Lieutenants H.F. Wardle, Herbert Smith, James E. Lewis, George Ratterman and Captain James Norman Hall who had previously been reported dead and was the first American officer captured by the Germans, all of whom Puryear had known. To pass away the time the men played cards, and an occasional package from home, received through the Red Cross, added to the comfort of all. The commanding officer of the prison camp was reported by Lieutenant Puryear as being one of the worst of the Huns, a man of mean disposition who 'bawled them out' in German every day by the clock, had their shoes taken away every night at eight pm and counted them in their beds with the guard. In spite of this, some of the officers planned an escape, details of which are given elsewhere, and succeeded in getting out by cutting through the wooden wall, but they were recaptured.

Puryear's mind was still bent on escape, but he was wiser than to attempt it here. He applied therefore for a transfer to the prison at Villengen. There was in the employment of the Germans, a civilian by the name of Pasteur, who had been married to an American girl and who owned property in New York. He was apparently the intermediary between the prisoners and the Germans and carefully reminded them: 'I am a German, be careful what you say.' Through this individual Lieutenant Puryear made his application for transfer early in September. Major Brown was also transferred. Another lieutenant who had a hole cut through his wall preferred to remain and take his chances of escape. First Lieutenant Carlisle Rhodes, who was in the group that had left Landshut, pretended that he was sick and escaped from the train, whereupon, when Lieutenant Puryear actually became ill, he got no sympathy and nothing but 'hell' from the guards. Lieutenant Rhodes was later recaptured. Lieutenant Puryear and the party, after two days in stuffy cars during which the German guards exercised the strictest rules, forcing them to keep their shoes off, giving them no food for one and a half days and allowing them to go to the toilet only every five hours, arrived at Villengen.

This was a new American officers' camp, fair according to the general standard, but better than others as it developed. It was 15 September when they arrived. The food supplied by the Red Cross was good and the clothing sufficient. After four or five days Puryear was informed by an interpreter that he had some good news for him. The news was that he was entitled to fourteen days' solitary confinement for his previous escape and since he had served only five of the days he would be given the pleasure of nine more days in jail. From 20 September to the 29th, he spent the time in a 6ft by 12ft cell, with nothing but a bed, table and chair, with a small window above him that let in a few rays of sun.

He was released on the 29th and by 6 October he had escaped from the camp. In the interim he did considerable figuring. It was 36 kilometres in a direct line to the Swiss border, but to the point to which he later tramped and crossed into Switzerland it was 65 kilometres, and he estimated that he must have tramped 100 kilometres in order to reach it.

Now to return to the plans for escape. The Americans had determined upon concerted action, and decided that they would select a night and all attempt to escape from the camp at several points at the same time. Two of them were in such a hurry that eleven others altered their plans and agreed to the same night rather than have their own chances spoiled by the special measures of discipline that would follow any one attempt. They waited for three nights for plans to develop before making the dash for freedom. Puryear had equipped himself with a hand-drawn map, made by a fellow captive, and with a small compass purchased from a Russian officer at a price of one stack of coffee, one box of Red Cross meat, one package of hard tack and an OD army shirt, the total of which looked like a million dollars to the Russian.

The men had carefully studied the defence of the camp. The barracks were located in an enclosure of about 800 by 200 metres, which was surrounded by a high board fence peaked with barbed wire. Outside that was a wire fence, and still further on a ditch set with barbed-wire entanglements. The main wire fence was about 9ft tall and on the inside was fastened with iron hooks intended to prevent people from climbing over it. Both inside and outside the camp were powerful electric lights and posts of guards of about 100 German soldiers, men of some age and limited vigour, set over the 200 Russians and 77 Americans confined there.

On the night of 6 October as stated, thirteen Americans were waiting impatiently, bent on escape. At 11.15 pm the lights flickered and went out (they had been short-circuited by an accomplice who had thrown chains across the wires at a preconcerted signal). Apparently there had been some suspicion among the Germans who were prepared for trouble; nevertheless, the Americans made their rush from four different points of the camp. The extinguishing of the lights was a signal for action. Three of the men, including Puryear, had posted themselves in a barracks window on the south side. As the lights went out they pulled from the window its iron grating which in advance had been carefully cut with a file, and Puryear jumped through to the ground.

Before this time they had constructed a 14ft ladder from bed slats, the rungs of which had been fastened in place with wire in the absence of screws. Puryear pulled the ladder through the window and placed it against the fence while Lieutenant Ticknor, a fellow captive, braced it at the bottom. By climbing to the top of this ladder it was possible to jump and clear the main fence, the low fence and the barbed-wire ditch in one leap. It was a starlit night, but dark. As Puryear scrambled up the ladder it squeaked and aroused the suspicion of the guard who was but ten steps away. 'Halt,' the German guard cried. Puryear was at the top of the ladder. 'Halt,' came the warning cry again. The American jumped, got to his feet and dodged behind a tree four paces away. The guard had seen him before he sought the protection of the tree. A second guard was approaching about thirty paces away. Puryear figured that he could not keep one tree between himself and two guards very long, but a desire to play fair and to still leave a chance for his accomplice who had not yet jumped from the ladder made him remain a moment in his place of hiding. Suddenly he ran past but 8ft from the guard. The stolid German followed his instructions and challenged him twice before shooting. The first time the fugitive was three steps away; by the time he could shout again Puryear was ten paces beyond and running a zigzag course. The German fired and missed. Another shot came from the other guard. The bullet whizzed by him in the darkness. On he sped until at length, just as both guns fired again, he stumbled into a ditch, which in the excitement he had forgotten.

'Forgetting about that ditch probably saved my life,' said Lieutenant Puryear later. 'The Hun thought he had winged me and immediately turned towards the others who were breaking out on every side. There was all kinds of excitement, guns were firing and men were shouting. I heard two more shots behind me, kept on running until my breath gave out about a quarter of a mile away. I went to a prearranged spot where we were to meet, and waited for fifteen minutes, during which time there were about fifty shots exchanged, I should judge. No one came, so I got down on my knees, prayed for luck and started off.'

In his travels towards Switzerland Lieutenant Puryear used the tiny compass that he had received from the Russian. Realizing that he would be travelling by night and that it would be difficult to get his directions in the dark, he had contrived to make the compass points visible by scraping the phosphorescent material from the face of his wristwatch and applying it to the compass needle. By this means he was able to travel in the dark and still keep himself constantly apprised of his direction. Frequently he would hear Germans approaching on the road, whereupon he would step into the woods to avoid them, as he was travelling in Russian coat and cap which formed a distinctive silhouette against the sky. One man, who caught him unawares, spoke to him in passing and Puryear replied, '*Gute Nacht*' in his best German.

The journey to the border was without unusual incident. On the night of 10 October, he came out south of Waldshut at about 11 pm. Believing he was near the Swiss border, he climbed the mountain to assure himself, having seen a picture of the town. The only element between him and freedom was the Rhine. It was only 200 metres across but the current was flowing at a speed of several miles an hour and Lieutenant Puryear had not been in the water for two years. He selected a point near a bend where the current would assist in carrying him to the other shore. Then he went into the woods, stripped off all garments but his underclothes and breeches, and gradually crept down to the bank, shedding a garment every few feet. At 05.30 in the morning he sprang into the river and swam it. It was about a fifteen-minute job, but the swift current was so great that eddies and whirlpools pushed him about and very nearly exhausted him before he reached the other side. He crept up the bank, stared back into Germany and cursed it. Several peasants approached, took him into their home and gave him food and clothing and he was later assisted by the American Red Cross.

Lieutenant Puryear was the first American officer to escape from Germany according to available records, but was preceded by three days by an American private.

In general he regarded his treatment in Germany as fair. Men were paid sixty marks a month by the German government, but had to spend fifty-two of this for mess and with the balance they could only buy two mugs of poor German beer.

'It was an experience,' said he, 'which I am glad I had, but could not go through again voluntarily.'

(From notes taken by L.H. Thayer, Second Lieutenant, AS.)

CHAPTER ELEVEN

First Lieutenant William W. Chalmers, USAS
94th Pursuit Squadron

At 08.30 am on 7 July 1918, I left the aerodrome of the 1st Pursuit Group near Rozoy, France, with a flight of 94th Aero Squadron Nieuports (Type 28) to protect a SPAD biplane machine piloted by 1st Lieutenant William Titus of the 1st Aero Squadron; the objective being a point some 12 or 15 kilometres north-east of Château-Thierry.

On our second trip to the objective, at about 09:30 and at about 4,500 metres altitude, four of us (including Lieutenants Coolidge, Meissner, Cates and myself) engaged and shot down in flames an enemy biplane machine. I paused to see the enemy aircraft crash thinking my friends still near, and before I could rejoin them I was attacked by two German Fokkers; my motor being damaged by the first burst from their guns. I continued to engage them until my motor was hit again and stopped entirely, and I was forced to land near Peuvarde [*sic*] about 15 kilometres N.E. of Château-Thierry.

German soldiers at once took me prisoner and the two aviators landed and conversed with me for some time in English and German. Then an *Oberleutnant* took me back 10 kilometres in a car and turned me over to an intelligence officer, who questioned me in English about the US Air Service in general and the 1st Pursuit Group in particular. As I was naturally reticent he answered most of his own questions and showed he knew almost as much as I about my own group, its officers, machines, individual records etc. This officer also took my coat, gauntlets, helmet, goggles, uniform, insignia, note-book, USAS identification card and boots – giving me in place of the latter a pair of French wooden shoes.

I then spent a day at Loupeigne, a week in a fortress at Laon, another week at Husson, and arrived at a prison camp at Kestart on 24 July. I escaped from this camp on the night of 27 July with Lieutenant Geoff Crowns of the 10th Field Artillery, and started south through the Black Forest towards Switzerland – walking at night and hiding during the day. We were captured again at about 10.30 pm on 5 August when almost to the Rhine, having passed Neustadt the night before.

Two armed soldiers and a civilian made the capture and we were too weak to offer much resistance.

As a penalty I was placed in solitary self-confinement from 6 August to 27 August at Rastatt, Karlsruhe and Villengen. From 27 August to 26 November I was given the freedom of the prison camp except for three days in October when I was held under a charge of bribery and found not guilty. Thirteen of us attempted an escape earlier in October, only three reaching Switzerland (Lieutenants Willis and Puryear of the Air Service and Isaacs of the Navy).

I cannot personally complain of brutal or harsh treatment at the hands of the Germans, though I saw many allied soldiers, especially the British at Laon, who seemed to be overworked and almost starved. The food given us was insufficient in quantity and of poor quality, but from appearances the Germans were living almost as poorly themselves and after getting into touch with the American Red Cross we fared very well indeed.

First Lieutenant Charles R. Codman, USAS
96th Aero Squadron

Second Lieutenant Charles R. Codman, a pilot of the 96th Aero Squadron, was taken prisoner while on a daylight bombing expedition against Conflans

on 16 September 1918. A flight of seven machines started on this expedition, but all but four fell out of the formation before crossing the lines. The remaining four aircraft bombed Conflans, but on the return trip were met by a flight of twenty-four German pursuit planes. Three of the aircraft were shot down in flames, while Lieutenant Codman and his observer Second Lieutenant Stewart McDowell were brought

Lieutenant Charles Codman, Lieutenant Henry Lewis, Lieutenant Robert Browning and Captain James Norman Hall (seated).

down out of control, with one aileron, the rudder and one-half of the elevator shot off. Both officers were wounded, Lieutenant McDowell seriously and Lieutenant Codman slightly. Lieutenant Codman states that he shot down three of the enemy aircraft before his machine was brought down, and this may be confirmed by the statements of three French aviators, also prisoners, who witnessed the fight (the pilots were from the French Squadron C-46).

Lieutenant Codman's aircraft came down in a spiral and crashed in a field near Conflans, in which were many German soldiers. The aircraft was immediately surrounded. There was no opportunity to set it on fire. The Germans gave first aid to Lieutenant McDowell, and he was taken to hospital. Lieutenant Codman was taken to some barracks in a small town near Conflans. From there he was taken by touring car to an Intelligence officer in the neighbourhood of Longuyon. There he was questioned for about three hours. Much wine was brought out. No force was used and the Intelligence officer was most polite. Next morning he was taken to Montmédy, a prisoners' camp, where he was placed in solitary confinement for three days, and from there he was sent to Rastatt near Karlsruhe and after three weeks at Rastatt was sent to Karlsruhe itself.

Above left: Prisoner-of-war camp at Rastatt.

Above right: The 'Listening Hotel' at Karlsruhe, as it is today.

Inside one of the huts in Landshut prisoner-of-war camp.

In the latter town he spent two nights in the famous 'Dictaphone Hotel' where he was kept with thirty or forty other aviation prisoners, about ten of whom were Americans. Later he was removed to the regular prison camp at Karlsruhe, where he received good treatment and where he stayed about a week. He was then taken to the Aviation Officers prison at Landshut, Bavaria. He was allowed to send one postal card on the 1st and 10th of each month and a letter on the 15th and 25th. In addition he could send all the picture postcards he desired and many photographic cards were given to him and the other prisoners as a sort of advertisement for the camp, these photographs largely being pictures of prisoners drinking or playing games. At Landshut he was inoculated against cholera, typhus and smallpox. He depended almost entirely on the Red Cross for food and had plenty of that. They remained at this camp until 16 November 1918. Newspapers were at hand every day.

On 7 November, a revolution occurred in Bavaria and most of the guards were taken away. The revolution, however, was a quiet affair, consisting largely of a political change, while King Ludwig was imprisoned in his castle. Herr Kurt Eisner, a poet and socialist editor in Munich, was made president of the Republic of Bavaria. The revolution lasted only about two hours. Everything had been planned in advance and many of the old regime officials retained their jobs. There was no saluting of officers in the streets.

In relation to other officers in the camp, the Americans were favoured. Lieutenant Codman stated that this was considered by American prisoners as propaganda for American goodwill after the war. Bavarians disliked the Prussians very much. Treatment at the camp was very good and the food was fairly good, the food situation in Bavaria being better than in other parts of Germany. No rubber or leather goods were to be had. Twenty-four American officers (flying) and a few each of the artillery and infantry were housed in Trausnitz Castle, where they were well quartered.

The Armistice came as a relief to the German people of the vicinity, but they were bitter regarding the conditions of the same, considering the paragraph regarding railroad carriages especially unjust.

On 16 November, all the prisoners were taken to Villengen except the Red Cross Committee, who stayed to check the Red Cross material. On this committee, in addition to Lieutenant Codman, were Captain James N. Hall, Second Lieutenant R.G. Browning and First Lieutenant Henry Lewis. The guards disappeared on this date and on the evening of 16 November, these four officers left the camp with a German corporal. They spent the night in a hotel in Munich where no one paid any attention to them and the next day they proceeded by rail with the German corporal to a point on Lake Constance from which they proceeded by boat and landed at Romanshorn on 17 November. From there they proceeded to Berne, where they spent some days with the American Red Cross, preparing necessary reports on their committee work. Then they proceeded through Geneva to France, arriving in Paris on 21 November.

First Lieutenant J.D. Fuller Jnr (pilot) Second Lieutenant Virgil Brookhart (observer)
135th Aero Squadron, USAS
(Both interned in Switzerland)
On the morning of 12 September, which marked the beginning of the St Mihiel Drive, both Lieutenants Fuller and Brookhart set out from their aerodrome near Toul on a mission for reglage [orientation] of artillery fire in the vicinity of Mont Sec. The weather was quite unfavourable owing to low-hanging fog and the south-west wind. At a height of 1,500ft they encountered thick clouds, and after five minutes progress in a west to east direction they became temporarily swallowed up in the clouds. By chasing holes in the clouds they managed to catch glimpses of the various towns over which they were passing. Though this presented some difficulties since it was their first flight together over the lines, they identified Nancy, and then found themselves over Thiaucourt (west). They were having such

STRIKE FROM THE AIR

difficulties that they decided to abandon their mission and started south-west with the Ourches aerodrome as a goal.

Climbing to 10,000ft, they proceeded for about half an hour in what they believed to be a south-easterly direction. When they came down they found they were over a range of mountains, and later discovered they had been near Mulhausen. They could see trenches as they neared the ground, and therefore ascended again and proceeded for some time towards the south-west, as they believed, and again came down to find themselves over the front-line trenches. It became apparent to them that a fairly strong wind was blowing them off their intended course. The wind at that time was westerly, and since they had been heading south-west, they concluded that the wind had been forcing them in a southerly direction and at the same time sweeping them constantly with an eastward inclination towards the Swiss border.

Finally they flew below the clouds again, and finding that they had left the trenches behind them they landed. Peasants and soldiers appeared from all directions, and as the country looked strange, they took off again with the intention of rising, but the motor died and they were forced to stop and land a second time. People crowded about them. They were not sure just what the trouble was with the motor, but as they had started to rise after the first landing, the Swiss soldiers had fired upon them, and they believed that a bullet had torn the jacket of the motor thus rendering it useless.

Enquiry showed that they were only 600 metres from the border in one of the projections of Switzerland into French territory and they believed that had they been able to proceed a few moments further they would have landed in French territory.

The Swiss authorities took charge of the two men and sent them to Berne, and thence to Lucerne. There they were informed of their rights; that is that they could either go free on parole, or not deciding on parole, could go to prison. It appears from the statements of both men that they were much chagrined over their internment, and realizing that they could not escape while on parole owing to the responsibility of the United States government to surrender them if they broke leave of honour, they preferred to take their chances of escape. Lieutenant Fuller in particular stated to the writer that he did not fancy the prospect of being interned in Switzerland for the period of the war, and therefore decided to take his chances in prison with the prospect of escape.

It was agreed, therefore, that Lieutenant Brookhart would go to the hotel at Lucerne on parole, while Lieutenant Fuller would enter the Military Prison at Andermatt near the St Gotthard Tunnel, and Lieutenant Fuller would reconnoitre the prison, study the chances of escape, and communicate his plans by code in letters to his comrade. It was planned that ultimately Brookhart would also come to the prison and they would escape together.

It happened, however, that by the time Lieutenant Fuller was able to make any substantial plans for escape the prospect of the signing of the Armistice was at hand. Having received no word from his comrade, Lieutenant Fuller decided to make his own escape single-handed. He was on the fourth floor of the prison. Near his cell was a toilet, from which opened a window overlooking the ground below. To this toilet he was ordinarily accompanied by a guard. He made it his habit to stay in the toilet room a longer and longer time each day, so that his delay on the night of the escape would not excite any suspicion of the guard.

The night that he chose in early November was dark and foggy. He cut his bed sheet into seven strips, which he tied together. These he tucked about his waist, beneath his pyjamas. Immediately upon entering the toilet he fastened one end of the bed-sheet rope to the window sill and the other end to his waist. Just as he commenced to let himself down, the guard knocked on the door. At the third floor the improvised rope broke and he fell a distance of 30ft, plunging onto his head and arms. He was severely cut about the face and rendered temporarily unconscious. He recovered consciousness, however, before anyone discovered him, and although lame and sore, he attempted to follow the course of escape which he had mapped out in advance. By careful work he managed to evade the two sentries at the mouth of the tunnel, but in making his way along, lost his candle and matches on which he had depended to guide himself through the thick fog. As he was coming out of the tunnel he was caught between two sentries, who halted him, took charge of him and turned him over to the authorities. For more than a week he was confined to bed, recovering from the injuries he sustained in his fall. Later he was released upon the signing of the Armistice.

Second Lieutenant Oscar Mandell, USAS
148th Pursuit Squadron

Lieutenant Mandell, while serving with the 148th Pursuit Squadron on the British Front, was shot down by ground fire and captured by the Germans. On the morning of 2 September 1918, he started from the aerodrome at Remesnil with four other machines for an offensive patrol over the lines. There was considerable ground haze with clouds at 2,000ft. After patrolling for half an hour they observed a flight of SE.5 machines ground-strafing further along the lines and nearby a patrol of Fokkers. Meanwhile, the

American formation had split up in the fog but they hung around waiting to jump the Fokkers in case they should attack the allied planes. Finally they got into a fight. Lieutenant Mandell shot down one plane, and was immediately attacked by two others from the clouds. They got above and he could not outclimb them into the clouds. He spent fifteen minutes zigzagging around in a circle until ground fire shot up his machine and stopped his engine. He came down 7 kilometres beyond the lines, crashing through some telegraph wires.

Two German infantry officers engaged him in conversation. They finally took him to dinner where they sat him down to good food and a bottle of wine and treated him courteously. He was finally taken to the regimental commandant in whose office he waited three hours. Then one of the German guards bade him 'Stand up for an Officer'; he looked at him and laughed. He was walked to the rear for six hours, but was stopped for a quiz by Intelligence officers at three different places. His fatigue and hunger gave the Huns an advantage over him, which they sought to use as a means of prying from him information about allied aircraft. They would order a fine meal, place it before him and then try to get him to talk. When he refused to reveal his country's secrets, they would remove the meal. Altogether Lieutenant Mandell made five attempts to escape and although none of them were ultimately successful, his persistence and courage constantly kept the Huns on the jump.

After two days at Sewarde where he received good treatment he was sent to Conde, which was the scene of his first escape. With a British officer by the name of Donaldson (Donaldson was in fact an American officer attached to a British squadron), he climbed through a window and dropped 15ft to the ground. They travelled rapidly and soon made their getaway to the lines. En route, about 03.00 am one morning, they came across a Hun aerodrome located at La Sentinel, south of Valenciennes. They were suddenly struck with the notion of trying to take out one of the German machines and flying it back to their own territory. They found an Albatros two-seater in a tent hangar and immediately got to work to get it out. They cut the canvas the full length and stripped it from the machine, but they were confronted by the difficulty of releasing it from a series of cables which held it in place. They worked on the job for nearly an hour, tinkering with the machine, loading and testing the guns and preparing the ship for an immediate flight when they were able to release her. By this time, however, it was 4.00 am and a German mechanic came whistling down the field, ready to start his morning task of preparing the machine for the Hun fliers. The bold captives still had one cable to remove from the wheel of the landing gear.

CHAPTER ELEVEN

Upon seeing the mechanic Mandell, who spoke good German, remarked in that tongue: 'Ah, here is someone to help us.' The mechanic, however, was not to be disarmed by the remark and immediately became suspicious. The two officers approached him and Donaldson seized him by the arms. The Hun struggled from the grasp of his enemy and pulled a small dagger from its scabbard. Lieutenant Mandell now jumped into the conflict and tripped the Hun but could not prevent him from jabbing Donaldson in the back with the dagger. The German jumped up with an agile movement, and started down the field for help. The officers knew better than to pursue him after the first five steps, and made their getaway.

'It was a damn shame,' said Lieutenant Mandell in an interview with the writer, 'for we had the machine all trimmed up and the guns all set, and we were going to run the ship up and down that aerodrome and clean out the whole bunch. As it was we made a getaway.'

The officers hurried along and got through the German lines to the edge of the water with which the Germans had inundated the land in the Douai salient. They were about to swim the overflowing river, after six days' energetic pursuit of safety, when a German patrol came along. They laid down in the dark and prayed for luck. Luck was in the air, but it went to the Germans who nearly stumbled over them. They were recaptured, sent back to Fresnes, court-martialled and given fourteen days' solitary confinement. They were now attacked by another Intelligence officer who discussed the war in its larger aspects, and informed Mandell that Germany was preparing to send a delegation to Japan to procure her assistance in case the United States became troublesome.

On 26 September Lieutenant Mandell escaped again with four others. Three of them started towards the Belgian border, but Mandell, in company with a British corporal made for Holland. They swapped their flying clothes with the French and Belgians who entertained them royally and secreted them by night. However, again luck was on the other side and as they were passing over the Holland border [*sic*].

Then Mandell was sent to Aachen where he spent four days, then to Karlsruhe for three weeks, then to Landshut which he left on 15 November for the officers' camp at Villingen. After three days there he was released and came back through Switzerland where the trainload of American prisoners received a wonderful reception at Geneva and Berne, where the people lined the railroad tracks.

The three other attempts at escape were very unsuccessful compared to the first two. In the interim he used to keep a little compass preparatory to future attempts, and when searched would carry it in his mouth. Regarding treatment, he stated that although he was occasionally subjected to insults, it was on the whole pretty good. Red Cross food and packages of Red Cross gifts were received frequently.

Second Lieutenant J.O. Donaldson
Att. 32nd Squadron RAF

I was taken as prisoner to Douai, and kept one night, but due to the heavy shelling by the English, was transferred the next day to a temporary prison at Conde. During the evening another American pilot was brought to the prison camp. This American, Lieutenant Mandell and I escaped that night by jumping out of the second-storey window of the prison and walking through the town. After walking all night, and about two hours before daybreak, we came to a new German airdrome. After making sure that there were no guards guarding this airdrome, Lieutenant Mandell and I attempted to steal a machine. After about two hours' work we managed to get a machine almost entirely out of its hangar, but finally had to take the whole hangar down to get the machine clear. Just as we were about to start the machine, a German came out for early-morning flying. We immediately got into a tussle with him, and during the tussle he stabbed me in the back and slashed up Lieutenant Mandell's clothing quite a good deal, but did not touch him, and we finally hit him on the head with a big electric lamp and ran across the airdrome.

We were not followed, and at the first French house we asked them to take us in. They dressed my wounds for me and gave us food for two days. At the end of the second day, German soldiers were to be billeted in this house, so we had to move on and although my wound was quite stiff, after once getting on my feet I could walk all right. After a number of adventures and being halted by sentries about eight or nine times, due to Lieutenant Mandell being able to speak German, he answered the sentinels as if he were a German officer passing and we passed safely. On 9 September we passed through all the German front-line trenches, and stayed in a shell hole in front of their front lines all day. We could see the English guns firing from where we were.

CHAPTER ELEVEN

Between us and the English lines there was a small stream dammed up at one end by the Germans. That night, on trying to wade across the stream we found it too deep and came back, and we were taking off our clothes to swim the stream when we were caught by a German wiring party in front of their front line. They carried us back to Battalion Headquarters. The German NCO who captured us was recommended by the Battalion Commander for an Iron Cross for catching us. After going through Division Headquarters, Corps Headquarters and Army Headquarters we were finally taken to Valenciennes. We were turned over to our old prison, but the guard refused to take us. Apparently they were afraid we would try and escape again, so they sent us to another prison across the street, where we were placed on bread and water for fourteen days.

On the eleventh day, Lieutenant Mandell and I started to think of means of escape. The only way we could get out of the building below was by passing through the roof. At the end of three days we had a hole sufficiently large for a man to pass through, and on the same day two other Americans came into the camp, Lieutenants T.E. Tillingham and R.A. Anderson. That night all four American officers and one British NCO, Corporal George Rodgers, crawled through the hole in the roof, down into the courtyard, over a wall on the other side, swam the canal and set out across country for the Holland border. We travelled for eight days, travelling in the night and sleeping in the daytime, getting food from friendly Belgians.

On the eighth day we struck Brussels and met some rich Belgians who could speak English. Here we were supplied with civilian clothes, maps and other little details that helped us on our journey. After staying two days in Brussels and looking over the airdromes but finding them too closely guarded to take a machine, we went out across country again to the Holland border. About twenty days from the time we left the prison we struck the Holland border. After reaching the border we were unable to cross for nine days, a friendly Belgian supplied us with insulated wire-cutters and also told us the exact location of the electric wire. Two days later we crawled up within 100 yards of the wire and due to the bright sunlight, we had to be very slow. It took us three hours to crawl to the edge of the wire, and as soon as the sentinel had come to the edge of his beat and went down the other end, we went up and cut the three lower strands of the electric wire. As soon as the sparks had ceased to come out of the wire, we ran across the wire and at the same time the German sentinel yelled and Lieutenant Tillingham claims he fired a shot.

In Holland we proceeded to Rotterdam and from Rotterdam to Le Havre, and from Le Havre back to England again. The total time we were in Belgium was about twenty-eight days. Two of the others, Corporal Rodgers and Lieutenant Mandell, departed from us at Brussels so only three of us escaped into Holland. The other two we believe are still somewhere in Belgium (dated 11 November 1918).

Second Lieutenant Howard C. Knotts, USAS
17th Aero Squadron

The following narrative, while only partly in the language of Lieutenant Knotts, will be noted to have been certified to be authentic in its essential respects and it is believed will be found of considerable interest and value to the Air Service, both with reference to the completion of data concerning the treatment of our officers while prisoners in the hands of the enemy and also concerning the abominations committed by the enemy which may be considered important for presentation to the present Peace Conference.

Lieutenant Knotts was a pilot in the 17th Aero Squadron, attached to the 15th Wing, Royal Air Force, British Expeditionary Force, and was

Lieutenant Howard C. Knotts USAS.

stationed at the time he was captured near the town of Sombrin, France (Pas-de-Calais). He was detailed for a ground-strafing expedition and left the airdrome at about 1.00 o'clock in the afternoon of 14 October 1918, in a Sopwith Camel Scout plane. The engine of his machine was damaged by machine-gun fire and he was obliged to descend near Colombes. He purposely descended at the point which he selected for the reason that it was within the zone of concentrated artillery fire, which he knew would soon damage his machine, making it unfit for further use. At that time he had nothing at his disposal to destroy it; therefore, he did not descend into the zone of safety which he could have otherwise reached with ease. This point was 3 or 4 kilometres beyond the enemy lines in their territory. He then planned the best manner in which to reach the British lines and attempted the practically impossible feat of negotiating the allied shellfire. He waited for available opportunities between shell bursts and walked and ran from point to point towards the allied lines, even crossing the enemy lines into no man's land where he discovered a sunken road, 8 or 10ft deep, running first east and west and then turning parallel to the lines north and south. In accomplishing this portion of the flight he was continually sniped at and two bullets penetrated his flying boots, fortunately without causing any injury. He then carefully reconnoitred and attempted to find a place of safety where he could await nightfall. He discovered a shallow parallel dugout in the side of the sunken road whose partition had partly fallen in, making it possible to creep from one to the other as will appear. Lieutenant Knotts entered the first of these parallel dugouts, hoping to hide there until nightfall and then cross over to the British lines.

He had, however, been discovered in his flight and noticed soon after he entered the first one, a German non-commissioned officer approaching to take him. This German soldier had apparently noticed him enter the first dugout and he looked cautiously into that one, but in the meantime Lieutenant Knotts had succeeded in creeping over into the other one. He immediately jumped upon the German soldier who had pulled his pistol and in the succeeding encounter, which developed for possession of the automatic, the German soldier accidentally killed himself with his own pistol. Other Germans, however, had witnessed the struggle and there ensued a pistol duel between Lieutenant Knotts armed with the dead German's automatic that still held eight or nine bullets, and four or five Germans similarly armed. In this encounter Lieutenant Knotts was overpowered by five Germans dropping down from the elevated side of the sunken road upon him in his awkward position. These soldiers stripped him immediately of his flying boots, flying insignia, watch, Sam Browne belt and ring and a guard of two of them marched him at pistol point to a lieutenant assembling a company in the line. This march was made over shell-shot country strewn with fragments of barbed wire, sharp stones, and the usual severe and devastated conditions of a shell-shot country, without shoes from 3.30 in the afternoon until approximately 6.00 in the evening. His feet became torn and swollen on the march so that later he was severely blood-poisoned in one foot and the calf of the leg, the ankle having been slightly wounded by a machine-gun bullet when he was shot down. He was immediately marched in charge of a guard of soldiers to Divisional Headquarters, 7 kilometres away. There were signs and other evidence that indicated that this was possibly the 33rd German Division. Here a German captain, who could not talk English, attempted to interview him, an attempt which failed. Then a poor interpreter interviewed him, but Lieutenant Knotts refused to talk.

It should be stated here that he had in his possession a flat purse with his identity card and about 140 francs in notes; also a deposit slip from a British bank, which the Germans had overlooked in the examination of his clothes. He carried nothing else. With the money, which he retained in his possession, he managed to bribe his German guard to purchase a pair of well-worn shoes for him. During this interview he was threatened and browbeaten by his interviewer who insisted that he must have carried secret papers and a British flying map, which they particularly wanted to find. At approximately 6.30 pm he was marched by one mounted Uhlan, sometimes at the point of a revolver and at other times when the guard was changed, at the point of a set lance, until approximately 3.00 o'clock in the morning without any food from the time of his capture. At this time he reached Maresches, France. His march was accomplished by four reliefs of guard and was made unnecessarily long because of its circuitousness. Lieutenant Knotts was particularly familiar with this country and is able to state precisely his east route which led to the outskirts of Valenciennes and thence south-east to the town of Maresches where corps headquarters for that front was located. He is unable to state which corps this was. Here he was taken to the Hotel de Ville and ushered into the presence of a brigadier general who was in bed. This officer could talk a little English and insisted on Lieutenant Knotts answering certain questions that would identify his unit. He also insisted that he must have secret documents and a map. Lieutenant Knotts replies to this general gave him no information whatever and so incensed him that he peremptorily ended the interview and ordered Lieutenant Knotts taken to an Intelligence officer. This was promptly done. The corps Intelligence officer was in the same building. He spoke English fluently. Lieutenant Knotts was here searched again and his pocket book, which was the only thing he carried in his clothing, was discovered. This interview was as futile as the other.

During the interview Lieutenant Knotts had noticed plenty of food and hot tea at hand and although he was asked if he had eaten, he was denied any of it. From here he was taken to the quarters of non-commissioned officers. They were in a state of carousel and desired to prove to him that they had plenty of food, with the result that he had an excellent meal contributed to by many of the soldiers from their own rations. Here he got good treatment for the rest of the night, a comfortable bunk being improvised. Lieutenant Knotts discovered that this guard comprised Prussian Guard troops (this fact might serve to identify the Corps). He slept until 8.00 o'clock in the morning.

At that time he was roused and began a march which lasted until 3.00 o'clock in the afternoon with a Uhlan guard, in a circuitous route which he can identify. He reached St Cast in the vicinity of Bavai at the end of the march. During this march the Germans gave him no food whatever, but a boy at the roadside gave him a hot baked potato and an apple. At the end of the march he was placed in a typical loft on the second floor of a building filled with German soldier prisoners confined there for mutiny. Lieutenant Knotts is able to state here as a matter of interest that there were approximately 100 of those soldier prisoners in his building and that practically every available building in the town had large numbers of such mutinous soldiers. It appears that there were so many of these soldiers mutinying daily, that it would have been futile to shoot them as fast as they came in. By this time Lieutenant Knotts' feet were in a frightful condition; moreover he was hungry. The Germans gave him no rations or medical attention, but one of the prisoners who proved to be sympathetic shared his rations with him and gave him some salve or grease and bandages that he applied to his feet with considerable benefit. He was imprisoned in that loft for the rest of that day, all that night, the whole of the next day and night. There were no sanitary conveniences. The place appeared to be free from vermin, however. No attention was paid to him during this time. In the meantime five former Australian prisoners who had attempted escape were recaptured and brought to this same loft, from which they in company with Lieutenant Knotts were escorted by a Uhlan guard to the town of Bavai the next day, approximately 5 kilometres away. That afternoon they entrained aboard flat cars loaded with airplanes. The flat car that Lieutenant Knotts was on was loaded with new Fokker monoplane fuselages. None of the other prisoners were on this car but there was a German sentry aboard. The wings of these planes were in the car behind with the five Australian prisoners. As the ride lasted until after midnight, it became pitch dark. The guard had been informed of Lieutenant Knotts' condition and paid very little attention to him, permitting him to move freely about the flat car. During his journey he watched his opportunity and climbed successively into the cockpits of each of the three Fokkers and succeeded in breaking one of the main cross-bracing struts in each of the fuselages, thus completely crippling the three machines under the very nose of the German guard. He then set fire to the aircraft. Food had been given to the six prisoners, consisting of a can of bully beef and a loaf of bread, but Lieutenant Knotts was not permitted to mingle with the other prisoners on the car behind and as they carried the bully beef he was unable to obtain any of it. He, however, had carried the loaf of bread, which was all the food he had until the end of his journey, Peruwelz in Belgium.

At this town they detrained and were marched to a supposed main *Stallelager* (Collecting Station), but this camp had been moved further back due to the rapid advance of the British, and Lieutenant Knotts and the five other prisoners were taken to the railroad station where they spent the night. They proceeded to Mons, Belgium the next day. No food was provided for this journey. This portion of the trip was made on a regular passenger train. Mons was reached that afternoon. From there the six prisoners were marched into the town to an ancient nunnery which had been converted into a Collecting Station at which there were approximately 200 British enlisted men and 6 British officers and 1 American officer. (This American officer was Lieutenant Walter Avery of the 148th Aero Squadron, attached to the same British Wing and operating on the same front as the 17th, Lieutenant Knotts' squadron.) Here Lieutenant Knotts was separated in a small room with the other officers, the living conditions being fairly good. No bunks or blankets were provided but the room was comfortably heated by a coal stove with fuel enough provided for a continuous fire. Here the meals were three in number each day. The morning and night meals consisted of plenty of German coffee and black bread and the noon meal was served by Belgian Red Cross workers provided with food by the American Food Commission. This was the fifth day of Lieutenant Knotts' imprisonment and was the first day he was permitted to wash. Moreover the Belgian Red Cross were permitted to provide the prisoners with a towel, soap, toothbrush and a package of dentifrice. The sanitary conditions were good. At the end of the fourth day here, meanwhile other prisoners coming in, all the prisoners at this Collecting Station were removed from the place with the exception of Lieutenant Knotts and two English boys retained as cooks.

During this four days' stay Lieutenant Knotts was taken each day to the quarters of a German Air Service officer who was a flight commander. He had breakfast with him each morning. He told him that his name was Schroeder and there were evidences that led Lieutenant Knotts to believe that this was his real name. This man later proved to be extremely familiar with the personnel, operating conditions and losses, particularly of our two squadrons on the British Front and of our American officers with British squadrons on the Front. Therefore Lieutenant Knotts' information concerning officers reported missing or dead might otherwise be impossible to obtain. He describes this man as about 5ft 7in in height, weighing about 145lb, with dark brown hair appearing black in the dim light. He was in the habit of wearing his hair as we associate generally with Germans, that is unparted, close-cropped both sides, the top brushed straight up, the crown graduated to an inch in length, but it is possible that in civilian life or at present he wears his hair different as appeared in a picture which he showed to Lieutenant Knotts, taken before the war which showed his hair long and brushed back from the forehead. It was a side-view portrait and did not show whether the hair was parted. This man could not have been over 30 years of age. His eyes were dark and flashing. His complexion was sallow. His nose was aquiline. He was always smooth-shaven in the presence of Lieutenant Knotts. His teeth were white and apparently sound. He could talk perfect English. Whether or not he had lived in the United States is not known to Lieutenant Knotts. He habitually wore a German second lieutenant's uniform with the brevet of an observer and eventually a pilot but, as is customary in the German Air Service, he still wore the observer's brevet. He wore the ribbon of the 2nd Class Iron Cross and the ribbon of either the State of Bavaria or the state of Hanover on the left breast and he wore the 1st Class Iron Cross in the usual position, left-hand side below the belt. The State ribbon was yellow and black mounted with gilded metal crossed sabres. Lieutenant Knotts believes that he must have been a second lieutenant as he stated and appeared to be, for the reason that in many conversations he exhibited chagrin at never having been promoted notwithstanding that he did meritorious service as was evidenced by his decorations and many conclusive remarks.

Lieutenant Schroeder's flight was stationed in the vicinity of Mons at this time. He told Lieutenant Knotts that he had served in the German Air Service in Russia during this war. He also asked Lieutenant Knotts whether he had heard of a German flying officer who had flown over the lines in a French machine, disguised as a Frenchman, landing upon a British airdrome, and had taken luncheon with the officers from a British Aero Squadron. Lieutenant Knotts believed he mentioned the number of the squadron, but inasmuch as he had never heard the story before and considered it fantastic he has forgotten its number, if it was mentioned. This is of note, however, because it corresponds with the facts known to you and others. This officer gave Lieutenant Knotts valuable information concerning the graves of two American flying officers, First Lieutenant Lloyd Hamilton and Lieutenant Gerald Thomas who are buried in the following British Artillery co-ordinates. Upon the map known as France, Sheet 57 C, Edition 2, scale 1/40,000, Lieutenant Hamilton's grave is north of Lagnicourt which is NE of Bapaume, Northern France; within the artillery co-ordinates 57 C, 18c, Lieutenant Thomas's grave is located upon British Artillery Map, sheet 51 A, Edition 1, Co-ordinates 51.A, 28 a. This officer fell from a height of 6,000ft in flames and was completely burned before reaching the ground. Lieutenant Knotts saw this personally on 22 September, so there will be burned remnants of the machine still there.

Lieutenant Knotts was never able to visit these graves but feels sure that the information given him is correct because it corresponds with known information. It will be found upon visiting these graves that Lieutenant Hamilton's machine burned up. Portions of the machine will undoubtedly be found nearby, according to Lieutenant Schroeder. He had complete information concerning all of the American flying officers with the British who had been taken prisoner and also concerning those who had been killed. This is proven by many facts which have been verified by Lieutenant Knotts since his return to the American Forces, related to him by Lieutenant Schroeder at this time, not known to Lieutenant Knotts until he heard them from this German officer. He had a portfolio with him with the names and full particulars concerning the status of all American flyers then with the British or who had been taken prisoner, killed, or wounded by the Germans and many others not with the British.

Lieutenant Knotts was not taken to this officer in any sense to be interviewed, but merely through his courtesy. He told Lieutenant Knotts that it was a hobby of his to know everything possible concerning American flying officers and that he was not an Intelligence officer; but this assertion would of course be proved untrue if his own statement that he was the German flying officer who had flown in a French officer's uniform to a British airdrome for the sole purpose of obtaining information was correct. Lieutenant Knotts knows nothing else concerning this officer which would be of value to identify him except that his flight was a two-seater flight comprising various types of machines. He told Lieutenant Knotts that he had one Hannover, 2 LVGs, 2 Albatros two-seaters, 1 Halberstadt. This officer being a flight commander was given considerable licence off duty and lived comfortably in a small, well-furnished house on the edge of the town of Mons, approximately 2 miles away from the Collecting Camp. Lieutenant Knotts was conducted to this house and returned by a guard during his stay there for breakfasts. He believes that if this officer could be identified and interviewed it would be productive of the greatest services to complete the investigation of data not now known concerning many of our officers reported missing or killed within the German lines whose graves are known only to him, so far as Lieutenant Knotts knows, unless it be shown that he was really an Intelligence officer, in which case it is probable that this data was also forwarded to the German Intelligence Bureau Archives.

At the end of four days' stay here, all the prisoners were moved with the exception of Lieutenant Knotts and the two British boys permanently retained there as cooks since March. Lieutenant Knotts was then transferred to a different room upstairs. Learning from the cook boys that the place was now guarded by a single sentry, and as his room was clumsily locked, he watched for a favourable opportunity that evening and escaped. Having become fairly well acquainted with the general directions during his visits to the house of Lieutenant Schroeder, and having learned of the advance of the allied lines to a point he thought he could reach by night marches, he struck off in that direction. He was favoured by rain and fog and walked fully 15 kilometres before dawn, hiding himself in a clump of bushes. Soon after daylight he shifted his position to a better point of vantage commanding a view of the main road which he had been following that night and was soon after taken prisoner by a German non-commissioned officer into whose arms he almost stepped. He was promptly returned to the Collecting Station and interrogated again in the same room from which he had escaped, this time better guarded. He remained here two days longer during which time several prisoners came in, and then was taken to Soignies where he joined the original group of prisoners from the Collecting Station at Mons then in a permanent prison camp known as 'English Prison Camp #19' (*Englander Geflagen Lager* #19), *Kommandur* Second Lieutenant Schulz. This was a reprisal camp and never a permanent station very long, being kept just behind the lines at all times, moving back as the lines moved back, locating in factory towns where buildings could be found big enough to accommodate 1,500 prisoners. The one selected here was formerly a tannery.

Lieutenant Knotts learned that this was a reprisal camp from many statements of prisoners who were so informed by the German guard. These prisoners were principally Australian and Canadians who were reputed by the Germans to habitually take no prisoners. There were 1,500 men at this Reprisal Camp at Soignies, 800 of whom were housed in a building where the officers were also kept, formerly a tannery. The sanitary conditions were indescribably vile and in fact continued so from that time on. The food conditions were intolerable. The meagre rations were weakening, there was no medical attendance, there was but one so-called doctor there for these 800 men who was actually one of the prisoners, a British stretcher-bearer knowing only the rudiments of first aid and nothing about medicine and surgery. Sicknesses of many different kinds developed. The great majority of the prisoners had dysentery. At night the men were obliged to relieve themselves in the yard or court for exercise, an enclosed space approximately 90ft square. They begged for permission to dig their own latrines, a request which was denied them. The stench was nauseating and permeated through the tannery. Many of the prisoners died. No bunks were provided and prisoners slept on the floor packed in like sardines, bodies touching. All of the prisoners had body lice. Lieutenant Knotts killed 167 of them from his own undershirt one morning, and about the same number that same afternoon. He states that it was impossible to kill them as fast as they propagated. No means whatsoever for cleaning the clothes were provided.

All this lack of sanitation was unnecessary, for in the town where the camp was progressively located, there was always plenty of available German medical skill. At one place the Germans were even preparing to take over the building in which the prisoners were located for a local German Military Hospital, but no medical assistance was given to the prisoners even here.

At one time Lieutenant Knotts together with Lieutenant Avery (the other American officer) and the British officers were placed in the meanest, darkest, most unsanitary, damp, cold, unventilated room available in the prison building, for the reason that they refused to sign paroles, the sole advantage of which appears to have been the promise of a bath. This illustrates well and typically the habitual and inhuman denial of common civilized, sanitary amenities which were always available to alleviate in some slight manner the miseries of the prisoners.

As a result of this intolerable and weakening treatment which he received in prison from the day of his capture until the early part of November, Lieutenant Knotts' wound became gangrenous and worse until his release on 10 November, at which time he was wholly unable to walk. This state of affairs was preposterous because it could have been avoided from merely elementary assistance and sanitary attention on the part of a doctor whose services could easily have been obtained.

From the time of his incarceration in Soignies until 15 November, Lieutenant Knotts and the other prisoners were frequently marched as has been stated above, always retreating further and further from the original frontier as it moved back. During these progressive marches the prisoners became weaker and weaker, some of them daily being unable to walk. They had to drag heavy wagons containing the plunder and equipment of a great variety of kinds, stolen or belonging to the German non-commissioned Guard, and one light military wagon containing food. Twenty-five men were detailed to drag one of these wagons. Sometimes some of the prisoners collapsed and were placed aboard the very carts they were assigned to drag. Their fellows gladly undertook the burden of this additional load. At one place the prisoners managed to obtain a carriage in some unknown manner and dragged these prostrate prisoners in it. The Guard was often very brutal.

The food wagon contained rations sufficient for every one of the prisoners, but the full ration was never issued, as was later proved. An inspection of the large remaining food stock, upon the fourth day of the march for which five days' rations were loaded into the food wagon, showed nearly one half the issued food remaining. This inspection was personally made by Lieutenant Knotts. On 15 November, the day of his release, none of the remaining food was given to the prisoners, their inhuman guards claiming that they needed it for their journey back to Germany.

From 11 November on there were many evidences of laxity in the German Guard towards the prisoners and mutiny towards their own officers. As they proceeded along the road the prisoners passed many German troops, abandoned by their higher officers. They encountered no higher-ranking officer than *Oberleutnant*. These troops were flying the red flag. The last day on imprisonment the group of prisoners with Lieutenant Knotts numbered only 150 to 200. The last day's march was from Maransart, Belgium, to Poucet. The place of their intended release was Holland. They intended to entrain at Liege, five days' march from Maransart. The prisoners were kept off the main roads to avoid encountering the many passing detachments of troops. On the fourth day's march only one half-day's rations were issued in the morning, comprising one loaf of bread for each seven men; nothing else. At Poucet the prisoners were all released without food or guidance. They were in a country, plundered, ruined, terrorized, without resources, were too weak to march further and were left in a local hospital. Five are known to have died since owing to their frightful condition. This place was 30 kilometres from Liege, 70 kilometres from the nearest town of Holland (Masterlink [*sic*]). Brussels was 10 kilometres away. The advancing allied army was 120 kilometres away (eight or ten days' march). An English captain took back 150 enlisted men and some British officers to the town of Hurmat, 2 kilometres away. Others left for an unknown route. Lieutenant Knotts and eight British officers being pitifully weak from their inhuman treatment at the hands of their captors begged to remain in the barn of the château, just back of which they had been released.

The owner of the château was a Belgian, the Burgomeister of the town of Boucet, and his wife proved to be of the noblest type of womanhood; sympathetic, humane, generous and courteous. It is believed only just that her gracious assistance to an American officer in distress be recognized officially by a letter of appreciation from the Military Authorities. It is believed by Lieutenant Knotts that a similar appreciation has already been sent by the British Military Authorities in acknowledgment of her generosity and ministrations to the five British officers housed at her home with him. The name of this woman is Madame Stanislas Seny Oury.

Here Lieutenant Knotts and the five British officers with him were cared for, nursed and fed just as if they were in their own homes. All the available local medical treatment was provided. Madame Seny herself nursed Lieutenant Knotts and it must be understood that for three or four days after these officers were taken into her home the Germans were going by there and some ten German officers and 900 enlisted men were being quartered each night in her château and barns so this care was given to the officers at the expense of having the livestock and the provisions of the farm plundered and stolen by the above Germans.

During this time, Lieutenant Knotts and the five British officers had been quartered in the service portion of the barn where heat, bathing and delousing facilities were provided and also a clean change of under and outer clothing. The only reason these officers were not taken into the château proper as was afterwards done, was because each night of the German evacuation, so many German officers were quartered in the house that hardly adequate sleeping accommodations were left for the Seny family itself. After the last of the Germans had gone by these officers were taken into the house and were treated as esteemed guests.

No allied troops came through this vicinity except one French division and that offered practically no transportation facilities to the prisoners to get back to the armies. It did offer them, however, the advantages of the French military post which was so slow that it brought no immediate results. After a period of three weeks all of the British officers had recovered and started back to their army which was then only 30 kilometres away, but Lieutenant Knotts was still unable to walk any great distances and was obliged to stay on until word was conveyed by letter carried by the gardener of Madame Seny to the American Section of the Permanent Allied Armistice Commission. The Commanding Officer was Major General Charles Rhodes, American Expeditionary Forces. The next day after the letter reached Major General Rhodes he sent a car with Captain White of the US Medical Services to Poucet so that Lieutenant Knotts was able to report for duty to the American Section of the Armistice Commission on 9 December 1918.

During his sojourn there he was given skilful medical attention. On 14 December, Lieutenant Knotts was ordered to report back to the 16th American Aero squadron through the Commanding General of the Third Army Wing Headquarters that were believed to be then at Coblenz, his orders read Coblenz. It was known that Lieutenant Knotts would be obliged to collect his personal belongings left at the squadron and probably be obliged to go immediately after that to a hospital before he was completely restored to health. He proceeded in compliance with his orders to Coblenz but found that the Army commander, Third Army, was at Hayson. Here he received verbal orders which sent him to report to the Army Air Service Commander stationed at that time at Treves (Trier) with which order he complied, reaching General Mitchell's office on 15 December 1918. From here he was ordered to proceed to Toul where he reported to his squadron, which moved the next day from Toul to Colombey-les-Belles. Lieutenant Knotts was immediately sent to Camp Hospital #5 at Barisey-la-Sete. Here he was obliged to remain six weeks, and on 26 January 1919, he left the hospital to receive orders for transportation to the United States which will be issued as soon as he has completed the special duty for which he was ordered to these headquarters.

Second Lieutenant R.A. Floyd
Ferry Pilot

Lieutenant Floyd on his first ferry trip from Orly to Colombey-les-Belles had the extraordinary experience of being lost en route and flying a brand-new Salmson plane into German territory. July 23rd 1918 was the date of his capture. It was his first flight in a Salmson plane, and his first voyage into the Colombey-les-Belles region, with the result that he knew neither his motor nor his maps. He represented that when he reported at Orly, he was formally introduced to the Salmson plane, informed there were some maps in the back seat of the machine and casually told that he should fly it to the First Air Depot. He declared he was unable to obtain from those on duty any special information of the plane or territory he was to fly over and that he was thus thrown on his own resources.

Under these circumstances he decided to follow another pilot. After some trouble in starting the motor he mounted into the air and flew for about an hour in a general easterly direction, but was unable to find the other machine which had started in advance of him. He returned, therefore, to Orly, for which, he declared, he was severely reprimanded. He set out next day and had considerable trouble in getting to Vinets which was ordinarily a stopping place for such trips. From Vinets there are two routes to Colombey-les-Belles; of these Lieutenant Floyd took the northern one which ran 15 to 25 kilometres behind the lines, as they existed. Unfamiliarity with the country caused repeated difficulty in finding his way, he said. Being in doubt as to what locality he was over he searched about for the large-scale maps, which would show the lines better, but was unable to find them. He kept on north and east following his maps, for about an hour. It became very cloudy and the mist hung low. He was lost. He decided that he would fly ten minutes and if he could not then orient himself he would land. He picked out a good field near Worchingenn [*sic*], Germany, spiralling down to it and in landing shot over the field. It proved to be a dummy Hun aerodrome. A German soldier, having spied him in the air, had hidden himself in an adjacent wheat field and when the machine had stopped jumped up 30ft away and captured him. The landing gear of the machine was smashed but otherwise the machine was in such condition as it would have been on delivery, with specifications in the rear seat.

Lieutenant Floyd was taken to the aerodrome of a new Fokker squadron where he dined with Germans who sought to discuss with him America's part in the war and showed him considerable knowledge about the American Air Service. He was kidded about Major Brown who landed the six Bréguets[1] in Germany, said Lieutenant Floyd, and was asked 'if our Liberty machines were going to act the same way'. Persistent efforts were made by the Germans to get information from the captive. When on 26 July no information was forthcoming, they made him take off his Sam Browne belt and confined him for seven days in a cell on German food of execrable variety. His orderly was a New Yorker

---

1. The incident regarding Major Brown and the landing of six Bréguet bombers in Germany is conflicting in its description of the incident. It is said that all six aircraft ran out of fuel and landed intact, their crews being captured. But in Lieutenant Codman's escape report, he says that there were seven aircraft of which three were shot down and the remaining four crash-landed.

fortunately and occasionally gave him French biscuits, which were a small source of nourishment.

He was taken next to an underground fortress at Strassberg where he met American enlisted men. The enlisted men's food was very poor and his was hardly better. He received two meals a day from a restaurant nearby and described the food as 'filthy', consisting of barley soup and blood sausages which turned his stomach. At Karlsruhe he was interrogated again and he lived for some time in the hotel there which was in a filthy condition and plentifully equipped with Dictaphones through which the Germans sought information of value, and he finally got to the camp at Landshut. From this camp he made his escape with three others: Lieutenants Doehler, Battey and C.W. Peckham of the RAF. It was a 'ragtime getaway'. For eight days they had worked to cut their way through the barracks door by the removal of certain screws from the panel and when at length they set to make their escape and were lined up on the contice ready to leap over the adjacent wall, they were discovered. They all jumped together and amid the ringing of bells, blowing of whistles and shooting of guns they cleared the 8ft wall and hustled away. They were pursued by the Germans and after running to the point of exhaustion were forced to climb trees where they remained while the Germans searched below. Lieutenant Floyd was at large five days and finally became lost in the swampy country and was captured at Erding on 15 September. He spent twenty-one days in solitary confinement and for singing *God help Kaiser Bill* with his comrades, he got three extra days.

Regarding his treatment, he said he had two books to read which were in the Red Cross package. Except when Red Cross food was received, their two meals a day were insufficient for nourishment as it was cold and damp in the stone jail.

In equipping themselves for the escape he said they used a German magnetic razor with which they magnetized needles for the entire group to be used in place of compasses when any one of them wanted to escape.

First Lieutenant Elihu H. Kelton
185th Pursuit Squadron

> On October 30th, 1918, at about 4:00 o'clock P.M. I left the 185th Aero Squadron at Rembercourt (1st Pursuit Group) in a Sopwith Camel (No.13) for the purpose of shooting down a balloon at Villers-devant-Dun. I arrived at the lines and patrolled until nearly dusk, searching for German bi-plane machines.

I then headed for the balloon but about 10 kilometres over the lines I saw a Fokker about 600 meters away and five more in the distance. I attacked and in the fight my motor quit. The Fokker shot up my machine on the way down so I landed out of control. When I came to there was a crowd of Huns around, two of whom were eagerly demanding in English when I thought the war would be finished. I was asked if I had any papers or arms but was not searched. They treated me very decently, giving me a cup of wine and cigarettes. In fact, the only expression of anger was by the pilot who shot me down. He seemed intensely peeved at first because I had spoiled his motor and forced him to land. He asked why I had attacked him.

That evening I was taken to several different headquarters where I was asked a few perfunctory questions which I did not answer. I walked to Wiseppe from where I was taken to Stenay in an auto. At Stenay a Captain of the German Intelligence Force gave me a very thorough cross-examination. I stayed at Stenay overnight.

On the afternoon of November 1st, I was taken to Montmédy and put into a fair little prison camp which however we had to evacuate the next day on account of the Americans shelling a bridge nearby. In this camp a French 2nd Lieutenant was put in with us but the two Frenchmen who were with us immediately suspected him and told us he was a stoolpigeon, so we were careful of our talk.

The next morning (Nov. 2nd), we were taken to the fortress on Montmédy where we stayed until November 6th, this room was full of cooties and fleas and we had very few blankets and very little wood. The food was always the same, roasted barley coffee and a day's ration of sour black bread for breakfast, cabbage soup for dinner, and more coffee and some uneatable vegetable jam for supper. On the 3rd of November, the Adjutant of a German Squadron invited us to tea. He was very cordial and asked no questions. His main object seemed to be to dispel our idea that Germans were Huns, Boche or Barbarians, although doubtless he was on the watch for any information we might drop. As far as personal treatment was concerned I have no complaint to make. My combination flying suit was the only thing taken away.

On November 6th we started for Karlsruhe – four American officers under charge of two guards. We arrived at Karlsruhe on the 7th and were kept in a bare hotel room two nights and a day. On the 9th we were questioned at the hotel by a man who was very stupid. Then we were taken to the prison camp in town. Here our Sam Browne belts were taken away, but we received an issue of clothing, toilet articles and food from the American Red Cross. We lived almost entirely on the Red Cross food.

The signing of the Armistice was marked with great celebration in the city and for some days rioting was feared. On the 18th we were allowed to go about the town under guard. On the 20th, as we could see no immediate chance of release, 1st Lieutenant Richard Aldworth (213th Pursuit Squadron), 1st Lieutenant William G. Caxton (41 Squadron RAF) and myself slipped the guard and as soon as evening set in we left town. We crossed the Rhine and walked until we reached Lauterberg, the first town in Alsace, at 4:00 A.M. We never had any serious difficulties. From Lauterberg hired carriages as far as Strasbourg which we reached on the 22nd November. Every town in Alsace seemed very enthusiastically French.

General Mitchell supplied us with funds and gave us permission to stay in Strasbourg a short time. We left by the first train to leave Strasbourg for Nancy (Nov. 30th). I rejoined my squadron and was re-assigned two or three days later.

I was paid sixty (60) Marks by the German government (in canteen money).

Second Lieutenant David C. Beebe
50th Observation Squadron

On 4 November at 1.45 pm, Second Lieutenant D.C. Beebe, pilot and First Lieutenant M.F. Lockwood, observer, of the 50th Squadron, 1st Observation Group, left the Clermont en Argonne Aerodrome, in a Liberty motor DH.4, as one of two machines forming protection for a third doing a contact patrol mission for the 77th Division. At this time the American forces were advancing so rapidly that the location of the first lines was unknown, even approximately, and this mission was instructed to cover a large area.

The formation of three machines passed Buzancy where no sign of activity was evident and proceeded north to Le Chesne at an altitude of

500ft. For a short time they circled about a large dam near Le Chesne until a single Boche mounted on horseback was soon in the town indicating that they were over hostile territory and that the lines were to the south. Formation turned south-east and almost immediately the machine of Lieutenants Beebe and Lockwood was hit by machine-gun fire, the engine stopping instantly. An attempt to resort to reserve gas availed nothing. At this moment the Hun trenches had not been observed by the mission. There was only one available field to be reached from this limited altitude which was then about 200ft and this field extended from east to west, to the south were poles and fences. As the machine glided to field both pilot and observer saw that they were landing parallel to the line of trenches. Though landing, the machine-gun fire continued, hitting the machine incessantly. As these were new positions and little artillery bombardment had taken place, the ground was not broken up extensively, permitting the disabled machine to land without crashing, 30 yards in front of the trenches. No friendly troops were in sight to the south.

Machine-gun fire did not cease except in pit opposite machine. Pilot and observer jumped out of machine, hesitated a moment but fire continued and then at the command of a Hun in nearest pit ducked to this place.

No violence was displayed but they were held in this pit until the other two machines circling above disappeared. The position consisted of disconnected machine-gun pits. At command pilot and observer crawled to a neighbouring pit and were led to an officer who, in French, requested identity cards, inspecting them, and returned them.

From here, they were led down the road and through the town of Tannay where a Hun soldier made a rush on them with an axe but was pushed away by the guard. At Reg. HQ considerable questioning was done here, principally in regard to the attack of the next day. (Observers combination taken.) From here they were led to Brigade HQ and then along the Aisne and the HQ of the 3rd Army Intelligence Dept., arriving about 1.30 am. At this place an *Oberleutnant* Brewer was Commandant who conducted the questioning in the presence of a stenographer who took down all that was said by the prisoners, who were separately questioned until 4.30 am. At 5.45 am captives were taken to the station where they joined another group of prisoners, an American lieutenant named Geo. Tiffany and four French officers and boarded a train for Carignan.

Neither of the prisoners had overcoats nor were they supplied with blankets during the trip to Libramont which was the new HQ for the retreating 3rd Army. Civilians furnished what food they had.

At Libramont this party of officers were the only officers present. They were questioned in a small room on the second storey of a schoolhouse. In a large room on the first floor were approximately eighty enlisted men, about forty Americans from the 77th Division, the remainder French. Neither officers nor enlisted men were supplied with blankets but slept on board frames. The food consisted of soup in the middle of the day and barley coffee in the morning and at night.

Almost daily questioning was conducted by *Oberleutnant* Brewer who said he had been a platinum manufacturer in Newark, New Jersey for fourteen years. Often Hun flyers were present. On the day before departure, a few blankets were given to the officers and a Hun army sergeant by the name of Ewald, who was formerly of New York, arranged to have food sent to the officer prisoners once a day from a hotel in town.

The Armistice came and all the prisoners were to be moved to a camp near Bouillon. A sergeant marched the party the 30 kilometres and as they were told they were to be held for two weeks more, the officers and many men succeeded in making their escape at night. The officers met outside of Bouillon and one of the party, a French captain, succeeded in getting all up to a castle above the town. The German guards searched all night for the party but in vain. The following day they marched all night to Sedan though stopped several times, but those not directly concerned with prisoners were too occupied to know what to do with them.

Sedan and the French outposts were reached by noon on 14 November and from there conducted by an American party back to Clermont and on the following day reported to the 1st Army HQ at Souilly. The officers were never searched but asked to show contents of pockets, and no souvenirs were collected from their persons. *Oberleutnant* Brewer kept the prisoner pilot and observer's identity cards. Many of the guards who had been in America expressed their intention of returning after affairs were settled.

First Lieutenant Brooke Edwards
20th Bombardment Squadron

On November 5th, 1918, the 20th Squadron made a bombing raid on Mouzon. Due to a strong south-west wind, the formation of eight Liberty-motored De Havilland 4s was blown far into German territory after the bombs were dropped. On the way back to the lines we were attacked by three patrols of German Chasse. We drove off the first patrol (Fokker D.7s with blue markings with white crosses). The second patrol brought down one of our planes in flames, and the motor of the plane in which Lieutenant Edwards (pilot) and Lieutenant Payne (observer) were flying was crippled by machine-gun fire, and fell behind the formation. When the third patrol attacked us, we were practically alone. The markings of the Fokkers of this patrol were black and white stripes. They ripped out our gas tank by machine-gun fire, and wounded Lieutenant Payne in the left arm, disabling him. The ammunition for his twin Lewis gun was almost exhausted. He turned to tell the pilot what the conditions were in the rear seat, when an explosive bullet struck the breech of the Marlin gun close to the pilot's head. He thought the pilot wounded and took control, putting the plane into a steep nose-dive. Three Fokkers followed, firing all the time, as the plane was still headed toward the American lines. It was necessary for the pilot to manoeuvre continually, and as the motor was barely turning over, the plane rapidly lost altitude. When we were very low, and close to the American lines, an enemy plane closed in on us and we shot him down. This made the second enemy plane we had shot down in combat. Due to the crippled motor and the manoeuvring necessary to escape the pursuing Fokkers, and to the strong wind ahead, we were unable to reach our lines and landed in the lines of the Wurtemburger Jaeger. A private rushed at the pilot and presented a Luger at his head while others grinned. A *Feldwebel*, however, ordered him back, saluted, and requested any papers we might have. We had no papers except a leave to Nice, and a permission to use explosive bullets. We were able to destroy this later, however, before the Germans found it. We were taken to a field dressing station, where Lieutenant Payne's wound was well and quickly dressed, and anti-tetanus injected. From there we were taken by an artillery officer, who later placed us on the cassons [*sic*] of his regiment and turned us over to the HQ at Louppy-sur-Loison, where we arrived on the night of the 5th November. We spent the night of the 5th in the orderly room of the Gruppe-Luppy, and were not fed until noon of the 6th, when we received some soup and bread with Lieutenant Henry Brown, who had been shot down that morning by Fokkers. We were taken that afternoon to Virton where a German Intelligence Officer gave us tea, but didn't question us very closely, as he already knew of the Armistice. He showed us, however, excellent pictures of American aerodromes, and surprised us with his knowledge of the First Day Bombardment Group. We were kept in a room at Virton for three nights and two days, the food being not good, but plentiful, and rations as issued to the guards. On the 9th two guards took us to Karlsruhe, by train, arriving the morning of the 10th. As we arrived, revolutionists with red bands on their arms were disarming all incoming troops. We spent the 10th in a room at the Europa Hotel at Karlsruhe, and taken to the permanent camp on the morning of the 11th. Here we were given American Red Cross parcels, good barracks, a French orderly and every consideration that could be expected. At 9.10 pm on the 20th, seven English officers and four Americans, Lieutenants Brown, Fulton, Payne and Edwards escaped from the camp by bribing a guard, stole a skiff from the Rhine bank, and landed at about 1.00 am 10 miles north of Lauterburg. We walked to a small village some 4 miles south of Lauterburg, rested there, and reached Selz on the night of the 21st. The Mayor of Selz showed us the greatest hospitality the members of the party were billeted, free of any charge whatsoever, with the Mayor, Cure and members of the Town Council, who were most kind. We reached Strasbourg on the night of the 22nd, and finally were able to get to Nancy by motor, reporting to Captain Zinn at Colombey-les-Belles.

Second Lieutenant D.D. Watson
8th Aero Squadron

Returning from a reconnaissance and bombing mission in Lorraine sector on evening of November 7, 1918, I was injured in the head by anti-aircraft fire. Unconscious for a while, exact time unknown, but at 6:15 P.M. Allied time, green rockets were fired and landing lights shown.

We had requested landing flares be shown on our return but did not think it was our field. It was very dark and misty and a strong south-west wind had blown us farther in than we reckoned on.

My pilot, 2nd Lieutenant Clark Robinson, attempted to land with weakened or shot controls and smashed into and through the German mechanics holding flares, and landed upside-down at the foot of a small hill, both being pinned under the wreckage.

When Germans pulled us out and carried us to officers' quarters, where my head was dressed, they then searched Lieutenant Robinson and questioned us both but made no threats on our refusal to talk. We had dinner with them which consisted of brown bread, roast beef, potatoes and dessert, some kind of pie. There was wine and beer but we were not pressed to drink. After dinner our flying clothes were taken from us and German overcoats given instead. They were not very clean but very warm. We were then carried to a guardhouse where we spent the night on wooden bunks.

Next morning after dressing my wounds we were carried to a railroad station Bernsdorf, and by train to Ranlach [sic], where I was put in a hospital and Lieutenant Robinson carried away under guard. The amenities were rather poor at this hospital, but I was treated kindly. I remained here until the morning of the 10th, when I was sent to Saargunen [sic]. I escaped from an ambulance there and went south on a freight train and crossed the lines south of Château Salines coming into the French lines at Arrancourt on the morning of the 12th at daybreak.

From my limited experience and observations food was comparatively scarce, the train service good, and discipline of the German army excellent. We were given good treatment and no insults were offered by either civilians or soldiers.

Second Lieutenant Clark Robinson
8th Aero Squadron

Controls weakened and Observer 2nd Lieutenant D.D. Watson wounded in head by archie [anti-aircraft] fire after dark 5:30 P.M. (Allied time), November 7th, while returning from reconnaissance of sector, and bombing archie batteries south of Metz with 24-pound Cooper bombs.

A mist had covered the river and there was a strong wind from the south-west. The plane was still in control and I headed south-west until 6.15. At 6.15 green rockets were fired to our left and landing lights shown.

I did not think that it was our field though I had asked for landing lights in case I got back after dark. The night was very dark; there was no moon. I thought we had crossed the lines. I attempted to land with the lights but when I throttled down the controls seemed to weaken.

A number of German mechanics were holding flares to show us the limit of the field and we accidentally ran into them. The plane landed upside-down at the foot of a hill; we were both pinned in and were pulled out by the Germans.

We were not mistreated. We were taken to the guard house where a doctor dressed Lieutenant Watson's wounds and we were then taken to the officers' house and were given a good dinner with the officers. We were not pressed to drink and no questions were pressed. We had crashed at a Fokker field near Bernsdorf.

We slept on bunks at the guardhouse and the next day were sent by automobile and train, under guard, to Ranlach where Lieutenant Watson was put in hospital. I was sent to the prison camp at St Aveld. My treatment there was very good though they had very little food.

At 7:00 P.M. on October 11th, thirteen French soldiers were sent back to France from the camp. I was dressed in a German overcoat and French helmet and had no difficulty leaving the camp with them. We were sent by train to Ouss and from there walked to Hinville [*sic*].

First Lieutenant B.B. Battle
91st Observation Squadron

Shortly after noon of 12 June, Lieutenant Battle left his aerodrome in a Salmson plane to fly as protection for another Salmson which was to take pictures. The photographic mission was accomplished without incident and the two machines were just crossing the lines on the return trip when Battle nosed his machine down and tried out his fixed gun. There was evidently some fault in the synchronization for at the first burst the propeller was shattered. Not having sufficient altitude to glide across the lines, he was forced to descend on the German side, landing between the first and second line of trenches. Bearing in mind that the first duty of a captured aviator is to destroy his machine, Battle endeavoured to set fire to his plane but the men in the trenches opened fire on him and he was forced to desist. He held up his hands as token of surrender but the fire still continued so he sought shelter in a shell-hole. Here he was taken prisoner by an infantry officer of the Bavarian division occupying that sector.

Having landed just in front of the village of Flirey, the nearest German headquarters were at Thiaucourt and to this place Battle was marched. During the four days spent at Thiaucourt, he was questioned on three different occasions but refused to talk. The Intelligence officer finally lost patience and threatened that, unless certain questions were answered, a note would be dropped over the lines stating that 'An American pilot, Lieutenant Battle, has been killed in combat.' He was told to go ahead and drop the note. Shortly afterwards, an armament officer entered and asserted that incendiary bullets had been found in the belt of the Salmson's fixed gun. The Intelligence officer then informed Battle that this was against the rules of warfare and that he would be shot unless he gave them all the information requested. This information was again refused.

Shortly afterwards, Lieutenant Battle was placed in a fourth-class coach and taken to Karlsruhe under the guard of an officer and three enlisted men. During the journey he asked to go to the toilet. This was granted but the guard was watchful and caught him when he attempted to escape through the toilet window. Arrived at Karlsruhe, Battle was sent to the now famous Karlsruhe Hotel, which was fitted out with Dictaphones. While here he fell ill but was refused a doctor. The food supplied sick prisoners was the same as that given to those in good health: thin soup, barley coffee and black bread.

After nine days in this hotel he was sent to a camp for British aviators at Landshut, Bavaria. Here he was locked in a small unventilated room with twenty other officers. A short period of exercise was obtained each day in a small, filthy courtyard about 20ft square. Food and living conditions were so bad that the officers requested in writing that they be moved to other quarters. After two weeks this request was granted and they were placed in an old castle nearby. The quarters at this place were better but there was slight improvement in the food until ten days before their departure when Red Cross food was received. During his stay here Battle attempted to bribe a German sergeant major to allow him to escape. This was reported and the American was punished by being placed in solitary confinement for eight days.

Seven weeks after he arrived at the castle, Battle was removed to the prison camp at Villengen. The trip was made by train and took two days. During this time the prisoners were allowed to visit the latrine only at eight-hour intervals. Their shoes were removed to prevent attempts at escape. They received one meal during the trip. The camp at Villengen was reached on 14 September.

On the night of 6 October, the prisoners short-circuited the electric light wires of the camp and Battle, in company with four American and one French officer, made his escape by climbing over the fence. He was fired on by the guards but received nothing more serious than a bullet through his haversack. The six officers separated and each took a different route. Lieutenant Battle travelled for five nights through the Black Forest, hiding during the day. He met many people during the evenings but they apparently supposed him to be some German wayfarer and he was only challenged twice. His food consisted of four pieces of hard tack a day. All went well until he reached the Rhine where he was captured by a police dog. He was immediately taken back to Villengen and put in solitary confinement for eighteen days. At the end of this time he was told that he had been tried (his presence at the trial was evidently considered unnecessary) and convicted of inciting mutiny. For this offence he was sent to Fort Kurstein, a reprisal camp near Berlin.

This place was never reached. At Cassel on 9 November, in the Grand Duchy of Hesse, the train was boarded by revolutionaries, among whom were a number of naval Marines, and the guards were disarmed and the prisoners freed. Battle struck up an acquaintance with a Marine who spoke English and who seemed very friendly. The two of them attempted to make their way to the Holland border but were stopped by an officer, and the Socialists who were in charge of the railway station ordered them back to Villengen. Lieutenant Battle talked to many of the Revolutionists and was told by all of them that the war was over and that he would be foolish to try and escape now as all prisoners would be released in a day or two. Discipline was very lax and he believed that if he had had any money he could have reached Holland with little difficulty.

Boarding a train in company with his acquaintance the Marine, Battle went to Frankfort. Here he met a German officer and got on very good terms with him by giving him some Red Cross food. They went into the station bar together and had some drinks. Everyone was drinking and talking of the revolution, rejoicing that the Armistice was signed or soon would be. A statue of the Kaiser and pictures of Ludendorff and Hindenburg were torn down.

Leaving Frankfort for Villengen, Battle tried to bribe the guard to take a route which would bring them close to the Swiss border. But the guard still possessed a strong respect for authority and wired ahead asking for reinforcements. When Villengen was reached a strongly-armed guard was waiting him and conducted him to the prison camp. It was necessary to remain in the camp until 25 November when nearly all the American prisoners were released. Lieutenant Battle went to Constance and remained there for three days receiving excellent food. From there the journey was made across Switzerland and into France.

First Lieutenant Merian Caldwell Cooper
20th Bombardment Squadron

First Lieutenant Merian C. Cooper was assigned to the US Bombardment Squadron at Maulan, France on 30 August 1918 as a pilot of a DH.4. One month later on 26 September 1918 with his observer Lieutenant Edward Leonard, they were part of a seven-plane patrol on a bombing mission of Dun-sur-Meuse, and had just completed the mission and were turning for home when they were attacked by a squadron of Fokker fighters. In less than five minutes five of the bombers had been shot down including Lieutenant Cooper's. As his aircraft started to burn, Lieutenant Cooper put the aircraft into a dive and then into a slide-slip to prevent the flames roasting him and his observer alive. His observer Lieutenant Leonard had been hit in the neck by a bullet and was bleeding profusely and Lieutenant Cooper's hand and face were being burned by the flames. The aircraft crash-landed and both crew members managed to extricate themselves from the wreckage. One of the Fokker pilots landed alongside the burning machine and accepted their surrender. Troops soon arrived and they were taken to a German field hospital and treated for their wounds. Later they were taken to another German hospital for further treatment and then to a prisoner-of-war camp for the rest of the war. At the signing of the Armistice, they were released and both returned to Paris, France.

Lieutenant Merian Cooper was assigned to duties in Paris with the US Air Service until July 1919, when Ignacy Jan Paderewski, the Polish premier, persuaded President Wilson to allow him to solicit volunteers from the US Air Service to help him form an air force and prevent the Bolshevik army from invading Poland. Cooper and seven other American pilots – Carl Clark, Edward Corsi, Arthur Kelly (96th Bombardment Squadron), George Crawford (20th Bombardment Squadron), Cedric Fauntleroy (94th Pursuit Squadron), Edwin Noble and Kenneth Shrewsbury – decided to volunteer to fight on the side of the Polish people. They were to fly combat and reconnaissance missions in support of the Polish ground troops. Their squadron was given the name the Kościuszko Squadron after

Tadeusz Kościuszko, the Polish patriot who went to America to fight for the Americans in their War of Independence.

The volunteers were inducted into the Kościuszko Squadron, Merian Cooper being given the rank of major. The squadron was a mobile one and consisted of a train of railway coaches, flat cars and boxcars for supplies and equipment, and as the area of action changed, so did the location of the squadron.

On 10 July 1920, Major Cooper was on patrol over the Bolsheviks' front line when he came under heavy ground fire, causing his engine to fail and force him to land. He was captured by the Bolsheviks and treated quite roughly as they didn't take kindly to mercenaries being involved in their struggle. Taken to Moscow, Merian Cooper was put into a prisoner-of-war camp for the second time in his career, this time for nine months. He made his escape at the beginning of April 1921 and after travelling for twenty-six nights he crossed the Latvian border and into safety. Transportation was provided back to Warsaw and at the end of May 1921, he returned to the United States.

His career after that is a matter of record, when he became one of Hollywood's outstanding film producers with films such as *King Kong* and *This is Cinerama*. During the Second World War he joined the USAAC, finishing the war with the rank of brigadier general.

First Lieutenant Alexander M. Roberts
74th Squadron RAF

On 19 July 1918 while flying with a patrol of British machines type S.E.5. from Claire Mairie Forest, Ypres to La Bassée at 0900 Lieutenant Roberts and others engaged enemy aircraft in combat. One of their members in ensuing manoeuvres brought down a balloon. Lieutenant Roberts attacked a two-seater and while observing the effect of his fire was set upon by a Fokker biplane and a triplane. A machine-gun burst penetrated the lower left wing and another crashed through the instrument board of the motor, tearing his sleeve. With engine trouble he was forced to a landing in a shell-hole. He was 10 kilometres behind enemy lines near Moorslede. He was captured by a German sergeant of a machine-gun company and was taken to Headquarters where he received fairly good treatment. While on the train between Liege and Aix-la-Chapelle he jumped to the ground and attempted to escape to the Dutch border which was only 6 kilometres away. He was recaptured while passing through a tunnel and started backward to the interior again. Upon his capture he was treated very roughly and threatened to the point that he believed they were about to shoot him. He passed through the prison camp at Coutray and landed at Rastatt. Here he escaped through a window on the night of 5 August with Hector Gray, a New Zealander, who had been in his squadron and also was a captive. The escape was effected at night just after the German sergeant had called the roll on the early morning of the 6th by making a rope of sheets and sliding 3ft from the guard as he passed. They spent seven days in the Black Forest but gave it up as they had no food and Lieutenant Roberts had sore feet, which made walking almost impossible. They were returned to a jail, Fremdenstatt, formerly the estate of some prominent German, where they were treated rather well. The meals were good.

(From notes taken by L.H. Thayer, Second Lieutenant, AS.)

From: Second Lieutenant Richard Fulton, AS
To: Chief of Air Service (Thro C.O. 1st Air Depot. APO 731-A)
Subject: My treatment as a prisoner

On November 5 1918, at 9:30 A.M. after having accomplished a bombing mission over the town of Mouzon, I was taken prisoner. My pilot was 1st Lieutenant Samuel Mandell. We fell from a height of 10,000ft 3 kilometres east of Stenay, which is north of Verdun. Lieutenant Mandell was badly wounded in the crash, his right leg being broken, his face smashed and his body crushed. I was obliged to leave him without the probability of medical attention, and because of his condition I believe he must have died.

I was marched to Infantry Headquarters, thence to four German Headquarters in widely separated parts of the town of Stenay. Dressed in my fur-lined flying suit, with a lancer on horseback immediately behind with a lance, ready to prod me, and apparent intent to humiliate me, I was marched on foot in public view of the population and soldiers of the town. From these headquarters I was thence marched on foot to Montmédy in the same fashion, from there thence about 5 kilometres further to what I believe was Headquarters of the 5th German Army which was reached the same night at 5.30 pm.

From this point I was slightly better treated. Eventually I was taken by auto to Virton, Belgium where I remained three days. On November 9th I left for Carlsruhe which was reached on November 10th, after 25 hours' train ride; and from there I was taken to a hotel in Carlsruhe and eventually to an officers' detention camp, from which I and three other American officers escaped by clearing three rows of barbed wire fence, where we found a boat and crossed the Rhine at one o'clock in the morning, reaching the Alsatian border at 5 o'clock, November 21st. Here we met officers in Allied Armies who assisted us, and we eventually reached Headquarters, First Air Depot, American E.F. on 27 November 1918.

R.W. Fulton

The following is a second statement submitted by Second Lieutenant Fulton:

While flying in a De Havilland 4 formation of eight (8) planes. On a bombing mission over the town of Mouzon on the morning of November 5th, 1918, we were attacked successfully by three patrols of enemy aircraft (Fokker D7 Type). The first and second of these formations were driven off without loss to our planes but the third attacked more viciously and in larger numbers. We had bombed our objective at 9:15 A.M. and were on our way to our own lines when the fighting took place. Here was a very strong wind blowing into Germany, which held us over enemy territory longer than usual. Two (2) of the leading ships in this German patrol were shot down by the observers in our formation. One of our ships was seen to leave the formation with white smoke coming from his gasoline tank and a Fokker directly on his tail. He fell a very short distance before bursting into flames, then fell from a height of 11,000 feet. The plane in which I was flying with 1st Lieutenant Samuel Mandell, pilot, then left the formation in a series of dives and side slips which clearly indicated it was out of control. The formation was flying at an altitude of 12,000 feet when we left it. After several unsuccessful attempts to get in communication with the pilot, I took hold of the controls and attempted to correct our position. It was possible to pull out of the dive somewhat but the aileron controls would not function. Although the pilot appeared wounded, he also tried to guide the ship and when we reached a height of about 50 to 75 feet above the ground we stalled the plane and fell off the right wing in a viree and crashed. This was the only way to come into the field as it was full of holes and covered with trees. I climbed out of my cockpit and found Lieutenant Mandell badly crushed and entangled in the wreckage. We were about halfway between the German front line and their artillery and due west of Stenay. The crash was about ten metres from the wreck and the opposite bank was lined with German troops, but they could not cross due to the fact that the bridge had been destroyed. After about 20 minutes or one half-hour's effort I succeeded in removing the pilot from the wreckage. He was unconscious and bleeding profusely about the face which was badly smashed, his right leg was crushed above the knee and broken below and his body slightly crushed. During this time, three (3) German soldiers had removed their clothes and swam across the canal. I made them understand that we were in need of medical aid and one of them secured a first aid kit which we used to tie up the pilot's face and did what we could for him. The Germans helped me in this work and were very considerate. They were very much interested in my gloves, Sam Browne belt and such leather goods which they took for themselves. An officer appeared on the other bank of the canal and after giving directions to the 3 men, with me they hurried me to a spot where a means of crossing the canal had been erected, leaving Lieutenant Mandell where I had placed him on the ground. This German officer spoke English and after explaining to him he assured me that medical attention would be given Lieutenant Mandell, but with the best of intention, I had little hope for his recovery.

I was marched under guard to what appeared to be Regimental Headquarters and from there to Stenay, with a Lancer on horseback directly behind me. At Stenay, we stopped at three places in separate parts of the town. The streets were filled with soldiers and I became an exhibit for their amusement. From Stenay, I was marched, still on foot with the Lancer behind me to Montmédy, a distance of about 12 or 15 kilometres. We passed through this town to a smaller village about 3 kilometres further which place I reached at 5:30 P.M. I had received a slight wound in the fight and was bruised in the crash and the march had been made in my heavy flying suit, so my condition was poor when this stop was reached. A little black bread and barley coffee was given to me, which was the first food since very early breakfast. The night was spent on the floor of this place, which I believed to be the Headquarters of the 5th German Army. During my march to the rear, the roads were badly congested with troops and the retreat had apparently become a rout as their organization was broken and there was a noticeable lack of discipline.

The next day, Nov. 6, I was taken by auto to Vireten [*sic*], Belgium where three other American officers and myself received a good meal and was interviewed by an Intelligence Officer. He apparently had seen the wreck of my plane and from it could tell my organization. He inquired my name, of several officers, in the 1st Day Bombardment Group, and appeared very familiar with the organization and personnel of it. Several pictures of airdromes were shown us including one of the Pursuit Group at Liste-an-Barrer [*sic*]. Comments were made on our ships and he volunteered some information concerning his own. It seemed that this officer realized that the war was practically over and for this reason did not question us much. From the evening of Nov. 6th until early morning Nov. 9th, I was confined in a small house of about 4 rooms in which there were other Americans. This house was guarded on the outside by armed soldiers. While at this place, a decoy was placed in my room. He was dressed as a French pilot but in Colonial uniform and said he had been shot down that morning by a patrol and wounded. His arm was tied up and on casually glancing at his flying suit, noticed that it had not been torn. When asked about this he showed me several small holes but they were in the opposite sleeve. He was removed shortly on the pretence of going to the hospital.

At 5.P.M., Nov. 9th, we left for Karlsruhe (Baden) reaching that place at 7 A.M. Nov. 10th, after a series of stopovers. The train we rode on was very long and crowded with troops on their way to the rear. On reaching our destination our guards were speedily disarmed by some reds who had taken possession of the station. We were marched under a Red Guard to a Hotel where we spent a day and on the morning of Nov.11th, were placed in an Officers' detention centre in this city. An issue of food and necessities such as razor, towel, change of underwear and etc., were received from the Red Cross (American). On the night of the 11th there was a demonstration in Karlsruhe, which could not be quelled by machine guns, but the air raid warning was blown and several anti-aircraft batteries fired several rounds which was successful in dispersing the mob.

Life at this camp was not at all bad. The Germans did not feed us sufficiently but we drew rations on Monday and Thursday from the American Red Cross, which was more than enough for our needs. On Nov. 20th seven (7) British Officers and four (4) American Officers decided to get away. The first man bribed a guard on the pretence of going to town and returning. We all followed one at a time over the three fences, which surrounded the camp and met outside at a predetermined place. This was at 9 P.M., and very few on the streets as they were all kept indoors at night. We found our way to a road leading south and hiked about 12 kilometres from Karlsruhe, thence to the Rhine. We found a boat close at hand and by making two trips across, succeeded in landing our entire party on the other side. This was at 1 A.M., Nov. 21. We walked the balance of the night and reached the Alsatian border at about 5.30 A.M. We

Allied prisoners of war at Karlsruhe camp.

met a German patrol of horsemen shortly after, but they did not stop us as they were looking for German stragglers and we told them that we were released prisoners. A small hotel was reached early morning Nov. 21 after walking all night. Three British Officers were forced to drop behind while in Germany, being unable to keep the pace. From Selz to Strassberg, we rode on the first transportation train, which was returning Alsatians who had been in the German Army, on the Russian Front. Two days were spent in Strassberg trying to secure transportation to the American lines, which was finally secured to Nancy from which place we reached our squadron the Headquarters of First Air Depot by train and thence, the Headquarters of First Air Depot. At First Air Depot, orders were received to proceed to Romorantin to await transportation to the United States.

The following is a report from the American Red Cross:

First Lieutenant Samuel Mandell, Pilot
29th Aero Squadron

Killed Nov. 5th 1918 at Martincourt on the Meuse (7 kilometres north-west of Stenay). Lieutenant Mandell was shot down in combat between twenty Germans and nine Americans. His leg was broken in the fall, but according to the French people of the village he was not otherwise wounded. His observer, who was not wounded, was led away to prison and Lieutenant Mandell was left by his plane from 10 A.M. until 5 o'clock in the afternoon when a German Captain came down to the across which Lieutenant Mandell was lying wounded [*sic*]. The German Captain took a rifle from a German soldier and fired a number of shots at Lieutenant Mandell, one of which penetrated his brain and killed him. The body was left unburied by the Germans for several days and the first American troops to advance in that territory buried Lieutenant Mandell. Lieutenant John S. Patit, Headquarters 56th Field Artillery Brigade stationed at Stenay when informed by us of Lieutenant Mandell's death had the

Lieutenant Samuel Mandell, USAS.

body removed and placed in the cemetery at Martincourt with a proper cross. He also had funeral services for Lieutenant Mandell by the Brigade Chaplain. A young man of the village, Marcel Pierrard worked all of one day removing the body, which was under water as the Meuse had overflown. We promised this young man 500 francs, which we are sending him and will notify his father of the same. The village grave-digger was instructed to place flowers and ferns on the grave and to keep them fresh. He can be recompensed by corresponding with the Mayor of Martincourt, M. Drouin.

First Lieutenant R.R.S. Converse
13th Pursuit Squadron
Late in the afternoon of the second day of the St Mihiel offensive (September 13) six SPAD machines from the 13th Pursuit Group left the aerodrome near Toul and commenced patrol of the lines between St Mihiel and Thiaucourt. The time for the patrol nearly over, they descended to 1,200 metres preparatory to start strafing the infantry on the way home when Lieutenant Converse, who was flying in the rear, saw a formation of seven scouts about 1,000 metres above him. At first he thought they were SPADs but when they got 'in the sun' he recognized the silhouette of the Fokker. Realizing from their actions that the rest of the formation had not seen the Huns but were probably watching the burning villages below, he dove past his leader, firing tracers past him to attract his attention. But the leader was engaged in watching the ground below and did not see the tracers. By this time the enemy had approached close enough to open fire, five of them diving down on the SPADs, the other two remaining above for protection. Lieutenant Converse turned and climbed back into the attacking formation. At this instant his motor went dead – whether from enemy bullets or just ordinary ill luck, he never learned – and he was forced to leave the combat. He later learned that three of the Huns had been put down in flames with his own plane as the single American loss.

The SPAD landed in a communicating trench about 4 kilometres behind the enemy lines and crashed the landing gear. Converse was immediately surrounded by an excited crowd of infantrymen – members of an Austrian unit – which had been rushed up to the line that day. He was handled pretty roughly, his flying equipment and belt were removed with scant ceremony. One enterprising private who had taken a fancy to the American's signet ring and finding it difficult of removal, started to hack off the offending finger. At this juncture the proceedings were interrupted by the arrival of an Austrian Captain of Cavalry. He placed a guard over Converse and had him conducted toward the rear, along a well-camouflaged road.

CHAPTER ELEVEN

The party had been proceeding on foot for some time when they were stopped by a German staff car which relieved the guard of their prisoner and took him into Mars-la-Tour and questioned at Headquarters. After spending that night in a small hut under heavy guard, Converse was marched to Jœuf in company with a cavalry private of an American unit. As they were passing the Air Service headquarters in Jœuf a German officer coming out of the building noticed the wings on Converse's tunic. He took the American away from the guard and to an Officer's Club where there were a number of Germans who spoke either English or French. They put questions but in a polite and indirect way. They gave their prisoner a book to look at – it proved to be a collection of photographs of Allied flying fields, and watched his face intently while he inspected it.

In the afternoon Lieutenant Kraft – the German officer who had appropriated the prisoner – took him to his quarters. Here the next four days were spent. Lieutenant Kraft was congenial but offered his guest very little in the way of food. Each day one French and two American fliers would be brought over to spend the day with Converse and his host, then taken back to their prison for the night. Why Converse was not kept in the prison also is a mystery.

On the fifth day the four of them were given a loaf of black bread between them and placed in a fourth-class coach for the trip to Karlsruhe. This was a two-day trip but they were given no additional food. At Karlsruhe they were placed in the notorious hotel there and left there for five days. The food was not fit to eat so a letter was sent to the British Red Cross who responded immediately and supplied them with wholesome rations.

Orders sending them to Landshut (Bavaria) came as a relief for it was felt that any change would be for the better. But Landshut proved to be just as bad. The food was unfit to eat and numerous vaccinations and inoculations did not add to the general joy. After two weeks Converse was again placed on a train and taken to Villingen. He had planned to make a dash for liberty on this trip but was forestalled by the removal of his shoes. And he found small chance for a getaway after arriving at the camp for Lieutenant Puryear – an American pilot – had just made good his escape and all the guards had been doubled.

In spite of the increased vigilance five of the Americans, including Converse, were able to start a move toward freedom. This was in the form of a tunnel which they planned to extend beyond the outer barbed wire. In the bath house was a disused room which had been boarded up and it was from this point that the tunnel was begun. An American private, working as bath house orderly, assisted by keeping guard and by heating a poker in the fire under the boiler, this red-hot iron being used to cut through the flooring. After this had been accomplished the poker was used for digging. At first the plan progressed very well but when a rock strata was encountered the work became extremely hard. They persisted, however, and managed to extend the tunnel a distance of 25ft when the news came that the German delegate had crossed the lines and that an armistice would be a matter of only a few hours. It was therefore decided to discontinue the tunnel as release would probably come within a week or two.

After the armistice, however, there were no signs of a speedy release so Lieutenant Converse and five other Americans made another attempt at escape. All prisoners were allowed to visit Villingen each day provided they gave their written word of honour each time that they would make no attempt to escape. One forenoon these six Americans remained behind when the others set out for the town. About half an hour later a wagon-load of cabbages drove up to the camp. When the guard opened the main gate to admit it Converse and his companions coolly walked past him, making some remark about going for a walk. They got a good start for it was not until three o'clock that afternoon that they were missed, the guard fearing to report that he had let them out. They made good progress and reached the Black Forest. Here they suffered great hardships as the snow was very deep and their clothing insufficient.

On the second day a Captain Green, 88th Infantry, became completely exhausted and could go no further. Converse volunteered to stay with him and the other four fugitives continued on their way. On account of the cold it was necessary to seek shelter so they walked 4 kilometres to the village of Furtwagoner [*sic*], arriving about midnight. They managed to arouse a German farmer who took them in and fed them. The farmer did not seem at all anxious to turn them over to the authorities but his son, a returned soldier, was not so considerate and reported them. They were immediately taken back to Villingen but were not punished and it was only a short time until they were released. They were sent to Constance, remained there for three days, then through Switzerland to Helgarde [*sic*], France.

First Lieutenant Ben E. Brown, AS
28th Pursuit Squadron

On the morning of November 6th, 1918, the 28th Aero Squadron was scheduled for a patrol of eight SPADs. Lieutenants Stonthes, McClung and myself were the only ones to reach the lines, the others turning back on account of engine trouble and for various other reasons. While flying at about 1,500 metres, we sighted an enemy biplane. Lieutenant Stonthes dove on the plane and then pulled up again. Lieutenant McClung went on down after the plane and I followed him. The plane dove towards its own side of the lines. When Lieutenant McClung pulled off it was evidently still under control and I followed it on down. I was diving straight down and began to manoeuvre to get behind the enemy plane. The German plane continued diving and as I came in behind it, it landed and turned over on its back. I pulled up with the intention of going back toward our lines when I was suddenly attacked from the rear by a Fokker. I did a quick turn and flew back under him and was attacked by a second Fokker. I had been surrounded by a formation of four enemy planes. I succeeded in getting into position to attack one of the planes but was forced to cease the attack by another Fokker behind me. We were fighting so close to the ground that I was unable to shake the Fokker from my tail. My machine was being shot up badly and I was shot in one finger, and while trying to get out of the machine-gun fire my machine went into a flat spin. I throttled the engine, straightened up as much as possible and crashed.

The German Infantry had pulled me out from under the machine and wrapped up my finger when I regained consciousness. None of my personal possessions were taken from me.

I landed near Louppy-le-Château and was taken to Virton that evening. I stayed at Virton about two days. I was sent from Virton to Karlsruhe. I arrived at Karlsruhe, November 10th, 1918.

I was not mistreated or insulted at any time. The food was of poor quality but of sufficient quantity, consisting of black bread, soup, cabbage and potatoes. While at Karlsruhe we obtained an abundance of American Red Cross supplies. After the Armistice we were allowed out of the camp on parole for four hours in the afternoon. On November 20th, 1918, eight of us decided to attempt to escape. The guards were very lax and we bribed one of them to let us out. We reached the Rhine near Selz at one o'clock that night. The next day we were far enough in Alsace-Lorraine so that we were able to obtain food and shelter. We reached Strasbourg on November 23rd, 1918.

Captain Elmer R. Haslett, AS
104th Squadron

Captured September 30, 1918, while on special duty with 104th Aero Squadron working with the 91st Division. In a Salmson plane. Very bad day, extreme wind velocity. Pilot – Lieutenant Raymond E. Davis, 104th Squadron. While over Jametz after being subjected to extreme anti-aircraft artillery and machine-gun fire for two hours, was attacked by four enemy planes, Fokker type, at an altitude of 350 metres. Opened fire on Fokkers at 400 metres with scattered burst of fifty rounds. Fokkers broke formation, three came to right and one to left, left Fokker got under my tail and three right closed in. Right gun jammed while firing into right Fokkers, left fired three shots then jammed. Just succeeded in getting right gun jam cleared, when left Fokker, under tail, put incendiary bullet in engine, flame broke out and pilot threw plane into a side-slip and miraculously landed. We jumped and ran, the Fokkers came down to 50 metres and continued to fire at us. Seeing the plane had not burned and that the side-slip had extinguished the flame, we ran back to the plane to set it on fire. The four Fokkers continued to fire at us from an altitude of 35 to 50 metres and fired not less than 12 to 14 hundred rounds. Pilot ran in one direction and I in another. I ran into five horsemen and stumbled and fell in the mud. One of these, who was an officer, pulled his gun and threatened to shoot me and demanded to know who had set fire to the plane. Asked me to disclose the whereabouts of pilot and upon refusal raised gun to shoot me, when a superior officer interfered.

Was taken to Montmédy, Headquarters of 5th German Army, then to prison camp, had soup only, the first day. In afternoon taken to Army Headquarters for examination. Intelligence officer produced pictures of our aerodrome and others in the vicinity and promised to drop news of our safety if we would disclose our location, we refused. Offered us liquor which we refused, offered us cigarettes, which we accepted.

After three days was sent to Karlsruhe and placed in confinement in a large hotel, better food but nothing extra.

Again questioned by a civilian Intelligence Officer, who gave the story that he was there simply for altruistic aims and only wanted to get information to cheer up our friends who might come later. Found later that Red Cross Committee had sent food for us to this hotel, which we never received.

Taken in three days to main Karlsruhe camp. After a thorough search and arguing for thirty minutes with an officer of the German Army, I finally had to give up my Sam Browne belt, although I told him that this was personal property and part of my uniform. He refused to give me a receipt for it. After a week at the Karlsruhe camp, attempted to escape. Was caught tunnelling under a fence and given a slight jab with a bayonet. I have no complaint to offer as this was justifiable, as I tried to go on out under the fence after the sentry had commanded me to halt. Placed in solitary confinement for three days after a thorough search. While in solitary confinement the authorities refused to allow me to receive any Red Cross food.

Bribed sentries to escape on third night and at four o'clock that afternoon, was taken away and sent down south to a camp at Landshut near Munich. After four days we were inoculated and vaccinated for Small-pox, Typhus, Typhoid, Para-Typhoid and Cholera. Was very weak from my second injection and ill with fever, when the officer commanding the camp sent for me and stated that the General had ordered that I should serve an additional sentence for attempting to escape at Karlsruhe. I protested vigorously to the commander and also to the prison inspector, as I had been told that my sentence was completed. In two days was taken to the County Jail at Landshut and put in a barren cell which was very cold and the bed was locked on the side of the wall. I beat on the door until the attendant came and I demanded that the bed be unlocked, as I was ill and must lie down. He refused to unlock it and after sending in a protest again, through the Spanish, Swiss and Netherlands Governments, to the German government, claiming illegal imprisonment, I was forced to lie on the cold cement floor from sheer weakness. In three hours the camp commander, with an interpreter, came and informed me that the General at Munich had decided that I need not serve my jail sentence, so

I went back to my Landshut camp. At this place we received 60 marks per month as pay and the price of our meals was 150 marks, therefore we had to draw on our banks to pay the difference. At Landshut they took all our clothes and gave us prison clothes, also gave us paper bedroom shoes, which they later charged us for at the current rate at that time of $2.80.

On leaving Karlsruhe, I deposited 76 marks in prison money, for which they gave me a receipt, and at Landshut they refused to accept and refused to allow it on my boarding account. I have never collected this money.

After the Armistice was signed, we were sent to Villingen. I tried to escape several times at Villingen to Konstanz and there released through the Swiss. The camp at Villingen also refused to give me credit for the money deposited at Karlsruhe.

First Lieutenant Herbert Wardle, AS
Ferry Pilot

On 26th of June 1918, in taking a plane from Lympne, England to Paris, France, I was taken prisoner. I went from Lympne, England, direct to Amiens, as I only had a map of that sector. From Amiens, I either drifted across the lines or the compass was a bit out of line. The day was very misty and cloudy. Had to fly at about 2,000 feet to be able to see at all. First noticed that I was across the lines when shot at by an enemy aircraft, and I turned immediately and started back. As I did, a shell broke about thirty feet in front of my motor, the concussion throwing the plane up on end. A piece of the shell had hit my meter and before I could right the plane, I was within a few hundred feet of the ground, when they turned machine guns on me bringing me down on a railway track. I was taken from the plane by German soldiers and taken to a dressing station. I had my nose broken, mouth cut and shins badly skinned. After leaving the dressing station, I was taken to the Intelligence Officer at Ham who told me that I had killed two of the machine-gunners. After leaving the Intelligence Office at Ham, where I was kept for four days, I was sent to St. Quentin, staying only a few hours in St. Quentin. Was sent fratner [*sic*] to a camp at Rastatt. From Rastatt I was sent to

Karlsruhe to the head Intelligence Officer. This Intelligence Officer is the main one for officer prisoners of war. They had about fifty officers of all nationalities in there at once, being confined about six to a room, some being kept there for weeks at a time before being questioned by the Intelligence Officer.

From that office I was sent to the camp at Karlsruhe. After staying there about two weeks, I was sent to Landshut with about one hundred Flying Officers, both British and French. This camp was called a quarantine camp. I escaped, along with Captain J.C. Clark of the RAF from the train as we were passing through some woods. When train stopped about a mile up the track soldiers were sent back in search of us. They caught me in a culvert. I was badly beaten by the soldiers with the butts of their guns all the way back to the train. After reaching Landshut I was put in the civil jail in solitary confinement, where I was held, without leaving one room, for thirty-one days. The only food I got during the thirty-one days was soup of miserable quality, one at one o'clock in the day and again at seven o'clock at night. I had no books, nor was I allowed to write any letters or notes to anyone in the camp at Landshut asking for food.

From this prison I was sent to the camp at Villingen very heavily guarded. Conditions at Villingen, as regard to food and clothing, thanks to our own Red Cross, were much better. We organized an escape by short-circuiting all the lights in the camp by throwing dummies over the wires. Out of the fifteen officers that attempted to escape that night, three got back to France – Lieutenant Isaacs of the Navy, Lieutenant Willis, French, and Lieutenant Puryear, an American aviator. After this attempt double guards were put on all over the camp, and I think if the war had kept on all Americans would have been removed from this camp and sent to Prussia.

After the Armistice was signed, perhaps two weeks before, the Germans changed around in their attitude towards the Americans, and treated them quite according to rules, but no more. All Americans from this camp were sent to Constance on the 24th of November. After being held there for four or five days were put on a train and taken to Switzerland, through Switzerland to Belgium and France.

First Lieutenant Karl C. Payne
20th Bombardment Squadron

On November 5th, 1918, the 20th Squadron made a bombing raid on Mouzon. Due to a strong south-west wind, the formation of eight Liberty-motored De Havilland 4s was blown far into German territory after the bombs were dropped. On my way back to the lines we were attacked by three patrols of German Chasse. We drove off the first patrol (Fokker D.VII, blue markings with white crosses). The second patrol brought down one of our planes in flames, and the motor on the plane in which Lieutenant Edwards (pilot) and Lieutenant Payne (observer) were flying was crippled by machine-gun fire, and fell behind the formation. When this patrol attacked us, we were practically alone. The markings of the Fokkers of this patrol were black and white stripes. They ripped our gas tank by machine-gun fire and wounded Lieutenant Payne in the left arm, disabling him. The ammunition for his twin Lewis machine guns was almost exhausted. He turned to tell the pilot what the conditions were in the rear seat, when an explosive bullet struck the breech of the Marlin gun close to the pilot's head. He thought the pilot was wounded and took the controls, putting the plane in a steep nosedive. Three Fokkers followed, firing all the time, as the plane was still headed towards the American lines. It was necessary for the pilot to manoeuvre continually, and, as the motor was barely turning over, the plane rapidly lost altitude. When we were very low, and close to the American lines, an enemy plane closed in on us, and we shot him down. This made the second enemy plane we had shot down during the combat. Due to the crippled motor, and the manoeuvring to escape the pursuing Fokkers, and to the strong headwind, we were unable to reach our lines and landed in the lines of the Wurtemburger Jaeger. A private rushed at the pilot, and presented a Luger at his head while others grinned. A *Feldwebel*, however, ordered him back, saluted, and requested any papers we might have. We had no papers except a leave to Nice, and a permission to use explosive bullets. We were able to destroy this latter, however, before the Germans found it. We were taken to the field dressing station, where Lieutenant Payne's wound was well and quickly dressed, and anti-tetanus serum injected. From there we were taken by an artillery officer, who later placed us on the caissons of his regiment and turned us over to the HQ at Louppy-sur-Loison, where we arrived on the night of 5th November. We spent the night of the 5th in the orderly room of the Gruppe-Luppy, and were not fed until noon on the 6th, when we received some soup and bread with Lieutenant Ben Brown, who had been shot down that morning by Fokkers. We were taken that afternoon to Virton, where a German Intelligence Officer gave us tea, but he didn't question us very closely, as he already knew of the Armistice. He showed us, however, excellent pictures of American Airdromes, and surprised us with his knowledge of the First Day Bombardment Group. We were kept in a room at Virton for three nights and two days, the food being not good but plentiful, and the same rations as issued to the guards. On the 9th two guards took us to Karlsruhe by train, arriving the morning of the 10th. As we arrived, revolutionists, with red bands on their arms, were disarming all incoming troops. We spent the 10th in a room at the Europa Hotel at Karlsruhe, and taken to a permanent camp on the morning of the 11th. Here we were given American Red Cross food, good barracks, a French orderly, and every consideration that could be expected. At 9:10 P.M. on the 20th, seven English officers and four American Lieutenants Brown, Ben. E., R.W. Fulton, Karl Payne and Brooke Edwards escaped from the camp by bribing a guard, stole a skiff from the Rhine bank, and landed at about 1:00 A.M. 10 miles north of Lauterbourg. We walked to a small village some 4 miles south of Lauterburg, rested there, and reached Selz on the night of the 21st. The Mayor of Selz showed us the greatest hospitality, the members of the party were billeted free of charge whatever, with the Mayor, Cure, and members of the Town Council, who were most kind. We reached Strasbourg on the night of the 22nd, and finally were able to get to Nancy by motor, reporting to Captain Zinn at Colombey-les-Belles.

Second Lieutenant Byron M. Battey
Serving with 48th Squadron, RAF

Lieutenant Battey was captured on 29 July 1918 while on patrol in a Bristol Fighter. He was serving with the 48th Squadron, Royal Air Force, with a patrol of six planes who set out from Bertangles, near Amiens. According to Lieutenant Battey, the machine in which he flew was an old one which had been used to some extent for night-flying. It was so untrustworthy that he had four times before had forced landings in it. On this occasion he had difficulty in keeping up with his formation and the flight leader failed to throttle down his machine. When he was thus separated from the patrol, six enemy Fokkers swept upon him and in the chase that followed, his engine failed, probably due to a defective safety valve, and he was forced to land near the third lines close to Foucaucourt.

It seems that Lieutenant Battey was flying with a French observer to whom he shouted to get out as they landed as it was his intention to try and start the engine and escape. The Frenchman, however, having an incendiary bomb in his hand, apparently lost his head and dropped it in the machine, whereupon Lieutenant Battey made a grab for it and buried it in the ground and jumped from the machine direct for the propeller to start to swing it. While he was in the act of swinging the propeller he was shot in the back by a machine-gunner. He rolled over and over to a nearby trench and attempted to escape and after a lively chase was cornered and made a prisoner by the Germans.

His wounds were given early attention, but during the process his money and clothes were stolen by bystanders. He was taken to an Intelligence officer who by various methods and liberal offers of cognac sought to draw from him information in regard to our aviation. Another trick of the Germans was to confront him by a civilian who represented himself as a writer of a new book on aviation, and desired information on British aeroplanes. Again he was taken to various British (German?) aerodromes and allowed to sit in some of the latest types of German machines and then inveigled into conversation during which they sought his opinion on the ships in comparison to those he had been flying.

In passing Lieutenant Battey remarked that he found the German Headquarters lying only 100 yards from the Red Cross building and which still bore this Red Cross, 'The emblem of safety from bombing'. When he remarked the fact to the Germans, they excused it by saying they had not sufficient time to remove the Red Cross insignia.

In his travels to the rear he lodged at Cartigni [*sic*] where he attempted to escape. Leading from the prisoners' quarters was a door, the wooden panels of which were arranged that they were able, by withdrawing a few screws, to put it in a condition where it was apparently of its original shape but, nevertheless, could be broken through in a few moments by removing all remaining screws. Several officers worked for a considerable period on this door in order to make it suitable for a means of escape. On several occasions the sergeant stood while Lieutenant Battey was working on the other side. His fellow officers organized a covering party in the form of a craps game coupled with a volume of hilarity which drowned out the scratching and scraping of the men who were at work. On one occasion they taught a German captain how to shoot craps while their fellow officers worked inside. It was on Friday, 13 September when two of them escaped by crawling through this space from which the panel was removed and made their way to freedom. They were dressed in military apparel and therefore quite different from other people; however, they successfully made their way through a number of towns until, after three days of freedom they were captured by a gendarme in Haag. While they were being conducted up a hill by the guard, Lieutenant Battey, 'faking' that he was exhausted, cut loose from the guard, effecting his escape again. With the aid of a needle which had been magnetized by a German magnetic razor he was able to find his way for another three days but was finally captured in the Austrian Alps.

He had headed for Switzerland and was almost at the point where he would swim the Inn River. The guard halted him at the railway track but he approached as if deaf until within a few feet of the sentry, then rushed by at full speed with the guard shooting behind him. He outdistanced the Hun and ran through various ravines through which the river flowed. He tried to swim it but the torrent threw him back onto land and in fact nearly drowned him. As he lay helpless upon a rock he heard a stranger coming up the ravine and he thought it was the German guard who had been warned of his presence by the unsuccessful sentry, but he was too weak to move. The German sergeant spied him and took him into custody and sent him back to jail in Landshut where he got twenty-five days, three of which were extra days for the offence of singing while on march. During his examination, stripped, he succeeded in retaining between his fingers tiny maps upon which he had depended for escape.

He next went to Villingen prepared with compass and maps, but he lost his maps during the last days at Villingen. The Americans built a tunnel through which they intended to escape.

They had a terrible time with the Americans there, said Lieutenant Battey. They called them 'Wild Americans' and could not understand why they were so reckless in trying to escape.

The escape at Cartigni, Lieutenant Battey learned later, had caused his fellow prisoners three months of their pay, so angry were the Germans. The German guard walked in and forced them to hold their arms in the air for many minutes with the threat of 'cold steel' ready to run them through.

(From notes taken by L.H. Thayer, Second Lieutenant, AS.)

Lieutenant C.W. Ford
103rd Aero Squadron (Pursuit) AS

I was on duty with the 103rd Aero Squadron (3rd Pursuit Group) and flying SPADs. Left airdrome (Lisle-en-Barrois) 12:45 o'clock, October 15th, 1918. Weather – rain, mist and clouds at 800 to 1,000 metres.

Lieutenant Keene Palmer and myself were flying in company. At about 1:55 P.M. my motor was hit by machine-gun fire from the ground, north of Grandpré (Argonne Forest), causing it to stop and I was too low to glide and reach my own lines. Turned over and crashed machine landing. Was taken prisoner by Hun Infantry troops and transported on a ration cart back to a town called Authie, which I presume was a divisional headquarters, and questioned by an Intelligence Officer.

Immediately after getting out from underneath my machine I looked up to see what Lieutenant Palmer was doing and saw him coming down in a vertical wing slip and disappear in a valley out of sight and apparently out of control. On reaching Authie I learned through the Intelligence Officer that he was dead. We both came down almost simultaneously and fell within less than half a kilometre of each other, and obviously both by machine-gun fire as were not being shelled and there were no enemy planes in sight.

I was taken from Authie to Stenay by automobile that afternoon to a place I imagine was an army headquarters and again questioned by Intelligence Officers. There were a lot of Infantrymen brought in while I was there and they questioned them regarding their regimental and divisional numbers, comparing their statements with a map of the sector, which they marked off into certain zones containing the numbers of various units, which they had identified. In each case where a prisoner was brought in from a new unit not previously identified this information was immediately telephoned to some outside quarter.

I was kept in Stenay for two days and then taken by automobile to Montmédy where I was out in prison and confined to a small room together with a 2nd Lieutenant (Infantry), where we were kept for eight days. This room was never opened except got one hour during lunch time, we never had any exercise. Nothing to eat except soggy black bread and a vile liquid called coffee which was served in a wash basin, and a little cabbage soup. Worst of all the cots were the filthiest imaginable. During our stay here we had no opportunity to wash, shave, brush our teeth or comb our hair, and although we complained bitterly many times to the officer in charge, nothing was done to remedy this evil. We were furnished with nothing to read. On the eighth day we were given a bath and our clothes fumigated and were then taken by train to Karlsruhe via Didenhoffen [*sic*] and Strassberg (the direst [*sic*] line through Metz was not used).

We arrived here at five o'clock in the morning and were put in a hotel, which I understood they used to take care of the overflow of prisoners going into the camp at Karlsruhe, which is situated in the centre of town. Here we were again interrogated by Intelligence Officers. That afternoon I was marched down with twenty-five other American and English officers to the camp. There we were kept for a week and then with about thirty other American officers was taken by train to Camp Villingen in Baden via Offenberg. It was here that I learned of the signing of the Armistice. However, the guards were not removed and in every sense of the word we were prisoners just as much as we were previous to the signing of the Armistice.

At 10 o'clock in the morning of November 29th, five others and myself walked out of the camp (Captain House, Safford and Green, 88 Infantry Division, Lieutenant Converse Air Service, and another Infantry Lieutenant whose name I do not remember). One of the Infantry Captains (House) who could speak a little German told the guard that we were going out and joining up with a bunch of officers who had left the camp about three-quarters [of an hour] previous on their usual morning walk. However, we were all prepared to make our escape and had food, maps and a compass with us. We walked all day through the Black Forest. Captain Green and Lieutenant Converse could not stand the walking so we left them at 10:30 o'clock that night and the four of us continued to walk until 4:40 the next morning. (I have learned that Captain Green and Lieutenant Converse were taken back to Camp Villingen.)

We rested all that day and resumed walking at seven o'clock that night, reaching and crossing a pontoon bridge over the Rhine at Brisach at about 5 o'clock the following morning. As there was nothing in the way of transportation there we continued walking, reaching Colmar about 7 o'clock in the evening but there were no trains running from there either. However, I met an American officer (a press correspondent) who introduced us to a French officer who had a touring car going into Belfort the next morning and volunteered to take us in.

On reaching Belfort (November 23rd) I telegraphed to General headquarters receiving a telegram in reply ordering me to report there immediately. Route followed – Villingen–Volrenbach–Furtwangen–Brend–Waldirek–Denzlingen–Eichstetten–Colmar.

In all instances where information was demanded and refused no force or coercive measures were taken. The living conditions at Karlsruhe and Villingen were not bad, the American Red Cross supplied us with sufficient food and tobacco to make us more or less independent of the prison fare, which consisted of black bread, cabbage, carrots, beets and a limited supply of potatoes.

First Lieutenant Carlyle Rhodes, AS
95th Squadron
Lieutenant Rhodes' statement follows:

On the evening of July 5th 1918, four or five other machines, Nieuport 28s, from the 95th Aero Squadron, and myself on patrol from Mézy to the Foret-de-Villiers-Cotterat, attacked a formation of enemy Fokker Rambler-place (Rumplers) airplanes. In the ensuing fight, one enemy machine was destroyed, the plane of Lieutenant Sidney Thompson. Shot down in flames and my plane shot down out of control. The rudder wires were cut by bullets. I crashed but was uninjured. Ran toward the sun, thinking because of the numerous shell holes that I was in 'No Man's Land'. Ran into the rear trench of German Infantry and was taken.

Treatment in Germany varied, depending upon the Commanding Officer of the Prison Camp. The first three months were much worse than the last two. The Red Cross parcels were our source of food. Lieutenant Wardle, retaken after an escape from a train, was badly beaten with rifle butts by the German guards. Lieutenants Floyd, Batty, Dohler were kept in solitary confinement twenty-one days with little to eat after escaping from Landshut, Bavaria. I was kept three days on a piece of black bread and water, and travelled three days on a train with only two plates of soup, one-fourth loaf of bread, small piece of sausage for the trip. Bought food ourselves. In Bavaria had very little space to exercise. At Villingen, Baden, camp was very good and we were well treated.

Information picked up was negligible. They killed many pilots in training, had flying Sergeants, used parachutes, liked new Roland (aircraft) for near ground, Fokker higher, thought new SPAD good.

(On 13 September 1918, Lieutenant Rhodes jumped off a train attempting to escape, but was recaptured.)

Appendix I

Members of Lafayette Escadrille N.124

Georges Thenault	18 April 1916–18 January 1918
Alfred de Laage de Meux	18 April 1916–23 May 1917
Victor Chapman	18 April 1916–23 June 1916
Norman Prince	18 April 1916–15 October 1916
James R. McConnell	18 April 1916–19 March 1917
Kiffin Y. Rockwell	18 April 1916–23 September 1916
William Thaw II	18 April 1916–18 February 1918
W. Bert Hall	18 April 1916–1 November 1916
Elliott C. Cowdin	18 April 1916–25 June 1916
Raoul Lufbery	24 May 1916–5 January 1918
H. Clyde Balsley	29 May 1916–18 June 1916
Charles C. Johnson	29 May 1916–31 October 1917
Lawrence Rumsey	4 June 1916–25 November 1916
Dudley L. Hill	9 June 1916–18 February 1918
Didier Masson	19 June 1916–8 October 1917
Paul Pavelka	11 August 1916–24 January 1917
Robert L. Rockwell	17 September 1916–18 February 1918
Frederick H. Prince	22 October 1916–15 February 1917
Robert Soubiran	22 October 1916–18 February 1918
Willis B. Havilland	22 October 1916–18 September 1917
Ronald Hoskier	11 December 1916–23 April 1917
Edmund C.C. Genêt	19 January 1917–16 April 1917
Edwin C. Parsons	25 January 1917–26 February 1918
Stephen Bigelow	28 February 1917–11 September 1917
Edward F. Hinkle	1 March 1917–12 June 1917
Walter Lovell	31 March 1917–24 October 1917
Harold B. Willis	1 March 1917–18 August 1917
Kenneth Marr	29 March 1917–18 February 1918
William E. Dugan, Jnr	30 March 1917–18 February 1918

Thomas M. Hewitt, Jnr	30 March 1917–17 September 1917
Andrew C. Campbell, Jnr	15 April 1917–1 October 1917
Ray C. Bridgman	1 May 1917–18 February 1918
Henry S. Jones	12 May 1917–18 February 1918
John A. Drexel	10 May 1917–15 June 1917
Charles H. Dolan II	12 May 1917–18 February 1918
Antoine de Maison-Rouge	28 May 1917–6 October 1917
James Norman Hall	16 June 1917–18 February 1918
Douglas MacMonagle	16 June 1917–24 September 1917
David McKelvey Peterson	1 June 1917–18 February 1918
James R. Doolittle	2 July 1917–17 July 1917
Louis Verdier-Fauvety	16 October 1917–18 February 1918
Christopher W. Ford	8 November 1917–18 February 1918

Appendix II

United States Squadrons in the First World War

Fighter Squadrons

The Lafayette Escadrille
L'Escadrille N.471
13th Pursuit Squadron
17th Pursuit Squadron
22nd Pursuit Squadron
25th Pursuit Squadron
27th Pursuit Squadron
28th Pursuit Squadron
41st Pursuit Squadron
49th Pursuit Squadron
93rd Pursuit Squadron
94th Pursuit Squadron
95th Pursuit Squadron
103rd Pursuit Squadron
135th Pursuit Squadron
138th Pursuit Squadron
139th Pursuit Squadron
141st Pursuit Squadron
147th Pursuit Squadron
148th Pursuit Squadron
185th Pursuit Squadron
213th Pursuit Squadron
638th Pursuit Squadron

Bombardment Squadrons

11th Bombardment Squadron
20th Bombardment Squadron
96th Bombardment Squadron
100th Bombardment Squadron
155th Bombardment Squadron
163rd Bombardment Squadron
166th Bombardment Squadron

Marine Day Wing

Marine Squadron No.7
Marine Squadron No.8
Marine Squadron No.9
Marine Squadron No.10

Observation Squadrons

1st Observation Squadron
8th Observation Squadron
9th Observation Squadron
12th Observation Squadron
24th Observation Squadron
50th Observation Squadron
85th Observation Squadron
88th Observation Squadron
90th Observation Squadron
91st Observation Squadron
99th Observation Squadron
104th Observation Squadron
135th Observation Squadron
168th Observation Squadron
186th Observation Squadron
258th Observation Squadron
278th Observation Squadron
354th Observation Squadron

Balloon Companies

1st Balloon Company
2nd Balloon Company
3rd Balloon Company
4th Balloon Company
5th Balloon Company
6th Balloon Company
7th Balloon Company
8th Balloon Company
9th Balloon Company
10th Balloon Company
11th Balloon Company
12th Balloon Company
13th Balloon Company
14th Balloon Company
15th Balloon Company
16th Balloon Company
24th Balloon Company
25th Balloon Company
26th Balloon Company
42nd Balloon Company
43rd Balloon Company
44th Balloon Company
69th Balloon Company

Appendix III

Air Stations

Operational Royal Naval Air Stations (RNAS)

Anglesey, Wales
Bangor, Wales
Barrow-in-Furness (Walney Island), England
Bembridge Harbour, Isle of Wight, England
Calshot, Hampshire, England
Catfirth, Shetland Isles
Cattewater, Devon, England
Chickerell, Dorset, England
Cromarty, Scotland
Detling, Kent, England
Dover, Kent, England
Dundee, Scotland.
Eastchurch, Isle of Sheppey, Kent, England
East Fortune, Scotland
Felixstowe, England
Fishguard, Pembrokeshire, Wales
Gosport, Hampshire, England
Grain & Port Victoria, Kent, England
Hornsea, Yorkshire, England
Houton Bay, Orkney Islands
Killingholme, Lincolnshire, England
Lee-on-Solent, Hampshire, England
Leuchars, Fife, Scotland
Manston, Kent, England
Mullion, Cornwall, England
Newhaven, Sussex, England
Newhaven, Sussex, England

Newlyn, Cornwall, England
Owthorne, East Yorkshire, England
Padstowe, Cornwall, England
Portland, England
Redcar, North Yorkshire, England
Scapa, Orkney Islands
South Shields, Durham, England
Stonehenge, Wiltshire, England
Tresco, Scilly Isles, England
Walmer, Kent, England
Westgate, England
Whitley Bay, Northumberland, England
Yarmouth, Norfolk, England

United States Naval Air Stations (USNAS)

USNAS Arcachon, France
USNAS Brest, France
USNAS Dunkirk, France
USNAS Fromentine, Italy
USNAS Ile Tidy, France
USNAS Killingholme, England
USNAS L'Aber Wrac'h, France
USNAS Le Croisic, France
USNAS Lough Foyle, Southern Ireland
USNAS Porto Corsini, Italy
USNAS Queenstown, Southern Ireland
USNAS St Trojan, France
USNAS Tréguier, France
USNAS Wexford, Southern Ireland
USNAS Whiddy Island, Southern Ireland

United States Marine Corps Air Stations (USMCAS)

USMCAS Le Fresne, France
USMCAS Ponta Delgada, Italy

Bibliography

A History of the Royal Air Force and United States Naval Air Service in Ireland, 1913–1923 (Irish Air Letter, Co. Dublin, Ireland, 1988. ISBN: 0-9508231-1-2)

Cooke, James J., *The U.S. Air Service in the Great War, 1917–1919* (Praeger Publishers, Westport, CT 06881, 1996)

Emmons, Roger M., *US Marine Aviation in France, 1918* (Marine Corps Aviation Association, 1976)

Greer, Thomas, *The Development of Air Doctrine in the Army Air Arm 1917–1941* (The United States Air Force Special Studies, 1985)

Hennessy, Juliette A., *The United States Army Air Arm: April 1861 to April 1917* (Office of Air Force History, Washington DC, 1985)

Jablonski, Edward, *The Knighted Skies* (Thomas Nelson & Sons Ltd, 1964)

Karolevitz, Robert F. and Fenn, Ross S., *Flight of Eagles* (Brevet Press, 1974. ISBN: 88498-022-7)

Knott, Captain Richard C., USN (Retired), *A Heritage of Wings* (Naval Institute Press, 1997. ISBN: 0-87021-270-2)

Sloan, James J., *Wings of Honor* (Schiffer Publishing, Atglen, PA, 1994. ISBN: 0-88740-577-0)

Van Wyen, Adrian O., *Naval Aviation in World War One* (CNO Washington DC, 1969)

Wise, S.F., *Canadian Airmen and the First World War* (Toronto University Press, 1986. ISBN: 0-8020-2379-7)

Index